PRAISE FOR
THE OPERATIONS ADVANTAGE

'This is a clear, simple and concise way of explaining the world of operations. The book lays the foundations and leads practitioners through the operations journey, imposing rigour on the ideas that underpin operations improvement. Nigel Slack brings his combination of common sense and deep functional experience to make the topic come alive.' **People Director: Finance & Supply Chain, AB InBev**

'*The Operations Advantage* is essential reading, not just for established companies, but also for high-growth start-ups. Filled with practical, applicable advice, this book shows that operations thinking can be a road map for creating sustainable high-growth service companies seeking predictable revenue.' **Dr Ben Betts, CEO, HT2Labs**

The Operations Advantage

A practical guide to making operations work

Nigel Slack

KoganPage

First published in Great Britain and the United States in 2017 by Kogan Page Limited

2nd Floor, 45 Gee Street	c/o Martin P Hill Consulting	4737/23 Ansari Road
London	122 W 27th St, 10th Floor	Daryaganj
EC1V 3RS	New York, NY 10001	New Delhi 110002
United Kingdom	USA	India

www.koganpage.com

ISBN   978 0 7494 7354 9
E-ISBN 978 0 7494 7355 6

British Library Cataloguing-in-Publication Data

A CIP record for this book is available from the British Library.

Library of Congress Cataloging-in-Publication Data

Names: Slack, Nigel, author.
Title: The operations advantage : a practical guide to making operations work
    / Nigel Slack.
Description: London ; New York ; New Delhi : Kogan Page Limited, [2017] |
    Includes bibliographical references and index.
Identifiers: LCCN 2017000784 (print) | LCCN 2017001132 (ebook) |
    ISBN 9780749473549 (alk. paper) | ISBN 9780749473556 (ebook)
Subjects: LCSH: Operations research. | Program management.
Classification: LCC T57.6 .S593 2017 (print) | LCC T57.6 (ebook) |
    DDC 658.5–dc23

Typeset by Integra Software Services, Pondicherry
Print production managed by Jellyfish
Printed and bound by CPI Group (UK) Ltd, Croydon, CR0 4YY

CONTENTS

ABOUT THE AUTHOR

Nigel Slack is Emeritus Professor of Operations Management and Strategy at Warwick Business School, an Associate Fellow of Said Business School, Oxford University, and an Honorary Professor at Bath University. Previously he was the Royal Academy of Engineering Professor of Service and Support Management at Cambridge University, Professor of Operations Strategy at Brunel University in London, and a lecturer in Management Studies at Oxford University. He worked initially as an industrial apprentice in the hand-tool industry and then as a production engineer, production manager and an operations director in the engineering and consumer durable industries.

He is an educator, consultant and researcher with wide experience in many sectors, including financial services, oil and gas, utilities, retail, media, professional services, general services, aerospace, FMCG, and engineering manufacturing. He is the author and co-author of many publications in the operations management area, including *Service Superiority*; *Cases in Operations Management*; *Operations Strategy* (with Michael Lewis); and *Operations and Process Management: Principles and practice for strategic impact*. His best-known publication is the market-leading text, *Operations Management* (with Alistair Brandon-Jones), now in its eighth edition, 2016, published by Pearson, a book that has been translated into several languages. His latest works include *Essentials of Operations Management*, again published by Pearson, and *The New CFO*, published by Kogan Page.

PREFACE

This book is about how you can make your operations better and how making your operations better will also make your business better. It does not address any national agenda, at least not directly. What it does do is to speak directly to those individual operations managers who are trying to succeed in a turbulent, competitive and probably ill-understood marketplace. It asks some simple, yet pertinent, questions that any company should be able to answer about its own operations; and at times it even offers some answers.

Success in business comes from doing those things that customers want (and are willing to pay for), and doing them better than any current or potential competitor. An operations advantage helps you to do both. It means delivering the things that your customers value and doing so in a way that supports the competitive sustainability of your business. Simple though it is to say that, anyone who has managed operations knows it presents both substantial intellectual and practical challenges.

It is those very challenges that make managing operations such an exciting subject. You cannot manage a successful operation without a well-founded understanding of what it is really like to try to do your best for your customers and for your business. Yet it is also an activity where knowledge of the underlying principles of operations management is vital. Without this knowledge it is easy to fall into the trap of becoming a management fashion victim – the belief that there is a simple single formula for operations success. There isn't one for managing operations (or for much else either for that matter). Sorry, but there just isn't. However, and it's a big 'however', there are some fundamental questions you should be asking yourself; some basic steps you can go through that will up the chances of doing the right things. That is what this book tries to do. It presents those steps in a straightforward manner that is based on the collected experience of the numerous managers from most types of business that I have worked with over the years and my many academic colleagues who have been generous enough to share their insights and research findings.

Nevertheless this is not an academic book (although written by an academic) in the sense that its sole concerns are with the abstract or theoretical, but it is unashamedly academic in the sense that it tries to make ideas, techniques and principles applicable enough to be useful outside the specific companies where they originated. So don't dismiss the contribution of academics: there is plenty of evidence that using their techniques and frameworks in your operations can bring significant advantage in terms of productivity, service and return on capital.

This book is also practical in that it treats real problems and is not afraid to be prescriptive where it seems helpful and appropriate. It is aimed at both the practising manager who can see beyond simple and simplistic remedies, and at the student of operations (aren't we all?) who is as interested in the rapidly accumulating weight of empirical evidence of what really works as he or she is in the more esoteric theories of operations. It certainly uses real examples to illustrate lessons that we all can learn from. Some are disguised to save embarrassment – particularly if they don't show a business in an entirely positive light. Yet, of course, it is those very examples that have the most to teach us.

ACKNOWLEDGEMENTS

Having worked both as a practising operations manager and an academic over, well, quite a few years, the people who deserve to be credited are far too many to be mentioned individually. So a more general acknowledgement is necessary. First, it is to the hundreds of often remarkable academics I have worked with, particularly in Sheffield, Oxford, Cambridge and especially Warwick. Second, it is to the thousands (as I said, quite a few years) of managers I have had the privilege of working with on executive education programmes and especially all the MBA students I have taught. I wonder if they ever realized that they were really teaching me?

Exploit the power of operations

'Operations' has this image problem. Too often it is seen as dealing with your routine, probably 'technical', low-level, and frankly dreary activities that obviously have to be done – but preferably by someone else. Worthy maybe, and even challenging, but neither exciting nor of direct interest to anyone outside the operations function itself.

Wrong. 'Operations' is how you make things happen. It is how you release whatever expertise you have so that your business can create value. It is through your operations that you serve your customers. It is through your operations that you use your resources to their best advantage. And it is through your operations that you make strategy into reality. It is how you make things real. It is how you navigate the translation from 'idea' into 'practice'. How could it not be important? It is how you can give your business a unique advantage – the operations advantage.

Why an operations advantage is essential

The operations function in most companies represents the bulk of its assets and the majority of its people. The problem is that, for some businesses, operations is just that – bulk, a dead weight, inertia dragging you back. But it really need not be. It is misleading, and harmful, to think of operations as mere bulk. It can be the business's central anatomy. Operations is the bones, the sinew and the muscles of the company. A healthy operations function gives the company the strength to withstand competitive attack, it gives the endurance to maintain a steady improvement in competitive performance, and perhaps most important, it provides the operational suppleness that can respond to increasingly volatile markets and competitors. That is what an operations advantage is.

A sickly operations function, on the other hand, will handicap a business's performance no matter how sharp its strategic sense. Many companies know the frustration of their best laid strategic ambitions rendered impotent because of their operations function's inability to translate their aspirations into the kind of effective action that they should be able to expect. Strategy only means anything when it can be translated into operational action. It remains an abstract set of aspirations if it is devised in an operational vacuum. Competitive strategy cannot hope to be successful in the long term unless it expects operations' role in creating a strategic advantage to be both pivotal and direct. This means more than simply acknowledging the limitations of its operations – though it will have limitations. It means that it must recognize the sheer strategic power that an effective operations function can give the whole organization.

This is not to say that a more conventional sense of strategic direction is unimportant. It is merely to stress that the environment for most companies requires both strategic wit and operations muscle. Sensible strategic direction is more than just important: it is a prerequisite for success. But it is not enough on its own. At the most basic level there is no better guarantee of long-term strategic success, nor is there a better defence against external surprises, than simply creating products and services better than anyone else. A healthy operations function gives the organization its operations advantage. A sick one is worse than merely indifferent; it condemns a business to perpetual mediocrity.

Now is the time to make a note about terminology. Throughout this book the terms 'the operation', 'the operations function', and 'operations' will be used more or less interchangeably. Also 'the organization', 'the business', 'the firm', and 'the enterprise' are used to mean whatever formal body (public or private) one is working for.

This is the first chapter and before getting into the necessary steps in 'making operations work better', we need to explore some preliminary ideas:

- How to exploit the power of operations to add value for all its stakeholders.

- How to exploit the power of operations to form a mutually supportive relationship between the two ingredients of any operation – resources and processes.

- How to exploit the power of operations to connect a strategic view of operations with the more traditional operational view.

- How to exploit the power of operations to plug you into your external supply network.

- How exploiting the power of operations depends on your ability to recognize and execute a number of key steps that you need to achieve an operations advantage.

Before that, a question: are you a casualty of the Red Queen effect?

A scientist called Leigh Van Valen, who studied the extinction of species, came up with the term 'the Red Queen effect' to describe how the struggle for survival never gets easier. The analogy comes from *Alice's Adventures Through the Looking Glass* by Lewis Carroll. Alice says, 'Well, in our country you'd generally get to somewhere else – if you ran very fast for a long time, as we've been doing.' To which the Red Queen says, 'A slow sort of country! Now, here, you see, it takes all the running you can do, to keep in the same place. If you want to get somewhere else, you must run at least twice as fast as that!'[1] And for many businesses, that is increasingly the state of the competition they face.

Improvements and innovations can be imitated or countered by competitors. In the automotive sector for example, few would deny that the quality of most products is significantly better than it was two decades ago. It reflects the many improvements in all auto firms' operations processes. Yet their competitive positions have changed relatively little. Those firms that have managed to pull ahead of their competitors have improved their operations performance *more than* competitors. Like Alice, they have had to run twice as fast. Where the pace of improvement has simply matched competitors, firms have survived, but not thrived. The implications for operations improvement are clear: if you are in an industry where competition is hotting up, improvement should be at the centre of how operations are judged.

Operations has the power to add value through its resources and processes

The whole purpose of having an operations function is for it to add value. Add value for its customers, add value for the business and its owners, add value for its staff, its suppliers, in fact all its stakeholders.[2] It does this by harnessing two vital ingredients of any business – resources and processes. Resources are the assets that you have. Processes are what you do: in other words, how you use your resources. Both resources and processes are fundamental to how any enterprise creates value. The central role of 'operations' is to manage the business's resources and processes so that they can add value through how they create products and services.[3]

The key word in this definition of operations (and how we think about operations generally) is 'create'. That is what all operations do: they focus on how the business creates, serves, moves, produces, manufactures, builds, fabricates, develops or constructs its offerings. Use whatever word works best for you.

Resources set the limits to what your operation can and can't do

Your operation's resources are more than what is shown directly on your balance sheet. They include not only your business's technology, equipment and facilities that form its physical fabric, but also its people (and their skills, enthusiasm and creativity), and its intangible elements (knowledge, supply and customer relationships, culture, etc) together with their intrinsic capabilities. Note that your operation's assets include not just your internal resources, but also the resources that you can conveniently 'get access to' (usually through your supply network). This means that your operation need not necessarily own the resources that it uses. It could have supply agreements that allow it to access resources as and when you have the need. In effect, an operation's ability to access resources is a resource in itself.

Figure 1.1   Operations resources and processes add value for your customers and your business

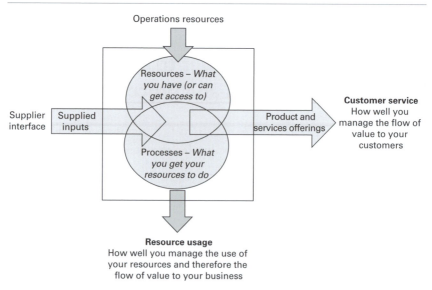

Operations resources

Resources – What you have (or can get access to)

Processes – What you get your resources to do

Supplier interface

Supplied inputs

Product and services offerings

Customer service
How well you manage the flow of value to your customers

Resource usage
How well you manage the use of your resources and therefore the flow of value to your business

Processes define how much of your resource's potential is realized

You cannot truly understand the potential and limitations of your operations by listing the resources you have. Your resources in themselves will not add any value if they are not used effectively. It is the relationship between your resources and the way they perform activities that adds value. That is what processes are: 'arrangements of resources and activities that transform inputs into outputs'.[4] In fact, the best way to think about your larger operation is as an input–output relationship such as that shown in Figure 1.1. As your supplied inputs (materials, information, customers, etc) pass through your operations they pass through your processes. Processes are the directions for how value is added – a kind of repetitive to-do list that specifies where, when, by whom and how things are supposed to be done. But do not make the mistake of thinking that all your processes need to consist of highly defined instructions. They can be looser than that. Processes are simply 'how you do stuff' with your resources. If appropriate, they could be defined in great detail, but they could simply require adherence to a set of broad performance objectives and leave the details to someone's professional judgement (as in many professional service processes for example).

Review your resources and processes

These definitions and 'abstract' models are worth thinking about, not because we want to be over-theoretical, but because it is important for all operations managers to go back to first principles. Doing so helps to clarify the fundamentals as well as providing a guide to the appropriate questions to ask. Even the simple model in Figure 1.1 prompts questions that any operations manager could find useful, and sometimes testing. For example, it focuses attention on the importance of evaluating your resources and processes. This is important because the health of your resources and processes will define how well your operation adds value. Inadequate resources and disorganized processes make for lousy operations. It makes a lot of sense to periodically review their fitness. Do you have the right resources? Appropriate skills? Appropriate technologies? Appropriate facilities and locations? Are they deployed in the right locations? Do you have enough to provide a reasonable service? (Even if the answer is 'no', it is worth debating the trade-offs between resource utilization and customer service.) What are, or will be, the main resource gaps now and in the future?

Similarly, with your processes: what are the key processes in the operation? (The ones that can have the biggest impact on revenue, costs and risk.) What are our processes good at? What are their weaknesses and/or vulnerabilities? How do we bring a sense of customer needs and expectations into our operations processes? How do we make sure that customer needs inform how we deal with suppliers? How might our processes cope with the ways in which the business might develop in the future?

Don't dismiss these questions as 'too obvious'. Very rarely do operations review and debate their resources and processes in a sufficiently systematic manner. Sometimes it is the most obvious questions that are the most powerful at understanding the real strengths and weaknesses inherent in an operation. The example of a European theatre lighting company gives a simple illustration of this.

CASE STUDY   A European theatre lighting company

Tables 1.1 and 1.2 show the (somewhat simplified) results of such a review carried out by a European theatre lighting company that had traditionally focused on designing the lighting arrangements and hiring the necessary equipment for theatrical and entertainment events, exhibitions and conferences. The company suppled almost any specialist lighting equipment, partly because it held a wide range, and partly because it had developed close relationships with other equipment hire firms. It was considering moving more into the more complex event management market (hence the review).

The founder and CEO of the business was clear that market opportunities were in flux. *'Competition is getting tougher in the theatre market because the large international lighting groups are able to provide lower-cost lighting solutions. Also, exhibition venues are increasingly developing in-house operations and encouraging exhibitors to use the in-house service. Margins are being squeezed in both these traditional markets. But the highest margin and fastest growing segment of our market is the larger integrated 'event' business. We believe we can differentiate ourselves by going beyond basic event organization. We already have great contacts in the industry, and we can provide aesthetically innovative event designs with novel staging and lighting solutions. The challenge is to adapt our operations to exploit this opportunity without sacrificing our traditional business.'*

Table 1.1   Resource review for European theatre lighting company

Resources	Strengths	Weaknesses
Equipment stock	Wide range in general theatre Large stock FX strobes	Need more integrated mix consoles? Increased range radio mike four ways?
Local sites	Strong in Benelux	Need two more in UK Expand Brussels?
Website	Visually impressive	Not sufficiently integrated with other systems
Configuration expert system	None	Needs upgrading/replacing Needs integration with website options
Lighting designers	Strong and experienced in Benelux	Need to recruit in UK Need more design expertise in UK Transfer staff?
On-site staff	Strong on regular conference/theatre work in Benelux	Need more event-experienced staff in all locations (except Amsterdam)
Event management	A little – in Amsterdam	Major gaps in all locations

Table 1.2   Key process review for European theatre lighting company

Processes	Strengths	Weaknesses
Routine hire delivery	Efficient process, experienced staff	Need faster inter-depot equipment transfer
Lighting design solutions	Reputation for creative designs at 'high art' end	Not always on-brief with routine work Can be slow in response to changes in client spec
Event organization	Amsterdam have developed an effective process	Only location with effective process is in Amsterdam
Equipment maintenance	Efficient process for basic equipment Good relationships with suppliers	Can be delays in resetting new integrated systems
On-site setup/ takedown	Strong on regular conference/theatre work in Benelux	Not always effective in coordinating with other teams
RFP response	Creative, high-quality proposals	Complaints are all about slow response

Figure 1.2 Your resources and processes can both limit and reinforce each other

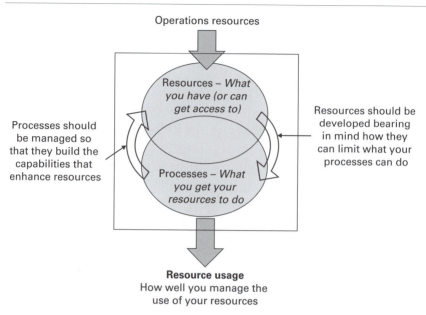

The interaction between resources and processes is key

Resources and processes are not physically separate; they are simply a way of thinking about what goes on in your operation. Moreover, resources and processes impact on each other. They can be both mutually supportive and mutually limiting. Your resources will constrain what your operation's processes are capable of doing. Just as important, the experience gained over time by your processes can add to the capability of your resources. That is what should be so special about your operations. They manage not just the nature and extent of your resources and processes, but also the interaction between them; see Figure 1.2.

CASE STUDY Whose responsibility?

The COO of an FMCG production site was telling his sad story. *'We knew that it was an important decision. The cost of these multipack machines is not trivial and we operate in a dynamic market where consumers respond to constantly changing offers and big retailers can demand their own packaging arrangements. So, given this, we emphasized to our Marketing colleagues the importance of having a reasonable prediction of market trends. "What," we said, "is the very maximum number of individual products that we will ever, ever, be asked to multipack for any, any, market?" And to be fair, they did take the request seriously. They took a month to come back with the answer. "Eight," they said, "eight is the maximum." Great. So we commissioned a machine that could multipack up to eight products and installed it. Within 18 months we got a request from Marketing. "Can you produce special 10-packs for the Canadian market?" When we reminded them of their previous advice, their response was, "Ah, but that was the previous Marketing team." The whole team had changed in the intervening 18 months.'*

That your choice of resources will limit what your processes can do is obvious. Technology, people or systems with inappropriate abilities or skills will restrict what your processes can do. So the lesson is to ask not only, 'What will this investment allow us to do?' but also, 'How will this investment constrain what we do?' The problem is that often you do not have a clear idea of what you may be asked to do in the future. Look at the example 'Whose responsibility?' This COO seems to have been very careful in looking to the future before committing to an expensive, and limiting, resource. Yet there is something of a backstory to this example. The COO in question did know that in that industry, the future was intrinsically unpredictable. Investing in that particular piece of technology was always going to be a gamble. You can't simply hand over responsibility to (in this case) Marketing. The real debate should have been about how much extra investment was worth the possibility of being constrained in the future – and it was that COO's responsibility to articulate and lead that debate.

What is often forgotten in the demands of running day-to-day operations is that how you manage your processes can enhance your resources. Well, it can if you run them in an intelligent way. Processes should not simply 'do what they do' without learning from what they do. Processes are too often run as unintelligent, non-learning and tedious activities – a 'tick-box' task, simply the routine checklist of how you do things. They are not seen for what they really are – the best source of learning you will ever have. In any medium to large business, thousands of individual transactions take place every few seconds. And every transaction is an opportunity to learn. All transactions involve doing something, then observing the result. They are a series of cause–effect activities, and linking cause and effect is what learning is all about. Processes are where learning happens (or should happen). If you are not exploiting the opportunity to learn from your day-to-day, hour-by-hour, or minute-by-minute process, you are indulging in one of the most egregious examples of waste in operations practice.

Understanding and exploiting the opportunities to learn from your processes can materially improve the resources from which they are made up. Look at the example 'It's a secret process', below. In this case, the original technology might have been genuinely innovative (in fact it was), but what is far more impressive is the company's ability to let its accumulation of knowledge about how to use the technology 'drip feed' into further incremental improvements in the technology. This mutual dependency of resources and processes is a particularly important point that helps us understand how operations improve their capabilities over time. It is also a point that we shall keep returning to later.

CASE STUDY   'It's a secret process'

The COO (yes the same one as in the previous example, as it happens) was adamant. *'Sorry, I can't show you around that department, the process is secret and company policy prevents any outsiders entering it.'* The product that was made in the department was an item that had been made by the company for decades.

Later the COO confessed: *'Frankly you could give the blueprints of the "secret" process to our competitors and they would not be able to make it as well or as efficiently as we can. That's what decades of producing it has given us: a knowledge of how to get the best out of the process. And it's that experience and confidence that allow us to modify the process every so often. We are continually pushing out the boundaries of what the process can do. Both our working methods and the technology itself are better than they were a couple of years ago. We continually develop the process.'*

Operations has the power to link the strategic with the operational

All great operations managers need to have a little bit of a split personality. One part of your personality needs to focus on detail. It needs to have a grasp of what is happening, and what should be happening, right at the workface.

The other part of your personality needs a more strategic vision. It needs to set the resource and process decisions that make up the bulk of an operations manager's role, in a wider and longer-term context. Much of what makes anyone a successful operations manager is how these strategic and operational perspectives are brought together. And this involves two core ideas of operations management.

The first is the input–output model illustrated in Figure 1.1. It is ideal to do this because it is a model that can be used at any level of analysis. Economists use it to measure the productivity of whole industries or even countries by comparing output to input. A business's return on investment calculations are, in effect, an output (return) compared to input (investment) calculation. Similarly, individual operations, departments or single processes need to be measured on what they produce compared to what they consume (in physical or financial terms). It's all about input–output.

The second idea is that of networks. A 'network' is simply a group of two or more sets of resources linked together by their inputs and outputs. Networks are central to operations because all operations are formed of networks. For example, there are the networks of people with their specific units of technology that form processes. There are the networks of discrete work centres or processes that make up whole operations. There are the networks of operations trading a complex mix of their offerings that form supply networks. Networks can describe any type of operations activity at any level of analysis, from strategic to operational. In fact, there is a hierarchy of networks at different levels that any operations manager needs to work with, from the supply networks at the strategic level, through to individual processes at the operational level. This idea is illustrated in Figure 1.3.

At a strategic level of analysis, your supply network can be defined by how things flow between all the operations in the network, including suppliers, suppliers' suppliers, customers, customers' customers, and so on. To understand the supply network of which you are a part, you need to know the capabilities of each operation in the network and the effectiveness of relationships between them. Working down this hierarchy of networks, each operation in the supply network is itself defined by how things flow between each of the processes within the operation. Understanding your operation means knowing the capabilities of each process in the operation and the effectiveness of the relationship between them. Even at the very operational level, each of your processes is defined by how things flow between the individual units of resource – the people and facilities that make up the process. And to fully understand your processes... well, you get the idea. The important point here is that at each level of analysis, you are effectively asking the

Figure 1.3 Two common threads run through all operations analysis from supply networks (strategic) to processes (operational) – the idea of input–output models and the idea of networks

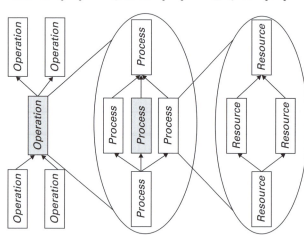

Strategic level of analysis

Supply networks describe how products and services flow between operations

Key questions....

- *What are the capabilities of each operation in the supply network?*
- *What is the effectiveness of relationship between them?*

Operations describe how things products and services flow between processes

Key questions...

- *What are the capabilities of each process in the operation?*
- *What is the effectiveness of the relationship between them?*

Processes describe how things flow between resources (people and technology)

Key questions...

- *What are the capabilities of each resource in the process?*
- *What is the effectiveness of the relationship between them?*

Operational level of analysis

same questions. What are the capabilities of each element of their network, and how effectively are they linked together as networks? The differences are really just a matter of scale and complexity.

One implication of visualizing your supply networks, operations and processes as networks is the emphasis it puts on the relationships between the elements in the network. Do people in each element have a clear line of sight from their part of the network to the end customer? Where are the bottlenecks inhibiting flow? What are the weak elements of the network? And so on. Value is added by the transformation that goes on within *and between* each element in the network. The organizational boundaries between each process are really secondary issues. If you feel that you are always reorganizing the responsibility for tasks between departments, you are not alone. Most businesses regularly move responsibility for tasks between departments. However, the underlying tasks and the processes that perform them change less often.

Operations has the power to plug you into the supply network

The idea that every operation is both formed of, and part of, networks has a further implication. Networks are linkages. They are the 'plumbing' that connects your business to the other players in your supply network. It is your operation that plugs you into your supply network. It can do this because of its unique perspective. Operations can define your relationships with your customers, your suppliers, your regulator (if you have one), and even your competitors. In fact, all the other players in your network. OK, you may say, surely other parts of the business are responsible for these relationships. Marketing and sales strike deals with customers. Procurement contracts with suppliers. Well, yes they may conduct the negotiations and do the deals, but it is operations that provides the channels through which they work. It is the people who run the operational 'mechanics' of how the day-to-day relationships with customers, suppliers, etc work, that define how the relationships actually work.

Remember, also, that in any supply network, the vast majority of the interactions are B2B interactions. Only the final 'retail' stage is B2C. (Even then, customers are generally 'processed' through their 'retail' operations.)

The point is that supply network relationships are essentially operation-to-operation connections – it is one operation interacting with another. This has consequences. It means that if you want to really understand other players in the supply network you have to understand their operations – their resources and their processes. And this realization is having an impact on how businesses think about their relationships. For example, this is how one Sales VP of an industrial chemicals manufacturer put the company's change in its attitude:

> We used to take what you might call the 'traditional sales' route to pitching our products. 'Look,' we would say to customers, 'this is why our products and our service are better than you can get from any other supplier.' And if we really had to match the other guy's price, we would do. Of course we still kind of do that, but now with a new slant. Now we also say, 'We run operations, you also run operations, how can our operations help your operations to work better?' We put our pitch in terms of how our products and services have a positive impact on their operations processes.

This is an approach that will work for any relationship in your supply network – 'How can my operation help your operation to work better?' And if the relationship is going to last and go deeper the benefit can be made mutual: 'How can our operations help each other to work better?' Figure 1.4 illustrates this idea. The logic works something like this:

- What is our customer/supplier/regulator trying to achieve? What are their operations objectives?
- How do their resources and processes give them the capabilities to achieve these objectives?
- How do their resources and processes constrain their ability to achieve their objectives?
- How can our products and services enhance the capabilities and overcome the constraints of their resources and processes?
- What could they do to help us help them?

Of course, the logic will not work like that when 'plugging into' competitors. Yet a similar logic can still be used. What are their objectives? What are the constraints and capabilities of their resources and processes? How can we develop our resources and processes so they exceed their capabilities and overcome any similar constraints? It is still using the operations perspective to get under the skin of another businesses operation.

Figure 1.4 Operations can plug you into your supply network by exploiting the nature of operation-to-operation relationships

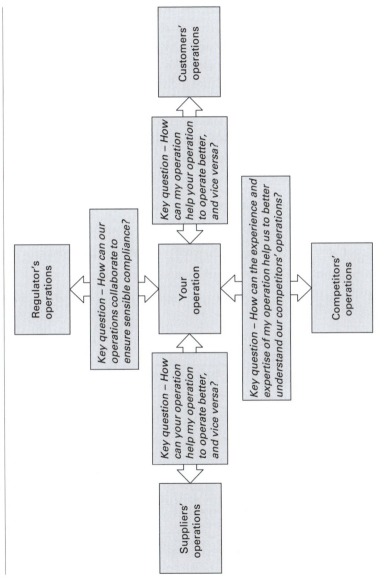

How to exploit the power of operations – the stages to an operations advantage

Running operations is complex; it needs practical guidance to help address the most significant issues that can make a real difference to how operations provides its advantage. That is what Figure 1.5 represents: a series of activities that will make operations work better. (They also represent the individual chapters in this book.) There are 10 of them, not counting this chapter, and they each contribute individually and cumulatively to making operations work. They are not '10 steps' necessarily to be followed sequentially, but the sequence does make logical sense. After establishing that there is a power within your operations function to be exploited.

The first three are the foundations, the prerequisites, to achieving an operations advantage:

1 Establishing an operations capability culture, *that lays the foundation for...*

2 Making your operations a strategic asset, *that helps to...*

3 Set your performance framework, *that sets the objectives for how to...*

   Support your operations advantage, specifically:

4 Resourcing your operation appropriately, *that provides the resources for...*

Figure 1.5 The stages to achieving an operations advantage

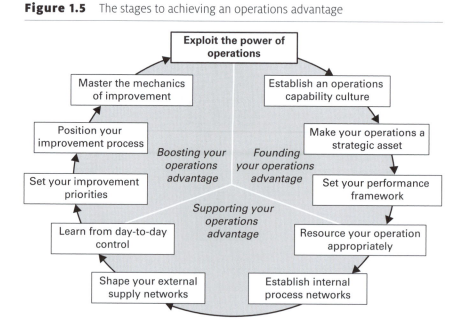

5 Establishing your internal processes networks, *which uses the same network approach as…*

6 Shaping your external supply networks, *that provides the context for…*

7 Learning from day-to-day control, *that supports how you…*

  Boost your operations advantage, specifically:

8 Setting improvement priorities, *that provide the basis for…*

9 Positioning your improvement process, *that will govern how you…*

10 Master the mechanics of improvement, *which supports your efforts to continue to…*

  Exploit the power of operations, and so on.

Now we look at each stage in more detail.

1 Establish an operations capability culture

Managing operations is considered by some to be a largely 'technical' subject that utilizes a logical, rational, sometimes quantitative, and methodological approach to improving performance. Well, it is, and hopefully unashamedly so. But this does not mean that 'softer', behavioural, even emotional issues should be neglected. On the contrary: the cultural context in which operations decisions are made will shape how these decisions are perceived, how they are analysed and what options are eventually adopted. Establishing an effective culture for the operations function is a prerequisite for everything else that operations managers will need to tackle, which is why it is the first topic that we treat in Chapter 2, *Establish an operations capability culture*.

2 Make your operations a strategic asset

For some in business the very idea of an operations strategy is a contradiction in terms. After all, they assume, to be involved in the strategy process is the complete opposite of those day-to-day tasks and activities associated with managing operations. Nothing could be further from the truth. They are confusing 'operations' and 'operational'; they are different words with very different meanings. For many *enduringly* remarkable enterprises, from Amazon to IKEA, and from Apple to Zara – how they manage their operations is central to their long-term strategic success. So a fundamental question should be: 'Does the way we manage our operations have a strategic impact? And if not, how can we make sure that it does?' This is the question that should be close to the starting point for all operations development. We examine operations strategy in Chapter 3, *Make operations a strategic asset*.

3 Set your performance framework

What is 'good' performance for an operation? Should it minimize cost? Should it maximize service and revenue? Should it sweat the operation's assets? Should it protect the business's reputation, its franchise to operate, and the environment? Should it balance short-term imperatives against long-term aspirations? Is it really possible to get all of the above? That's where the problem lies – being good at some aspects of performance often involves sacrificing other things. Yet, over time, some operations do manage to raise their game all round. That is the key issue: how should your operation overcome the trade-offs between the various aspects of performance? Over time they must work on developing the capabilities that encourage mutually reinforcing levels of performance. These are the questions. How do you identify appropriate performance characteristics? How do you measure each aspect of performance? How do you manage the trade-offs between performance objectives? These are all examined in Chapter 4, *Set your performance framework*.

4 Resource your operation appropriately

All operations have the basic responsibility of deciding how big they should be; in other words what capacity they should have. Partly this will depend on how much you do in-house and how much is outsourced. But one thing you can't outsource is uncertainty around demand. Even in relatively stable markets, demand will go up and down, sometimes surprisingly. So, whether as a result of intrinsic uncertainty, or relatively predictable fluctuations, demand will vary, and as demand varies, the operation will have to decide how to resource itself to cope with the variation, in particular how it flexes its capacity (or not). A number of resourcing options are available. One could simply keep capacity level and let the operation's resources absorb demand. Conversely, one could constantly adjust resourcing levels in an attempt to match demand with capacity. It may also be possible to influence demand itself to reduce the need to change capacity. Probably all three of these approaches will be necessary, either together or at different times. But which one? And when? This is what we shall be looking at in Chapter 5, *Resource your operation appropriately*.

5 Establish internal processes networks

Internal processes are the building blocks of any operation. Just as the output from a process is limited by the effectiveness of its worst stage, the success of the whole operation is limited by the performance of its least effective process. Configuring internal processes involves designing each process and integrating individual processes to form an effective internal 'process network'. This is why good process design is necessary. It is also why it is too important to be regarded as a mere technical task to be performed by junior staff. No matter how senior you are, you have a responsibility to get involved in the details of how your processes are shaped. It demonstrates the importance of the activity, it refreshes your understanding of why processes behave as they do, and it is just too important to neglect. We examine the key issues in process design, including the influence of volume and variety, in Chapter 6, *Establish internal processes networks*.

6 Shape your external supply networks

Internally, processes are linked together to form an internal network. Externally, operations link together to form supply networks. Your operation cannot act in isolation. Everything is connected. Every operation is part of a far larger system of linked operations – suppliers, customers, competitors and collaborators. All are connected by agreements, contracts, relationships, mutual understandings – and sometimes, mutual misunderstandings. Some authorities argue that, as economies become more competitive, turbulent, globalized and technology-enabled, supply decisions become especially critical. The performance of an operation will be governed not only by what it does itself, but also by what it buys-in, where it buys it from, and how it develops and runs its critical external connections. Therefore, a key responsibility for any operation is managing these connections to provide the appropriate combination of efficiency, service and flexibility. We deal with how these external connections, and the purchasing activity that plays such an important part in their management, can contribute to the performance of the operation in Chapter 7, *Shape your external supply networks*.

7 Learn from day-to-day control

Controlling operations means monitoring their performance, judging whether their performance is on track, and intervening to change things if necessary. It sounds routine, but that is missing an important point.

Day-to-day control is not as restrictive, or as dull, as it sounds: it can be the engine of improvement. Control implies intervention, and intervention presents the opportunity to observe what happens as a result, and observing these consequences is the basis of learning, and learning is essential for improvement. But control is not always a straightforward activity. All manner of problems can make it a challenging undertaking. How, for example, should operations be controlled when objectives are ambiguous, or knowledge of how the operation works is partial, or when the operation deals in 'one-offs'? These ideas of how the control activity can be the driver of improvement, and how it can cope in a more complex environment are dealt with in Chapter 8, *Learn from day-to-day control*.

8 Set your improvement priorities

Almost all businesses measure performance, but not all businesses use the information to prioritize their performance improvement. Prioritization is the step that links operations performance with operations improvement. Without some form of prioritization there can be no direction to improvement. Time, effort and expense will be wasted in areas where greater return is available elsewhere. The question is, how should priorities be set? Two approaches are commonly used; both are perfectly valid, but when they are brought together they give a powerful guide to where priorities should lie. The first approach is to focus on what customers find important – what customers find important must surely guide what any business finds important. The other approach is to focus attention on those aspects of performance where one's own performance is below that of competitors. Any improvement here will close any competitive gap that is harming your prospects compared with rivals. Again, a perfectly valid argument. Yet bringing these two approaches together provides much more nuanced guidance. This, and advice on how the trade-offs integral to any prioritization are outlined in Chapter 9, *Setting improvement priorities*.

9 Position your improvement process

Improvement comes from closing the gap between what you are and what you want to be. So, unless you are perfectly satisfied with every aspect of your operations (or you are remarkably complacent) you should always be interested in the improvement activity. Performance improvement is the ultimate objective of all operations management; it's also wildly popular: who doesn't want to be better? It has become the subject of numerous ideas that have been put forward as particularly effective methods of ensuring improvement. Starting with total quality management (TQM), we have worked through continuous improvement (CI), 'lean' operations, business process re-engineering (BPR), Six Sigma, Lean Six Sigma, and so on. None of these is a total answer; none is the ultimate panacea – the silver bullet that guarantees perfection – but nor are any of them without at least some merit. Most significantly, they all overlap, to some degree. Positioning your own improvement process means understanding each of these ideas and their constituent elements, and deciding which of these elements is right for your conditions. This is the subject of Chapter 10, *Position your improvement process.*

10 Master the mechanics of improvement

Operations improvement, if nothing else, is a practical business. Sooner or later any operations manager *at any level* who wants to really have an impact on how well improvement is accomplished needs to get involved in the mechanics of how improvement happens at the workface. Positioning one's improvement process is, of course, a necessary first step. The secret of making these various approaches to improvement work lies not just with their particulars, but how we use them in practice. And central to the practice of improvement is the idea of the improvement cycle. Whether the improvements being sought are incremental but continuous, or radical and innovative, there is a cyclical process that can guide how improvement can be realized. The relative emphasis placed on each part of this cycle, and the way each part is interpreted, will need to be adapted, depending on what type of improvement you want, but the underlying principle of the cycle will hold good. Yet despite the often-demonstrated efficacy of improvement cycles, much well-intentioned improvement just does not take hold. Why? It is usually because operations managers have neglected to develop the essential organizational behaviours that provide the environment for improvement to flourish. The steps in the improvement cycle, together with advice on how to develop these appropriate behaviours (and a questionnaire that will identify which behaviours you need to develop) are presented in Chapter 11, *Master the mechanics of improvement.*

What each chapter will give you (and your operation)

Each chapter in this book represents one step in a series of actions that all operations managers can take to improve their operations. Following them will not necessarily guarantee an operations advantage, but it will certainly help. Just as important, ignoring them will seriously damage your chances of achieving it.

Chapter 2 – *Establish an operations capability culture.* An operation that understands the importance of developing a capability culture that takes an 'operations perspective', that moves from a role of implementing to supporting to driving the competitiveness of the business, that can discriminate between different operating conditions, has an external orientation, and can recognize the new agenda for operations.

Chapter 3 – *Make operations a strategic asset.* An operation that has an operations strategy that reflects business strategy (top-down), connects with market requirements (outside-in), learns from its operational experience (bottom-up), and develops its resources and processes to give strategic advantage (inside-out).

Chapter 4 – *Set your performance framework.* An operation that is able to assess its performance at three levels: the 'societal level using the 'triple bottom line' approach, the strategic level by assessing its effect on costs, revenues, return on capital, risk and its ability to develop capabilities. and the operational level by assessing its quality, speed, dependability, flexibility and cost efficiency.

Chapter 5 – *Resource your operation appropriately.* An operation that is capable of deciding how many resources it should have in the short and long terms, both to cope with normal and forecasted variations in demand and as a result of intrinsic uncertainty, and can decide the best way to cope with these fluctuations.

Chapter 6 – *Establish internal processes networks.* An operation that has well-designed and connected processes that are appropriately resourced and configured, and link together to form an internal process network where process managers have a clear understanding of their line of sight forwards to customers and backwards to suppliers.

Chapter 7 – *Shape your external supply networks.* An operation that can decide what it buys in (as opposed to doing it in-house), where it buys it from, and how it develops and runs its critical external connections, and can manage the agreements, contracts, relationships and mutual understandings between operations and others in the supply network.

Chapter 8 – *Learn from day-to-day control*. An operation that can learn from all the ways it monitors and controls all its activities, and can manage the process of building the knowledge and capabilities that can potentially come from the learning.

Chapter 9 – *Setting improvement priorities*. An operation that has a good grasp of what its customers find important, especially in terms of its qualifying factors, order-winning factors and possible 'delights', and can judge its performance against competitors, and can bring them together to prioritize individual aspects of operations performance.

Chapter 10 – *Position your improvement process*. An operation that fully understands the various approaches to operations improvement, and the elements contained in each approach and can relate their view on the positioning of their improvement process to whether they want to adopt an incremental or radical approach and a prescriptive or methodological approach.

Chapter 11 – *Master the mechanics of improvement*. An operation that can use a 'problem-solving' cyclical improvement process, and can identify the organizational behaviours that maximize the chances that improvement will really take hold, and be able to detect which behaviours it needs to develop further.

Principles are generic... solutions are not

One final point before moving on. The basic contention of this book is that, a) the operations function is hugely important to any business, and b) by doing the things outlined in the steps that form the chapters, you will be able to derive competitive advantage from your operations function. So here is a question you should be asking: 'Why should all these steps to an operations advantage apply to my particular operation?' You may say, 'My operation is different.' I know everyone says that, but to some extent it's always true. My particular set of competitors, customers, suppliers, funding constraints, group strategy, organizational culture and shared history, are unique. How can one set of directions be as right for me as they are for operations with a completely different set of circumstances?'

The answer lies in a simple line: *Principles are generic... solutions are not.* Any solution to whatever operations-based concerns you have will indeed depend on your circumstances, but they should be based on a sound understanding of the basic principles that underlie the way operations respond to the way they are managed. A principle is a basic idea or rule that explains or controls how something happens or works.[5] A solution is more specific and relates to a particular set of circumstances. This is not to say that one cannot be prescriptive about the best way to apply and adapt principles, but even when advice is couched in seemingly prescriptive terms, it should be treated as advice on how to employ general principles, not in any way as a route to some kind of dogmatic solution. In fact, summarizing in the form of practical prescriptions is a useful way of making sure that principles remain truly practical, hence the following section. (Each chapter is summarized in the form of some 'practical prescriptions' that are intended to provide applied guidance to how operations can work better.)

Practical prescriptions

- Do not let anyone undermine the potential of operations to give a significant competitive benefit to your business.

- Do not let any other function think that 'operations' is only of concern to the operations function. All functions of the business have an operations element because they all have resources and processes. They all have something to learn from how operations should be managed.

- Have high expectations of your operations function. Expect them to contribute positively and significantly to the current and future performance of the enterprise.

- Regularly perform a critical review of the resources and processes in your operation, assessing their strengths and weaknesses.

- In this review, assess the extent that your resources constrain or enhance how your processes can operate, and how the experience gained from running your processes allows your resources to extend their capabilities.

- Think networks. It allows you to assess your operation's strategic position in terms of the capabilities of all the operations in the network (including yours) and the relationship between them.

- Think networks again. It allows you to assess your operation in terms of the capabilities of its processes and the relationship between them.

- Take an operations perspective on the other 'players' in your supply network. Think about all supply network interactions as operation-to-operation relationships.

- Consider the steps outlined in this chapter (and developed in the rest of this book) and assess how much contribution each activity makes to your (actual or potential) operations advantage.

Notes

1 Lewis Carroll (1871) *Alice Through the Looking Glass*

2 Added value, as used here, is 'the increase in those perceived benefits that satisfy a need or expectation'

3 Slack, N, Brandon-Jones, A, Johnston, R and Betts, A (2015) *Operations and process Management*, 4th edn, Pearson

4 Slack, N, Brandon-Jones, A, Johnston, R and Betts, A (2015) *op cit*

5 *Cambridge English Dictionary*

Establish an operations capability culture

The prevailing culture amongst any business's operations managers matters – a lot. Their fundamental viewpoints, attitudes, behaviours, beliefs, habits and even biases make a massive difference to achieving an operations advantage. Establishing a culture for your operation that fully embraces its potential and capability must be close to the starting point for developing an operations advantage; see Figure 2.1. That is what this chapter is about: developing those aspects of your culture that will lay the foundations for all the subsequent stages and boost their chances of contributing to an operations advantage. It includes how you should view the scope and role of your operations, and how some key characteristics of your operations will make a real difference to the way they should be managed. More broadly, it will examine the emerging challenges faced by operations managers and how their beliefs, knowledge and behaviour should match the role that the operations function plays within your organization.

Culture?

What do we mean by culture in the context of operations? There is certainly no shortage of either academic or popular material that treats the concept of organizational culture, yet no single authoritative definition has emerged. Nevertheless, we all kind of know what we mean by it. Put simply, it is what it feels like to be part of an organization. It is what you assume about how things get done, rather than what is necessarily formally articulated. It is what you know really happens rather than what is supposed to happen. It is your organization's shared values, ideology, pattern of thinking and day-to-day rituals. In the words of one well-known writer on the subject, it is 'the way we do things around here', it is 'the organization's climate'.[1]

Figure 2.1   This chapter looks at how to establish a capability culture

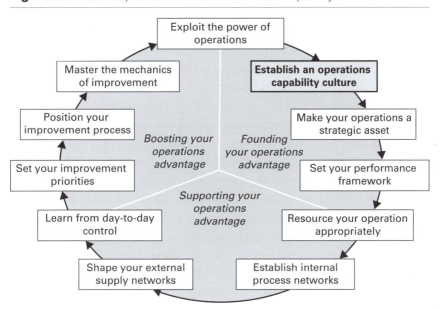

Culture is about style. It is less about what you do than how you do it. It is a notoriously slippery concept to pin down. It responds to myriad signals given out (intentionally or not) by leaders – by reward systems, by reporting responsibilities, and especially by how decisions are made. That is what makes culture such a subtle, elusive, but tantalizing thing. It is also something that is built slowly, but can be destroyed quickly. There is no big knob marked 'culture' on the side of the office, factory, hospital or whatever, that you can turn to give the 'appropriate' culture.

Can the idea of 'organizational' culture apply to a single function like the operations function? Yes, of course it can. If not, there would not be such interest in overcoming those cultural differences between different functions that can, if not managed, lead to what some academics call 'cultural fragmentation'. While there may well be elements of an organization's culture that are shared across all parts of the enterprise, different functions are very likely to have their own subcultures. The question here is what culture holds the best chance of the operations function, specifically, contributing its full potential. This is what we call the *capability culture*.

What is a capability culture for your operations?

The clue is in the name – capability – the ability to deliver the desired result. Essentially the idea of a capability culture is fairly straightforward. It simply means that everything that the operations function does is geared towards building the capabilities that will encourage the business as a whole to reach a sustainable competitive advantage. It means that the operations function can bring something exceptional and distinctive to the business; exceptional in the sense that its performance is outstanding when compared with competitors or similar operations, and distinctive in that it is willing to be original and innovative in how it achieves this performance.

A capability culture for operations values both excellence and originality. Partly this means building your resources (technology and people) so that they have appropriate competences (skills in the case of its people, features or attributes in the case of its technology). But it also depends on your integration of these skills and features with knowledge, attitudes, broad understandings and organizational structures that allow your operations function to respond to changing circumstances. More than this, a capability culture means that every activity of your operations function is treated as an opportunity to learn, enhance operating knowledge and therefore improve its performance. It means that your operations are always intent on synthesizing new knowledge from day-to-day experience.

What does a capability culture involve?

First, you will need to address attitudinal factors. Particularly important is how everyone in your operations function see themselves, and how they articulate their role and their contribution to the business. More than this, if you want to form a foundation for developing such a culture, there are additional basic elements that you will have to master. You should:

- Be able to articulate the operations perspective (particularly the importance of the way resources and processes are developed) to others in the business.
- Understand how the beliefs, knowledge and behaviour of your operations managers need to develop as their role becomes more central to the business by moving from implementing to supporting to driving the strategy of the business.
- Be able to clarify and distinguish between the needs of the various products and services produced by your operation's processes.
- Take an external orientation to getting inspiration for new ways of working in your operation.
- Understand how the 'operations agenda' may change and the resulting consequences for managing the operation's resources and processes.

These are the points that form the rest of this chapter.

CASE STUDY Capability culture at W L Gore[2]

Bill Gore worked at chemicals giant DuPont, but he was frustrated. He had come to believe that the company's corporate culture was stifling innovation, especially in the exploitation of PTFE (polytetrafluoroethylene). So, at age 45 and having obtained a licence for the technology, he and his wife Vieve started the business in their garage in Delaware. Now W L Gore has become a global business with facilities in locations around the world manufacturing and selling a range of innovative products, virtually all of which are based on just one material (expanded polytetrafluoroethylene). It also has become famous for how its culture supports and encourages the company's innovation-based strategy.

On almost every level Gore is different to other global companies. It has what it calls a team-based, flat lattice organization that fosters personal initiative. There are, says Gore, no traditional organizational charts, no chains of command, and no predetermined channels of communication. Instead, team members communicate directly with each other and are accountable to the other members of their team. Groups are led by whoever is the most appropriate person at each stage of a project. Associates (not employees) are hired for general work areas. With the guidance of their sponsors (not bosses), associates commit to projects that match their skills. The company's stated aim is to provide an environment that combines freedom with cooperation and autonomy with synergy.

Project teams are small, focused, multi-disciplined, and foster strong relationships between team members. Personal initiative is encouraged, as is 'hands-on' innovation, which involves those closest to a project in its decision making.

Leaders may be appointed, but are defined by 'followership'. More often, leaders emerge naturally by demonstrating special knowledge, skill or experience that advances a business objective. Even the Group's CEO (one of the few people with a title), Terri Kelly, 'emerged' in this way. No shortlist of preferred candidates was interviewed; instead, along with board discussions, a wide range of associates were invited to nominate people they would be willing to follow. 'We weren't given a list of names – we were free to choose anyone in the company,' she says. 'To my surprise, it was me.'

Associates adhere to four basic guiding principles, originally articulated by Bill Gore:

1 Fairness to each other and everyone with whom we come in contact.

2 Freedom to encourage, help, and allow other associates to grow in their knowledge, skill, and scope of responsibility.

3 The ability to make one's own commitments and keep them.

4 Consultation with other associates before undertaking actions that could impact the reputation of the company.

Gore culture is also reflected in its evaluation and reward procedures, which are egalitarian yet performance-driven. There is no 'boss' to decide what you should be paid. Everyone is your boss. And everyone is rated by those they work with. After all, these are the people who know what they've done and how they've interacted with colleagues; compensation is based on this rating. There are no detailed measures: people are simply asked to say who's making the biggest contribution. Similarly, the company's approach to economies of scale reflects its culture. Bill Gore believed in the need 'to divide so that you can multiply'. So when units grow to around 200 people, they are usually split up, with these small facilities organized in clusters or campuses. Ideally a dozen or so sites are close enough to permit good communication and knowledge exchange, but can still be intimate yet separate enough to promote a feeling of ownership.

'Operations' is a state of mind

Asked to talk about their business, Marketing people are likely to explain how different segments of the market are served. An HR professional will talk about organizational structures and skills. An IT person may attempt to clarify how information systems talk to each other (or not). The way each of us sees our organization reflects the nature of our specific responsibilities. We can describe organizations in terms of their organization chart that shows how resources are allocated and where lines of responsibility lie. We could also describe an organization in terms of where knowledge and information resides or how the political system works, with both formal and informal groupings exercising decision-making influence. In operations we think in terms of the added value we create between the inputs and outputs of our processes. Which is why we used the input–output model (Figure 1.1) in the previous chapter.

One problem with using such a general model of operations is that it doesn't exclude anything; it applies to any business, any function and any process. At different levels of analysis everything is an input–output system. But that is also the strength of the model: it establishes the idea that 'operations' is a way of looking at all human undertakings. It underlines the idea that 'operations' is as much a state of mind as anything else. For sure it is not the only way of looking at human undertakings, and like those Marketing, HR and IT professionals, we commonly take other perspectives. Each of these perspectives has its uses. None is 'right' as such. No single perspective (including the operations perspective) is necessarily 'better' than another and no single perspective on organizations will ever tell the whole story. However, taken together, these different perspectives allow us to understand the full richness of the reality of how organizations work in practice.

Here, of course, we are focusing on one perspective – the operations perspective – and its contribution to a capability culture. It may not be the only way of looking at organizations, but it is an important one, and one that is widely misunderstood. It is a perspective with enormous utility. More important, without an operations perspective that embraces a rich understanding of the resources and processes that go to make up an operation, any culture change will be severely inhibited. How can you change things if you don't understand the mechanics of how they work? The trick is to focus on the nature and role of your resources and processes – the 'operations perspective' – while accepting that this is but one of many ways of looking at your business. It is a prerequisite for establishing an operations advantage.

A capability culture moves you from implementing to supporting to driving

An essential part of achieving a capability culture is how you see your role. Ideally, all operations managers should be confident of their ability to enhance the contribution they make to their enterprise. However, regrettably, many see their role as simply maintaining a 'business as usual' steady state. A capability culture means moving beyond a state where operations contributes relatively little to the success of the business (other than not exerting a negative influence) to a position where you are directly responsible for a large part of its success. This means that you should be able to, progressively, 'implement', then 'support' and then 'drive' strategic improvement. See Figure 2.2.[3]

Implementing strategic improvement

The most basic role of operations is to implement strategic improvement. It is the skill that moves the operation from simply 'keeping the show on the road' and trying to avoid having a negative impact on the business, towards

Figure 2.2 A capability culture should move operations from implementation, through supporting, to driving performance

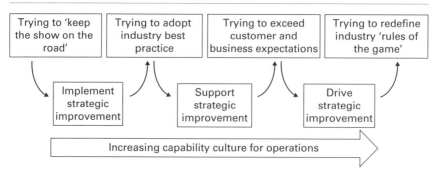

being able to match the best examples of operations performance and practice in the industry. Implementation is a basic skill for all operations. After all, you cannot touch a strategy, you cannot even see it; all you can see is how the resources and processes behave in practice. Without it no improvement is possible. Without effective implementation even your most original and brilliant strategy will be rendered ineffective.

Supporting strategic improvement

Supporting strategic improvement goes way beyond simple implementation. This does not mean that implementation becomes any less important; the skills that define these roles are cumulative; they build on each other, as well as being sequential. The supporting role means developing the capabilities that allow the organization to improve and refine its strategic goals. It means you are competent at linking everything within the operation to achieving your strategic objectives – both external customer objectives and internal business objectives. So, for example, if you want to be the first in the market with product or service innovations, your resources and processes must be developed to be capable of coping with constant innovation. You must develop processes flexible enough to handle novel tasks, organize your staff to understand new technologies or ways of working, develop responsive relationships with your suppliers, and so on.

Driving strategic improvement

The most difficult but most rewarding role of operations is to act as a leader of change, driving strategic improvement by giving the organization a unique and long-term operation advantage. To achieve this, your operations must have a firm sense of the long term. If you are at this stage, you should be forecasting, or at least speculating on, likely changes in markets, competitors and suppliers. Using this, you should be developing the operations-based capabilities that will be required to compete under future conditions. (We call this the 'new operations agenda', and will discuss it later.) Your operations at this stage will be innovative, creative and proactive. They will drive strategic improvement by deploying their unique operations capabilities to be one step ahead of the market. Again, it is worth stressing that adopting a driving role in no way implies that implementation and support are less important, and it certainly does not mean that senior operations managers should abandon their concern for the more operational aspects of their role.

Moving to a capability culture is a cumulative process

Don't think that you can jump straight to this final 'driving' stage. In the example, 'Walk before you can run', a COO failed to understand that moving towards a capability culture for operations is a cumulative process. In operations, there is a natural inertia to resources and processes. They can be organizationally 'heavy'. This does not mean that can't be moved, but failing to recognize the existence of this inertia, failing to learn to walk before you try to run, is counterproductive.

CASE STUDY Walk before you can run

The new COO had been appointed with one aim in mind. The people at Group had made it clear: '*Your new division is important and has been broadly successful, yet we believe that it has become complacent. Moreover, it acts as if it were an independent entity. It is not. It needs to realize that it is a part of something bigger and become more of a corporate player. We believe it has the potential to reach even higher levels of performance, and you are the person to take it there.*'

In line with his brief, the new COO set about making the changes he thought necessary. The Executive Committee for the division was slimmed down, and instead of including all departmental heads, was reduced to what the COO called 'a high-powered group of like-minded people who accept the need for change'. In fact, most departmental heads had been prepared for some degree of change (some more than others, admittedly) and initially were looking forward to more energy from the top. He also tightened up performance and appraisal systems and introduced what he called 'super-stretch targets' that required an increasing number of commercially viable innovations each quarter.

What he did not do was try to understand what the various parts of the business actually did; what expertise they relied on, what processes they followed, and what knowledge they valued. One of the departmental heads commented: *'He thought it was all about structure, systems and targets. He didn't take the time to get to know what we did or how we did it. He said that to him "leadership" was all about having "clarity of vision" and "putting the systems in place to achieve that vision". Well, that's OK as long as it fits with what we have to do to serve our customers. These basic things were ignored.'*

Some things did improve in the short term, at least on paper. The number of commercially viable innovations did increase, but only slowly, and the real impact of the innovations was limited. As one departmental head put it: *'He measured outputs without understanding the inputs, he just never got to grips with what was really happening in the engine room of the business.'* Others were more understanding: *'Look, he wanted to make an impact quickly, the problem was that he confused seriousness with urgency; he wanted us to run before we could walk.'*

Believe, know and behave

It's always going to be difficult trying to pin down exactly what it is about a particular culture that explains its power to create exceptional operations. A strong, pervasive culture shapes everything that happens in the business, but it often does it by stealth. It isn't a matter of taking a 'culture template' and simply filling in the boxes. It's far subtler than that, and it's difficult to articulate precisely. As was said of one organization with a particularly strong culture (a university as it happens); 'From the outside looking in, you can't understand it. From the inside looking out, you can't explain it.'[4] But what about a capability culture for operations? It is best summed up by what the operations team *believe*, what they *know* and how they *behave*. It is these three elements of operations culture, belief, knowledge and behaviour, which provide the foundations for how it contributes to the business and how capable it is to improve over time.

1 What operations should believe

Using the word 'belief' is something of a double-edged sword. In one sense it means 'an acceptance that something exists or is true, especially without proof'. Here we certainly don't invest the word with any quasi-religious 'faith without proof' sense: there is ample proof that operations can have a positive impact on businesses. But, by 'operations belief', we do mean that the people within your operations function should hold firmly to, and have confidence in, their ability to be a force for good in the business. One could summarize this 'core belief' as having total confidence in the idea that operations can have a transformational impact. But there are progressive degrees of holding such a belief, and the nature of how operations interprets this core belief will get progressively more developed as the role moves from implementation, through supporting, to leading strategic improvement:

- To succeed at the *implementation* role – your operations should believe that, because they can seriously impede successful improvement, they have a responsibility to avoid the glitches that undermine smooth execution. They need to hold to the idea that professionalism and reliability are the key to making an effective contribution.

- To succeed at the *supporting* role – your operations should believe that they have a responsibility to interact with and fully understand all other functions' strategies and their implications for operations. Similarly, they have a responsibility to explore, translate and interpret the implications of their strategies for other parts of the business.

- To succeed at the *driving* role – your operations should believe that they can develop capabilities within their operations resources and processes that offer a unique and long-lasting strategic advantage. Moreover, they can develop capabilities that are difficult for others to copy because they are based on the knowledge gleaned from their experience.

2 What operations should know

What should the operations team know? The tempting answer is 'everything', or at least 'everything about operations'. Sorry! No one does, or ever will. However, it is a central assumption (and belief) of this book that the more you understand about how operations can be managed, the better your management of operations can be. One could summarize what the operations function needs to know as the underlying principles that govern how resources and processes work Only with a thorough understanding of the objectives, concepts, tools, and techniques of operations management will your operations function ever contribute fully to the success of the business. The real question is: what knowledge do you need to master? This will depend, to some extent, on your industry and market positioning. But also, again, different types of knowledge will be prioritized as the role of operations moves from implementation, through supporting, to leading strategic improvement:

- To succeed at the *implementation* role – your operations should know at least the basic project management skills that will allow it to introduce change, on specification, on time and on budget. Also, because implementation is likely to be more successful when conditions are predictable and stable, issues such as risk and reliability management, and the foundations of quality management will help to preserve your operating stability.

- To succeed at the *supporting* role – in addition to an appreciation of how the underlying principles of operations management work, the operations team should know how to translate strategic objectives into specific operations work streams. This will almost certainly require careful coordination between different functions and processes within functions. So an understanding of how internal customer networks should operate will be vital.

- To succeed at the *driving* role – your operations must actively be building new capabilities, partly by learning from your own operations experience; partly by being inspired by what knowledge other operations are accumulating. You should therefore be able to connect your regular control procedures to capture the learning from each control intervention. Also, you must establish mechanisms to accumulate this learning and turn it into the kind of process knowledge that builds into strategically important capabilities. (We deal with this extensively in Chapter 8.) In addition, you will need to be able to manage the whole innovation process and integrate it into the efforts being made on operations improvement.

3 How operations should behave

Knowledge is one thing; action is quite another. The most knowledgeable managers in the world will be totally useless unless they take appropriate action based on their knowledge. This is true, of course, for all managers: the way operations managers should behave is not fundamentally different from any effective manager. The popular and academic literature has for decades been full of 'key behaviours' for effective leadership, and they don't seem to have changed much for years. 'Don't micromanage your team, empower them while still being available for advice.' 'Be a coach to your team.' 'Be clear and results-oriented, but help the team to see how they can achieve them.' 'Have a clear vision and strategy.' 'Always communicate; both ways – and listen to your team.' 'Support open discussion and listen to the team's concerns.' All of these are what one commentator called 'forehead-slappingly obvious'. Yet all are undeniably good managerial sense. Perhaps a more important question is, which of these points are the more important, and under what circumstances?

CASE STUDY Google's plan to build a better boss[5]

When Google (which knows something about data mining) began analysing performance reviews, feedback surveys and information on its top-manager awards, it correlated phrases, words, praise and complaints to find out what its employees really valued in their managers. It found that what employees valued most were steady, consistent managers, who made time for one-to-one meetings, who helped team members solve problems by asking questions, rather than dictating answers, and who took an interest in their lives and careers.[6] Certainly the idea of consistent behaviour, as opposed to flopping about changing priorities every week or following the last thing somebody talked to you about, is a point that experienced operations managers will recognize. Even when circumstances do dictate a change in priorities or direction, it is best done within a coherent set of long-term objectives or 'overarching framework'. In fact, that is a reasonable summary of the core guide to what should govern appropriate operations management behaviour – consistency, within a coherent set of objectives or overarching framework.

Again though, different types of behaviour may be appropriate as the role of operations moves from implementation, through supporting, to leading strategic improvement:

- To succeed at the *implementation* role – your operations managers are likely to be focused on keeping to plan, and when necessary modifying plans to reflect changed circumstances. This will necessitate constant monitoring of progress (or the lack of it) and continual updating of all involved, so avoiding potential misunderstandings.

- To succeed at the *supporting* role – your operations managers, once again, must engage with other functions to debate, explore and investigate the implications of operations improvements on their plans. But, because this role will almost certainly mean establishing operations skills, it is also important to follow up on the way new ideas, techniques and operating practice are used.

- To succeed at the *driving* role – your operations managers will need to take on an increasingly educational role. New operations capabilities will need explaining in a strategic context. By this stage, far more than before, you will have moved on from simply representing the interests of the operations function and be at least an equal partner in overall strategy formulation and execution.

Table 2.1 summarizes the beliefs, knowledge and behaviours of a competence culture as operations moves from an implementation role, through supporting, to a leading role.

Table 2.1   What operations should believe, what it should know and how it should behave as it develops an increasing competence culture

	If operations is able to successfully implement strategic improvement	If operations is able to successfully support strategic improvement	If operations is able to successfully lead strategic improvement
What the operations function needs to believe: *That operations can have a transformational impact on the business*	• Professionalism is a key quality. • Colleagues can depend on you to keep your undertakings. • The unexpected is the enemy of smooth implementation. • Keeping your promises is the way to contribute.	• We have a responsibility to fully understand all other functions' strategies and their implications for operations. • Similarly, we have a responsibility to explore the implications of our strategies on theirs. • Interact, integrate, implications and interpret.	• We can develop capabilities within our operations resources and processes that offer a unique and long-lasting strategic advantage. • We can develop capabilities that are difficult for others to copy because they are based on how we have learnt from our experiences.

(Continued)

Table 2.1 (*Continued*)

	If operations is able to successfully implement strategic improvement	If operations is able to successfully support strategic improvement	If operations is able to successfully lead strategic improvement
What the operations function needs to know: *The underlying principles that govern how resources and processes work*	• Basic project management skills. • Risk, reliability and quality management.	• The underlying principles that govern process performance. • How to translate strategic objectives into operations actions. • How internal customer networks should operate.	• How capabilities develop by learning from operations experience. • How operations can manage innovation.
How the operations function needs to behave: *Consistently, within a coherent set of objectives*	• Constantly monitoring progress. • Constantly communicating so as to avoid misunderstandings.	• Establishing operations skills and following up on the way they are used in practice. • Debating, exploring and interacting with other functions.	• As the coach/ tutor helping other functions to deliver their services.

A capability culture does not make 'one size fit all' – the four Vs

A capability culture means understanding differences. Should all your operations, or parts of your operation, be managed in the same way? No, of course not. Operations differ, but not in the way you may think. Obviously different operations serve different markets and use different technologies. But these obvious differences are a distraction. What really matters is that different operations have different 'operating conditions', and four of these in particular have a major influence on how your operations should be managed, and therefore the underlying culture of the operations function. They all begin with V, which is convenient:

1 The *volume* of products and services you produce. If you manage high-volume operations, you will have a high degree of repeatability that low-volume operations don't. You are likely to value the systemization of activities, have a relatively high degree of task specialization, and use specialist technologies dedicated to a relatively narrow range of activities. A key driver will be your operation's efficiency and cost performance. Yes, I know, they always are key drivers, but particularly so if your operations are high volume. That's *why* they are high volume.

2 The *variety* of products and services you produce. If you manage high-variety operations, you will have to manage a wide range of different activities, changing frequently between activities and employing a wide range of skills, with 'general purpose' technology. You are likely to value flexibility, particularly the flexibility that enables customization and a wide range of products or services. Variety control should be important to you, as well as policing the boundary of what you are willing to do for your customers. High-variety operations are invariably more complex and costly than low-variety ones. Cost control has to be balanced with flexibility.

3 The *variation* in demand for your products and services. If you have high demand variation, the volume you need to produce is variable and/or unpredictable. This means that resourcing levels have to be underutilized or constantly adjusted. Sometimes you will need to provide a 'capacity cushion' that can absorb unexpected demand. Either way, this usually means relatively high costs. Conversely, low variation means you have predictably constant demand, which is generally easier to manage. Your resources can be geared to match demand and activities can be planned in advance, resulting in relatively low costs.

4 The degree to which the your operation's value-adding activities are *visible* to customers. Visibility indicates how much of your resources and processes are 'experienced' directly by customers; how much they are 'exposed' to customers' scrutiny. If you have low visibility, you can be more 'factory-like'. You can create your products and services when it is

convenient for you (rather than having to respond to customer requests immediately). You may want to use this time buffer to achieve high utilization in your resources. By contrast, if you have high-visibility operations, the creation and consumption of your offerings will be more or less simultaneous. Not only does this make high capacity utilization difficult, it also requires your staff to have customer contact skills that manage customers' expectations and shape their perception of performance. All of this means that high-visibility operations tend to have higher costs than low-visibility ones.

If you look at these four 'operating conditions', you may notice the odd one out – volume. The type of attributes associated with high variety, variation and visibility are all fairly similar. If your operation is like this, you will probably value traits such as flexibility (because you are required to do many different things or operate at many different levels), and responsiveness (because you are more exposed to customer demands). By contrast, if you have low variety, variation and visibility, you will probably put more significance on such attributes as control, conformance and systemization (because you are able to exploit these things to increase efficiency). However, volume is different. It works the other way round. It is high volume that requires conformance and control to boost efficiency and low volume that allows for greater flexibility and complexity. Figure 2.3 illustrates this idea.

Different characteristics, different cultures

The four operating conditions go a long way to explain not just why different operations need to be managed differently but also how their prevailing

Figure 2.3 Volume, variety, variation and visibility operating characteristics determine the extent to which operations have an agile or efficiency culture

	Agility culture	Efficiency culture	
Low volume ←	Flexible	Controlled	→ High volume
	Complex	Conformance	
High variety ←	Diverse	Formality	→ Low variety
	Accommodating	Systematic	
High variation ←	Responsive	Ordered	→ Low variation
	Adaptable	Constant	
High visibility ←	Exposed	Buffered	→ Low visibility
	'Front-office'	'Back-office'	

culture will be shaped. The closer you operate towards the left of Figure 2.3 – low volume, with high variety, variation and visibility – the more you will need an agility culture that emphasizes 'front-office' style attitudes (even if your operation is not strictly 'front-office') of flexibility, responsiveness and customer-facing skills. If you operate more towards the right of the scales – with high volume and low variety, variation and visibility – you are probably partially protected from having to respond in real time to immediate customer requests. You are likely to be better off developing an efficiency culture that emphasizes those more 'back-office' type attributes of conformance, control and systematization that are possible with a more buffered operation.

CASE STUDY The four Vs in a legal operation

One medium-sized law firm in the UK reorganized its operations based on the four Vs with separate teams (and processes) for each of its service offerings. Listen to the Managing Partner: *'Establishing separate processes for each type of service has allowed us to discriminate between what each team should be aiming for, and how they need to improve. For example, look at the contrast between how we manage our Family Law and Litigation practices. In the Family Law team we help people through the trauma of divorce, separation and break-up. All clients are different, and everyone has to be treated as an individual, but we have devised a high-level procedure that still allows plenty of latitude to customize our advice while making sure that we haven't forgotten anything. Of course, some relatively routine work is less interesting but we try to make sure that everyone has a mix of work so they can develop their professional skills. This team has adopted an open-plan office arrangement centred on our specialist library of family case law.*

'By contrast, the Litigation team handles the bulk collections of debt by working closely with the accounts departments of client companies. It has developed a semi-automatic approach to debt collection. Staff input data received from their clients into the system; from that point everything progresses through a predefined process, letters are produced, queries responded to and eventually debts collected, ultimately through court proceedings if necessary. The details of each case are sent over by the client; our people input the data onto our screens and set up a standard diary system for sending letters out. We know exactly what is required for court dealings

and have a pretty good process to make sure all the right documentation is
available on the day.'

This firm has discovered that the challenges of designing processes that
are appropriate for each of these two extreme services are very different.
'Litigation' services are high-volume, low-variety, with relatively low variability
and visibility. Here economies of scale are exploited, activities can be
systematized and may lend themselves to automation, all of which can be
exploited to reduce transaction costs. By contrast, 'Family Law' services are low-
volume, high-variety, with medium variation and high (and delicate) contact with
clients; high visibility in other words. This type of process cannot attain very low
transaction costs. However, they do require enough inbuilt flexibility to cope with
the wide variety of activities expected of them. Figure 2.4 summarizes the relative
characteristics of the two processes.

The law firm example shows that the impact of the four Vs is the same
on individual processes as it is on whole operations. Within your operation, you could have a range of different types of processes. Neither whole
operations nor their constituent processes are all the same and (again,
this is the important bit) should not all be managed in the same way.
An operations advantage is as much about the art of discrimination, of
distinguishing between different types of process and their needs, as it
is about manipulating the details of how you design and run them. The
key issue here is not just that your operations and processes will differ,
that's fairly obvious. It is that one should not use the same approach to
managing operations and processes that have wildly different objectives
and characteristics.

Figure 2.4   The relative volume, variety, variation and visibility operating
characteristics of 'Family Law' and 'Litigation' for the law firm

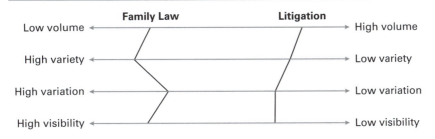

A capability culture has an external orientation – get out more!

If you manage operations, it is easy to become focused almost exclusively on internal issues. After all, that is what you are dealing with most of your time. Yet a capability culture requires not only in-depth understanding of your own resources and processes, but also the ability to set them in a wider context. An obvious way to do this, as well as tapping into a source of stimulation and inspiration, is by visiting other operations. Put another way: we all need to get out more. All operations managers can gain some kind of benefit from seeing other operations directly, but relatively few of us actively seek opportunities to do so. Although it is often derided as 'industrial tourism', visiting other operations can be a potent way of providing operations with fresh and challenging ideas. You need not make them formal benchmarking exercises (which we will discuss in Chapter 9) but such visits can spark alternative ways of looking at how your operations can be organized. However, if the potential of such visits is to be realized, there are a number of guidelines you should follow:[7]

- Make sure that your objectives are clear. If you don't know why you are visiting, you won't know what to focus on.

- Have an 'organizing framework' with specific questions that can structure your observations and accelerate learning.

- Make sure that whoever visits the operation has sufficient experience to make meaningful comparisons with similar operations. Do not let seniority outweigh experience.

- Focus on practices rather than on numbers. A visit is the opportunity to see how things actually get done. Quantifications and diagrams charts can be useful but are no substitute for seeing things happen in practice.

- Keep an open mind. The learning that occurs during a visit can be unexpected. You may go to see one process or aspect of the operation, yet end up being inspired by something completely different.

- Do not limit your observations either to your own areas of expertise (or on those things that the host operation is the proudest of).

- Do not be immediately judgemental. What can seem strange or ineffective may become more understandable, and useful, when put in a broader context.

- Avoid the temptation to visit only operations that are similar to yours. All types of operation share some of the same problems and they may have adopted methods of solving those problems that you can adapt to your own circumstances.

In fact, you can take this last point even further. Every day we walk through, experience, ride on, use and buy from a whole range of different types of operation. How often, one wonders, do we ask ourselves how these everyday services manage their quality, develop their people, cope with fluctuations in demand, struggle to understand their markets, measure their performance, and generally face the same issues that are common to all businesses? Whatever challenges you face in your operations, someone will have the same ones – but worse. Seek them out and learn, if only from their mistakes. The task is to go into any business and come out with at least one new idea that is worth considering for your own operation. In fact, it is not that difficult. The real difficulty is failing to find any useful new ideas.

A capability culture recognizes the new agenda for operations

It is something of a cliché, 'the world is getting increasingly competitive', but certainly in the operations field there has been a lot happening. Some of it is in direct response to 'demand-side' issues. In many industries there is increased cost-based competition while simultaneously customers' expectations of quality and variety have increased. Few businesses outside pure commodities can still focus exclusively on providing standardized offerings to meet what are assumed to be customers' needs. Increasingly globalized markets mean more demand for higher variety or totally customized offerings. Rapidly developing technologies are leading to more frequent updating of our offerings. Customers have increased ethical and environmental sensitivity, and the regulatory and legislative environment is not getting any lighter.

As well as these 'demand-side' developments there is a whole set of 'supply-side' innovations. The most obvious is the impact of new process technologies, most of them digital. The dramatic effect of these technologies is radically altering the operating practices of almost every industry. They are changing the way operations create their products and services, serve their customers, relate to stakeholders and involve their workforce. According to one study on the impact of digital, 'every business is, or soon will be, a digital business'.[8] Just as important, globalized supply markets are opening new options in how operations source input goods and services; there must be few operations that have not at least considered purchasing from further afield. But while bringing opportunities for cost savings, a bigger supply market also brings new problems of long supply chains, supply vulnerability and reputational risk.

If you are to ride these demand- and supply-side pressures, you will need to develop responses to them in the form of a 'new agenda' for operations. Parts of this agenda will be approaches and practices that have always existed but that you have adapted to fit new circumstances. For example, supplier selection has always been a part of operations management, but now, in addition to cost, quality and delivery performance, we also need to focus on assessing suppliers' underlying capabilities, consider supply vulnerabilities, and so on. In the same way, our process improvement has always tried to eliminate wasted effort, but now we need to be far more ruthless in eliminating waste in all its forms.

Some elements of the new operations agenda require a more fundamental response from us; for example, the increased possibility of automating our routine 'vanilla' processes, harnessing algorithmic decision making, exploring how best to manage the interface between human workers and new technologies, beefing up cyber-security protection, and so on. Other responses may need us to be more conceptual; for example, operational practice being linked to strategic objectives through formally structured 'operating models', employing servitization ideas to integrate our service and product offerings, mass customization to overcome the cost–variety trade-off, the use of 'supply ecosystem' concepts, and so on.

Keep practice and possibility within sight of each other

Perhaps most importantly, this new agenda means that, as an operations manager, you can no longer simply wait and react to developments as they become obvious. Rather, you must take a far more proactive role in keeping practice and possibility within sight of each other. Certainly you must be aware of what ideas are emerging in the worlds of technology, consultancy, even academia. Scanning these worlds for potential insights is a prerequisite for widely informed improvement. Definitely you should be able to assess the potential of new ideas. In particular, you should be able to work with the germ of an idea to adapt and modify it until it makes sense in the context of your own operations. Try using a template something like that in Table 2.2 to think through what might develop to form the new agenda for your operation. The categories can be whatever is appropriate for you of course; don't necessarily use the ones in the table. But do follow the implied logic, which is:

1 Think critically about the limitations or constraints implied by the current state of things.

2 Speculate on future possibilities, how things might develop in the future.

3 (Most importantly) consider the implications of possible futures for how you will need to manage your operations.

Table 2.2 Considering the implications for you of the new operations agenda

What could be on the operations agenda for the future in...	Current constraints	Future possibilities	Implications
Market demands, for example: • *Competition/ consolidation* • *Emerging products/ services* • *Demand variability* • *Customization* • *Pricing* • *Ethical sensitivity*			
Distribution, for example: • *Geography* • *Service levels* • *Channels* • *Network structure*			
Technology, for example: • *Features/attributes* • *Economies of scale* • *Integration* • *Flexibility* • *Capital requirements* • *Security/risks*			
People, for example: • *Skills availability* • *Integration with technology* • *Organization structure* • *Flexibility* • *Location*			

(Continued)

Table 2.2 (*Continued*)

What could be on the operations agenda for the future in...	Current constraints	Future possibilities	Implications
Supply base, for example: • *Number of suppliers* • *Emergence of new suppliers* • *Capabilities of suppliers* • *Location of suppliers* • *Integration with suppliers*			

A final word about the capability culture for operations

You don't change the culture of any function, and certainly not of the whole business, by simply saying that it must change. It's a subtle and difficult task that demands a coordinated and coherent effort. There is plenty of advice on culture change out there, often stressing the importance of leadership, vision, mission and so on, which, of course, is important. It is clearly more difficult to establish any culture change without the active support and involvement of the organization's leadership. But it is a mistake to think about (or even worse, act on) operations culture independently of the activities, tasks and decisions that all operations managers engage with. In the complex, often uncertain, and detailed world of operations, culture and 'routine' decision making are intertwined. Certainly a capability culture, as we mean it, is not predominantly a top-down affair. It starts with, and is actually based on, how things are done at the operational level of the business. It derives from what is learnt from the everyday business of running the operations' resources and processes. It is just as much 'bottom-up' as it is 'top-down'. That is why all the activities of operations management (and therefore all the topics in this book) have their role to play in establishing a capability culture: all these activities are part of how the business can, and should, learn.

Practical prescriptions

- Do not dismiss the importance of the culture of the operations function. It governs how effectively all the steps to achieving an operations advantage can be pursued.

- Critically assess the culture of your operations function. Does it support and develop the capability to bring something exceptional and distinctive to the business?

- Always take an 'operations perspective' that focuses on a rich understanding of the resources and processes of the business, while also understanding that it is one (albeit important) perspective of many.

- Aim to develop a culture that encourages confidence of the operations team's ability to continually enhance their contribution to their enterprise – the competence culture.

- Consider the culture of your operations in terms of their beliefs, their knowledge and their behaviour.

- Use Table 2.1 to judge where you are in the progression of operations contribution, from implementation, through support, to leading.

- Do not treat all operations and processes in the same way. Distinguish between them in terms of their volume, variety, variation and visibility. Manage them accordingly.

- Be aware of how supply-side and demand-side changes will require you to adapt your operations and processes.

- Get out more. Take inspiration (and ideas, but be careful) from other operations, even ones outside your industry. If you stay open-minded, it's difficult not to find useful new ideas.

- Recognize that markets, technologies, key skills, the supply base and the environment in which you operate are changing. Don't wait until these changes are upon you before considering their implications and how you should respond to them.

Notes

1 Schein, E M (1999) *The Corporate Culture Survival Guide – Sense and nonsense about culture change*, Jossey-Bass, San Francisco, CA

2 Sources include: company website; Roberts, D (2015) At W L Gore, 57 years of authentic culture, *Fortune,* 15 March; *The Sunday Times* Best companies to work for (2009) W L Gore & Associates (UK)

3 There are several versions of this type of 'progression' scale. This one owes a lot to Hayes, R and Wheelwright, S C (1990) *Restoring Our Competitive Edge,* Harvard University Press, Cambridge, MA

4 Spence, R M with Haley, R (2009) *It's Not What You Sell, It's What You Stand for,* Portfolio Hardcover, London

5 Google's 8-point plan to build a better boss, retrieved June 2015, https://www.google.co.uk/about/careers/lifeatgoogle/build-a-better-boss.html

6 Bryantmarch, A (2011) Google's quest to build a better boss, *New York Times,* 13 March

7 Upton, D and Macadam, S (1997) Why (and how) to take a plant tour, *Harvard Business Review,* June

8 *HfS Research* (2014) BPO on the brink of a new generation: technology transformation, March, p 2

Make operations 03 a strategic asset

It is an exasperating coincidence that the words 'operat*ions* management' and 'operat*ional* management' are so similar. They are not the same; they are very different.

'Operational' is the opposite of strategic. We all understand, more or less, what strategy means. It means long term, it means guiding the enterprise in its business environment, it means working with abstract, even philosophical, ideas; and it means that something is really important. When you hear the word 'operational' on the other hand, you take it to mean detailed, localized and, if only by implication, not as important as strategic. In fact, 'operational' is hugely important, but we'll come to that later. 'Operations' (as opposed to 'operational'), as we explored in Chapter 1, is how you manage your resources and processes. You can look at 'operations' from either a strategic or an operational perspective. In this chapter we look at how your operations should have an important strategic role, in fact it should be central to the strategy of your whole business.

Achieving long-term competitive success through the driving force of a great operations function is never easy and takes time, but, as we said in the previous chapter, it must start with expectations. If we expect only mediocrity from our operations function, that's exactly what we get. Yet, if we expect operations to inspire the whole firm – well at least that creates the possibility of achieving it. So, after establishing a capability culture for operations, a business should be in a position to start shaping its operations strategy; see Figure 3.1.

The four elements of making operations a strategic asset

As an operations manager you must do four things to make operations into a strategic asset:

1 Your operation must contribute directly to the business's overall strategy (the top-down element).

Figure 3.1 This chapter looks at how to make your operations a strategic asset

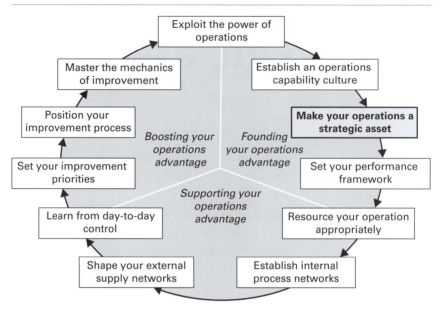

Figure 3.2 The four elements of operations strategy

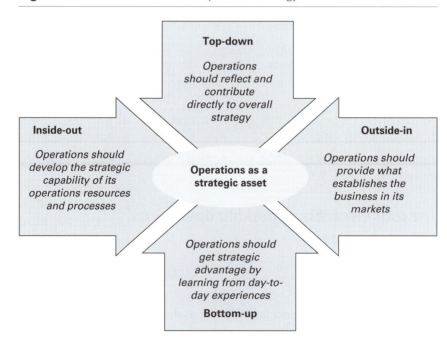

2 Your operation must provide the things that establish the business in its markets (the outside-in element).

3 Your operation must get strategic advantage by learning from your day-to-day experience (the bottom-up element).

4 Your operation must develop the strategic capabilities of its resources and processes (the inside-out element).

Each of these elements is important and each is a necessary condition for a truly strategic operation. They are sometimes called the 'four perspectives on operations strategy' or the 'four elements of operations strategy' and are illustrated in Figure 3.2. It's worth looking at each of these elements in more detail, because we will be returning to them several more times.

Your operation should reflect and contribute directly to overall strategy – top-down

Your operations function is one amongst many functions, all of which need to be aligned with business strategy and all of which should be pulling in the same strategic direction. So the first and most obvious strategic contribution that your operation can make is to confirm that all its decisions reflect the strategy of the business as a whole. This is the 'top-down' element of operations strategy. Classically, a functional strategy, like operations strategy, is supposed to be the last connection in a set of logically linked strategic positions, starting with corporate strategy and working through your business strategy, finishing up at functional strategy. Corporate strategy allocates resources to each business. Business strategy sets out the individual mission and objectives of the business, and defines how it intends to compete in its markets. Operations strategy sets out how the function will contribute to the strategic objectives of the business.

All this may seem a bit 'textbook', but don't dismiss the central idea – that to fully understand strategy at any level one has to be able to understand how and why it is what it is, before deciding how you can improve it. In effect, the top-down element of operations strategy is a process of translating the requirements for each level of strategy into a form that makes sense to the level below. Or, to put it another way, how can each level of strategy contribute to the level above? It is a question that can give both clarity and some rigour to any operations strategy. A good strategy at any level should provide clarity and connection. It should make clear what objectives operations should be prioritizing, and reveal how they are to be achieved.

Correspondence and coherence

Never be tempted to think that deriving an operations strategy from a business strategy should be a relatively straightforward planning activity. If it feels like it is, you are missing something. It is during the translation from business strategy to operations strategy that all the ambiguities and conflicts that are buried within most businesses strategies will be exposed and will need to be resolved. You may find that your business strategy is painted in broad brushstrokes. It may point the business in a general direction, but it cannot spell out every detail; that is what functional strategies are there to do. Your operations strategy, like any other functional strategy, should take the general thrust of your business strategy and translate it into 'what it means for the operation's resources and processes'. Or to put it another way: 'Is there a clear *correspondence* between your business and your operations strategy?' This means making a clear, logical and explicit link between all the activities of the operation and the business strategy in which it operates. (See Figure 3.3.)

However, this vertical logic from your business strategy to your operations strategy is not all that is needed. Your operations strategy also needs to be *coherent*, within itself and with the strategies pursued by other functions. Within your operations strategy coherence means that there should be a logical 'horizontal' connection and consistency. Put another way, the

Figure 3.3 Correspondence and coherence are the two requirements of the top-down element of operations strategy

choices you make should not pull it in different directions. For example, if you introduce new flexible technology that allows products or services to be customized to individual clients' needs, it would be 'incoherent' to devise a performance measurement system that ignores the possibility of customization, a supply network strategy that fails to develop suppliers to understand the needs of high-variety customization, and so on. In other words, all decisions should complement and reinforce each other in the promotion of the operation's objectives.

Between an operations strategy and the other functional strategies, coherence means that your operations strategy should be compatible with and support other functional strategies. This is clearly important, although it often requires some strong top-down direction, or at least a strong planning process, to make sure that it happens. Obvious examples of great functional coherence are the successful 'low-cost' airlines like Ryanair and Southwest Airlines. Low prices and well-defined value-based marketing are supported by technology standardization, robust, low-variety operations and sophisticated IT systems.

Your operation should provide what establishes the business in its markets – outside-in

Your operations function is the supplier to its markets. It should help to establish and maintain its desired market position by providing the levels of service, innovation and cost that outclass competitors, or at least keep up with them. The key question to ask should be, 'How well do we help the business to compete in its markets?' This is the 'outside-in' element of operations strategy.

Meeting, or even exceeding, market expectations should usually be a prime goal of any operation. It is, of course, a necessary requirement of successful operations to fully understand what drives customers' behaviour and then let that understanding guide the development of its resources and processes. But do not think that the relationship between markets and the operations that serve them is simply a matter of markets dictating how operations should behave. Remember that your customers will behave, at least partly, on how you (or your competitors) have treated them in the past. The reality is that it is always a two-way street between your markets and your operations. If your consumables supplier's 24-hour delivery service sometimes takes longer, you order sooner than if their service were more reliable. If the supply of particular parts is erratic, you may respond by holding higher inventory levels. In other words, your customers (and markets more broadly) may set the agenda for how operations should be managed, but the way that operations perform also shapes the assumptions (and therefore the behaviour) of customers. For an example of this, see 'How Zara shapes customer behaviour'.

CASE STUDY   How Zara shapes customer behaviour[1]

There are few better examples of operations performance shaping customer behaviour than Zara, part of Inditex, the Spanish garment manufacturer and retailer. Amancio Ortega Gaona founded the wildly successful fashion company, Inditex, back in 1963. Now, Zara, the largest Inditex division, accounts for around two-thirds of total Inditex sales. Although the first Zara store was simply intended to be an outlet for surplus production, a more fundamental lesson was soon learnt – there were benefits in having, in the words of one Inditex executive, *'five fingers touching the factory and five touching the customer'.* This 'virtual' vertical integration gives significant control of the whole design/production/supply/retail process and because of it, Zara is able to offer cutting-edge fashion at affordable prices: its operating model exerts control over almost the entire garment supply chain.

Famously, Zara is able to get from the design stage to having garments for sale in its shops in two to three weeks for its most fashionable items. This means that Zara can offer its fashionably exclusive (yet low-cost) products while still holding very low levels of inventory – typically only a few pieces of each item – and this could mean that a store's entire stock is on display. Indeed, it is not unusual to find empty racks by the end of a day's trading. Importantly, this creates an additional incentive for customers to buy on the spot, because if a customer chose to wait, the item might be sold out and may never be made again. So Zara can both carry less overall inventory and have fewer unsold items that have to be discounted in end-of-season sales. Items that remain on the shelves for more than two or three weeks are normally taken out of the store and shipped either to other stores in the same country or (rarely) back to Spain. Also, because of the fast supply, the stock (and the clothes) can change every two or three weeks, giving another reason for customers to return and spend.

In an industry where discounting means that the average product fetches only around 60 per cent of its full price, Zara often manages to collect almost 90 per cent. However, this approach means that stores are completely reliant on regular and rapid replenishment of new designs.

Figure 3.4   The outside-in element of operations strategy translates the
requirements of the market into a set of operations performance
objectives

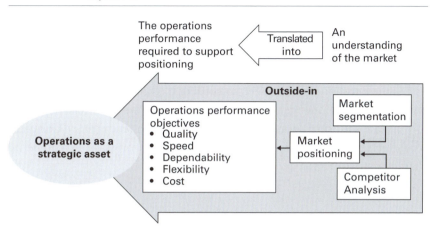

The essential point is that your operations strategy must reflect your
intended market position (see Figure 3.4). It sounds straightforward. The
hitch is that the concepts, language and, to some extent, philosophy used to
help marketing people understand markets are not always useful in guiding operations. The result is that descriptions of what markets need often
need 'translating' before they can be useful to operations. Take the idea of
market segmentation, for example. Even the most evangelical marketer will
admit that market segmentation is a simplified version of a reality that is far
less clear-cut. A necessary simplification maybe, but a simplification nevertheless. In reality all customers are different, yet segmentation brings some
kind of order by grouping similar(ish) customers together. What can make
segmentation difficult if you're an operations type is not the act itself, but
what is chosen as the basis of segmentation.

Segmentation matters to operations people too

Marketing specialists often say segmentation helps the business to 'develop
products and services that are appropriate for particular segments'. Right –
but only partially so. It should be broader than that. Segmentation should
provide the basis for all the things you need to do to get your offerings to
customers and not just be confined to product and service characteristics.
This includes what you outsource, how you design your internal processes,
how you organize your supply chain, how you manage your improvement trajectory; in fact everything about how you manage your operation.

Market analysts have a bigger responsibility for the internal workings of the business than they sometimes realize.

Theorists provide us with many ways to segment markets: by their demographic, geographic, psychological characteristics, and so on. But the outside-in element of operations strategy is a translation process. What should matter is how easily the segmentation characteristics can be translated into clear directions for the operation. For example, needs-based segmentation is the clustering of customers according to common sets of needs, and purchasing behaviour (generally used in a B2B context) is relatively easy to translate into operations objectives; see the case study 'Dow Corning's Xiameter service'. By contrast, segmentation based on (say) psychometric characteristics offers operations little guidance.

CASE STUDY   Dow Corning's Xiameter service[2]

For years Dow Corning was a silicone business with a market position built on service and technical excellence. Customers had been willing to pay top prices for pioneering technology, premium products and customized service. Yet as the market matured it became clear that some customers were becoming increasingly price sensitive. The premium price strategy was under attack both from large competitors that had driven down costs and from smaller competitors with lower overheads. This was when the company adopted a 'needs-based' approach to segmentation, attempting to identify the basic drivers for customers' purchase decision. It revealed four segments that could be plainly related to the operations requirements for serving them:

1 *Innovative solution seekers* – who wanted innovative silicone-based products.

2 *Proven solution seekers* – customers needing advice on existing proven products.

3 *Cost-effective solution seekers* – customers who may even pay premium prices for a product if it could mean taking costs out of their business by improving their productivity.

4 *Price seekers* – experienced purchasers of commonly used silicone materials wanting low prices and an easy way of doing business with their supplier.

Each of these segments held a distinct message for Dow Corning's operations: 1) for innovative solution seekers, work with customers' R&D to develop new products; 2) for proven solution seekers, help sales staff to exploit the range of existing products; 3) for cost-effective solution seekers, give sales staff a thorough understanding of customers' processes and help to match their requirements with appropriate products; 4) for price seekers, do whatever it takes to keep the costs of manufacturing and delivery as low as possible. This price seeker segment was the most challenging. Dow Corning's sales to this segment were small and declining, yet the segment represented around 30 per cent of the total market for silicones, and was expected to grow significantly.

Dow Corning's solution was to create a new service offering that was unambiguously targeted at this segment, and allowed its operations to provide exactly what customers required. Called 'Xiameter' (rhymes with diameter), it was a 'no-frills', limited availability service with low prices that could only be accessed on the web (drastically cutting the costs of selling). It offered only regular products, at minimum order quantities, without any technical advice. Delivery times were sufficiently long to fit individual orders into the operation's existing manufacturing schedule.

The Xiameter offering presents a classic illustration of how the 'translation' logic that connects the requirements of the market to operations activities works. It goes something like this:

First – *segment the market.* In the silicone market, the most challenging segment for a 'technically premium' firm like Dow Corning is the 'price seeker' segment.

Second – *understand how well you are currently serving the market segments.* Competition is tough in the market because competitors are not carrying large sales and R&D overheads.

Third – *decide whether each market segment is worth serving.* This 'low price' market is worth pursuing because it is large and growing. And the company has manufacturing expertise and high production volumes, and potentially could compete.

Fourth – *what would operations have to achieve to allow the business to compete?* For price-seekers, be able to supply good product at low cost, but abandon the technical advice service – most customers in this segment don't need it.

Fifth – *what does the operation have to do to achieve these things?* For Xiameter, make it clear that it is a 'no frills' service (hence the new Xiameter brand), and eliminate excess overheads (hence web-based sales). Do not allow customers to ask for anything that increases costs (hence limited product range, minimum order quantities and delivery times that do not disrupt production schedules).

Performance objectives

The final stage of the outside-in analysis, as illustrated by the Xiameter example, needs more explanation. It is the stage that identifies the *performance objectives* for the operation. Performance objectives are the aspects of operations performance that satisfy market requirements and therefore your operation is expected to pursue them. Generally, they include the following (though obviously their relative priorities will differ):

- *Quality* – the 'performance' of products and services (specification quality) and their consistency of 'performance' (conformance quality).
- *Speed* – the elapsed time between requesting and receiving products and services.
- *Dependability* – the chance that products and services will be delivered as promised.
- *Flexibility* – the extent and cost (or time) of the operation's ability to change, including the introduction of novel methods, products or services.
- *Cost* – the resources consumed to create products and services.

The important performance objectives for the Xiameter offering would be cost, specification and conformance quality, and delivery reliability. We will look further at performance objectives in the next chapter.

Focus – operations can't do everything (well, not at the same time)

The Xiameter story is also a lesson in how you can avoid one of the great dilemmas of operations strategy – how you set clear performance objectives for operations when you produce several offerings, all of which compete in their markets in different ways. (The Xiameter service positioned itself to be ultra-convenient for what the operations did anyway.) Is it possible for an operation to be excellent at achieving many different (and sometimes conflicting) objectives simultaneously? We will go into this in more detail in Chapter 9, but the simple answer is, no. Operations are usually capable of achieving great performance when they concentrate on a relatively narrow set of objectives, not when they try to do everything. In other words, be truly great at the few things that matter rather than mediocre at everything. This idea is called *operations focus*, and is both powerful and proven.

Chip away at the bits you don't need

There is a story about the 16th century genius Michelangelo. He was asked how he managed to convey such beauty in his masterpiece sculpture of David. He is supposed to have replied, 'It's easy. You just start with a block of stone, and chip away those bits that don't look like David.' That is what operations focus is. You chip away the stuff you don't need and focus only on those things in the operation that are important in achieving those objectives that one (or one set) of your offering requires. This allows you to invest in the equipment, systems and procedures that can be designed to achieve a more limited, but targeted, range of tasks for a smaller set of customers.

Segment your operations to reflect market segmentation

The implication of focus is that, to serve separate markets well, you need separate (or at least partly separate) operations, each of which can support the specific market position of the subset of offerings that it produces. In fact, operations focus is very close to the idea of market segmentation. Just as market segmentation breaks diverse markets down into smaller, more consistent markets, operations focus breaks down complex resources and processes with a whole range of different skills and technologies, to create dedicated and targeted mini-operations. In effect, this is segmenting your operations to match the way you segment your markets.

Just as in marketing there are continual debates on the best way to segment markets, so in operations there are similar debates as to the most sensible way to focus your operations. Although the benefits of operations focus can be very significant, the major problem is that what is a sensible basis for segmenting markets does not always map onto the ideal basis for segmenting operations.

For example, a food service company operating in continental Europe has a plant that prepares menu dishes for its restaurant customers. All its products are essentially similar insomuch as they involve the batch preparation of food that is packed either in an aluminium container or a heat-resistant polymer container. Yet the company's plant has two quite distinct sections. This is how the plant's operations boss explains it:

> It seems strange at first. All our products are technically similar. They use
> the same technologies; and involve similar (although not identical) skills and
> ingredients. The reason that we separate them is that they serve different types

of customer and so need to focus on different objectives. The larger section produces for our larger customers such as AutoRoute service stations chains. These products and the volumes involved are agreed several months in advance with our corporate sales team, and some lines have been produced for years with little change to their recipes. Obviously these customers expect very competitive pricing and absolutely reliable delivery schedules.

Our other section has a very different set of customers. There tends to be more of them and they are, on average, far smaller. Often they are individual family-owned restaurants that want frequent new (and often seasonal) lines. They are served by our regional sales teams who can tempt them with innovative or unusual dishes. Margins tend to be higher, but we need to be constantly introducing new lines, often with little notice. However, the wider range and constant change do affect utilization. That was the most difficult lesson to learn when we split the plant. You can't judge parts of the plant serving different markets using the same criteria.

Your operation should get strategic advantage by learning from day-to-day experiences – bottom-up

Putting your operations strategy together should not be just a top-down affair. Not all decisions that turn out to be of long-term importance come top-down from senior management, or even the staff who support senior management. Some important ideas 'emerge' from those seemingly routine activities that happen every day in all businesses. Anyone who has sat on the board of a company knows that not all ideas come from its august deliberations, or even the advice of those with responsibility for formulating strategic action. Your business can move in a particular strategic direction because your ongoing experience of serving customers at an operational level convinces you that it is the right thing to do. There may be no high-level generation of strategic ideas in the classical fashion. Instead, a general consensus emerges, often from the operational level of the organization. The 'high level' strategic decision making, if it occurs at all, may simply confirm the consensus and approve the resources to make it happen effectively.

Letting strategic ideas emerge from the operational level of your business is not an abdication of responsibility; it is simply an acceptance that great ideas can come from those who work at the sharp end of the business. In fact, it would be a dereliction of duty if you did not do everything you could to encourage good ideas emerging from day-to-day experience. It would be to waste one of the richest sources of practical and grounded understanding that you have access to. Every action, every decision, in fact every transaction made by your operation's processes is an opportunity to add to its knowledge. From a bottom-up perspective, making your operations into a strategic asset means: 1) developing the mechanisms to capture the learning that should come from your routine operations activities, and 2) transforming that learning into strategically valuable knowledge.

One of the great advantages of developing an effective bottom-up element to your operations strategy is that day-to-day experience is often where trends first show themselves. Especially in a volatile or turbulent business environment, this is important. The other three elements of operations strategy can take time to detect trends in how markets are moving. They are often part of a hopefully effective, but bureaucratic, internal planning process, while the bottom-up element is more direct. It draws on everyday experience. It senses what is happening 'on the ground'. It plugs you into reality.

Figure 3.5   The bottom-up element of operations strategy is to learn from day-to-day experiences and converting the knowledge gained into strategic capabilities

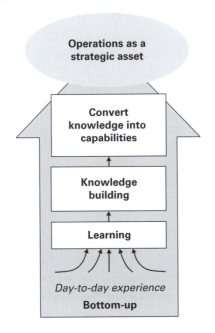

That is the essence of the 'bottom-up' element of operations strategy; see Figure 3.5. The key question is, 'How good are our operations at learning from their day-to-day experiences and converting the knowledge gained into strategic capabilities?' The idea of operations contributing to strategy by learning from its experience is so important that a whole chapter (Chapter 8) is devoted to it.

Your operation should develop the strategic capability of its operations resources – inside-out

The bottom-up element of operations strategy focuses on how your processes can learn from what processes do best – dealing with day-to-day activities. The 'inside-out' perspective is similar, but different. It is similar, in the sense that it deals with how your operations can bring something unique to your business's capabilities; and it is different in that it directly questions what your operation has (its resources) as well as what it does (its processes). Its aim is ambitious – to give your business capabilities that your competitors don't have. The key question for this element of operations strategy is, 'What can your operation do that your competitors can't?'

For too many businesses, the answer is, 'nothing'. Even if your operation does not have any unique capabilities, it should at least be striving to gain some kind of advantage from its resources and processes. If one accepts this, two further questions are relevant. First, what resources and processes does your operation have that should be contributing to your capabilities? Second, how are the decisions that you make within your operation contributing to developing and supporting these capabilities? Figure 3.6 illustrates this. Again, this element of operations strategy is partly a translation exercise: translating an understanding of your operation's resources and processes into potential capabilities and identifying your decisions that help to transform potential into real capabilities.

The VRIO framework

By far the most useful (and most common) way of evaluating potential capabilities is to use what has become known as the VRIO framework. It was first developed in the 1990s[3] and identifies the four features that your operation's resources and processes must have if they are going to give a

Figure 3.6 The inside-out element of operations strategy develops the capabilities of the operation's resources and processes

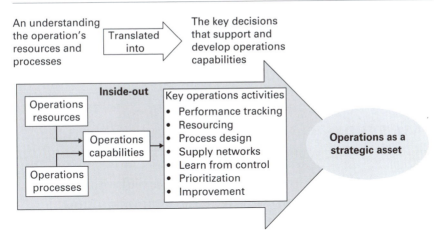

sustained operations advantage. Operations' resources and processes must be 'Valuable', 'Rare', imperfectly 'Imitable' and the business 'Organized' to capture their value. The key questions to ask are these.

1. *Do you have valuable operations capabilities?* Can you identify specific and definable competitive value in your resources and processes? Do they help to exploit opportunities in the market, or defend against threats from competitors, and if so, exactly how? If they do one or both of these things, then your resources and processes are strategically valuable; if not, they are a weakness. Remember though, it is relatively unusual for valuable operations capabilities to be gained from 'off-the-shelf' resources. If competitors can acquire (say) the same piece of process technology as you, it cannot be valuable in the long term. This is why it can be best to look at the operation's intangible resources as a source of strategic value. Also, what counts as valuable depends on the markets in which you are competing. Resources and processes that have value in one market, at one point in time, will not necessarily be valuable in other markets or at other times. If markets change, what counts as 'valuable' may change.

2. *Do you have rare operations capabilities?* In other words, do you have, or have access to, resources that your competitors don't? Management theorists often define this idea of 'rarity' as when a business has a resource that is unequivocally unique, and is likely to remain so in the foreseeable future. That is a bit extreme: for all practical purposes, a resource is 'rare' if it is at least in short supply, if not unique, and likely to remain so. For example, if you have a member of staff with (currently) unique or exceptional skills,

eventually someone somewhere will be able to match or even exceed his or her skills. Yet this will take time. So resources and processes that are rare and valuable will give a business, at the very least, a temporary advantage. Even if competitors 'catch up' with your once-rare resources and processes, it is a mistake to neglect them. Parity with competitors is better than falling behind.

CASE STUDY   Is your capability really a capability? Don't fool yourself

Don't be fooled into thinking that a competitive position you have adopted, or worse been forced into, necessarily represents a 'capability'. Listen to what the COO of this automotive part manufacturer has to say about how his business competes: *'We really believe in customer service. Our customers have scheduling issues of their own so they really appreciate our ability to be adaptable. We are far more willing than our competitors to be flexible in terms of order size and deliver times. That's our great strength, the willingness and the ability to do whatever our customers want.'*

The following would be a more honest evaluation of their competitive position. *'Our competitors have a product range that is at least as good if not better than ours. Their quality is also better. Consequently, we are forced to take any orders that we can get, no matter how small, how inconvenient or how much they impact on our costs.'*

The reality is that this business's operations are no more flexible than its competitors'. It is forced to offer flexibility to its customers because of weakness in the specification and quality of its products. In this case flexibility isn't a competence; it's a final act of desperation.

3. *Do you have operations capabilities that are costly to imitate?* Do you have resources and processes that competitors cannot imitate, purchase or find a suitable alternative to at a realistic cost or in a realistic time frame? Notice here that 'imitability' can be either because competitors can copy your resources and processes directly, or because they can find an acceptable substitute for them. Your business may have 'difficult to imitate' capabilities because they are legally protected through patents. More likely in the operations function, they could have been developed over time through the incremental build-up of your implicit operating knowledge.

If your business has a particularly clever idea (say, a technological break-through), and you incorporate it into your products, what is the first thing your competitors do? They 'reverse engineer' the product to discover all they can about it. It still may be difficult for them to come up with a direct copy or a substitute, but they will have a starting point. Contrast this with incorporating a similarly clever technological innovation into your resources and processes (rather than your products). Now, the innovation is far less visible to competitors, far less obvious and, one would assume, far less easy to imitate.

4. *Are you organized to capture the value of operations capabilities?* Do you have within your business the systems, culture, capacity and motiva-tion to exploit any capabilities embedded in your resources and processes? Your business may have valuable, rare and inimitable capabilities, but if you cannot exploit them, you are falling at the last fence.

What does it take to make the most of your operations capabilities? Partly, the answer lies in the formal reporting and control mechanisms in the business. Are your operations people aware of their role in developing and exploiting capabilities? Are they required to explicitly articulate and debate them? Is the idea of capability development formally included in reporting routines? Partly it is also down to the informal and cultural environment of your business, and here, with no apology for the repetition, it's a matter of developing a capability-based operations culture, as outlined in the previous chapter. Also, having your operation's activities running in a smooth and efficient manner helps in being able to exploit capabilities. Certainly it is difficult to recognize, let alone exploit, potential competitive advantage if you are constantly distracted by having to work round faltering processes.

In summary then, the 'inside-out' perspective on operations strategy is concerned with making sure that your resources and processes are valuable, rare and inimitable and that the operation is organized to exploit them. Remember though, all these things are time-dependent. A capability may be valuable now – but for how long? Your competitors are not likely to stand still. Similarly, rarity and inimitability are not absolutes and with time can be undermined by competitor activity. Even the ability to exploit capabilities can erode if operations leadership is lacking. Also, although the conven-tional order in which to treat each of these elements is as we have done here (which is why it's called the VRIO framework), it maybe is best to think of the 'O' of 'organization' to be a necessary prerequisite. After all, without the ability to exploit operations capabilities, they have little worth. At least with effective organization there is the potential for your operations resources

Figure 3.7 The four features of the VRIO framework[3]

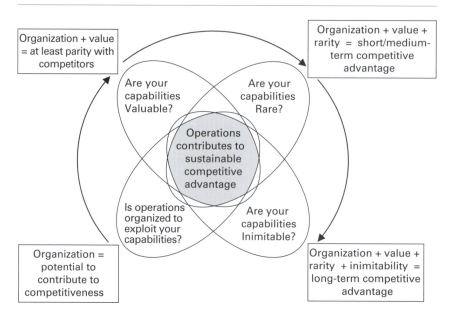

and processes to enhance your competitiveness. If your capabilities are also valuable, then parity with competitors should be possible. With the addition of rarity, a short- to medium-term competitive advantage is likely. Add inimitability to this mix and competitors will find it difficult to match capabilities in anything but the long term. This sequence is shown in Figure 3.7.

Bringing it all together

It's worth repeating that the top-down, outside-in, bottom-up and inside-out elements of an operations strategy are not alternatives. Each is important, each is necessary, but each is different; that's the point. None of these four elements alone will fully develop your operation's potential to be a strategic asset. That's why they are all needed, in all their ambiguities, to give the whole picture of how your operations should be a strategic asset to the business. It is also why putting an operations strategy together is largely a matter of integrating and aligning these four elements.

It is never easy. Two issues are particularly important to how effectively you can manage the process, and how difficult you will find it: 1) the role of senior operations managers in the process, and 2) the clarification of the logical links between the four elements of an operations strategy.

What role should you play in putting an operations strategy together?

A central question in making operations a strategic asset is what role you should play in putting your operations strategy together. Once again, the four elements come to our aid. They are not only a guide to what needs to go into your operations strategy, they also form the framework of what role you should play. Two questions may go a long way towards helping you with this.

First, *do you want to be predominantly top-down or bottom-up?* If your view of how operations' strategic contribution should be guided is predominantly top-down, you are likely to take an ordered and planning-based approach to strategy development, emphasizing the implementation of overall company strategy. Conversely, if you take a bottom-up view, you are more likely to favour an evolving model of operations development where individual parts of your operations together contribute to the overall building of operations as a strategic asset.

Second, *do you want to be predominantly outside-in or inside-out? Or put another way, do you take a market requirements or an operations resource focus?* If you take a market requirements view of operations development, you are likely to focus on the explicit performance achieved by each part of your operation and how far that performance serves to satisfy the operation's customers. If you take an operations resource focus, you will probably want to emphasize the way in which each business operation develops its capabilities and successfully deploys them in its marketplaces.

You can use your answers to these two questions to help identify the appropriate role (or more likely, mixture of roles) that you should play in the ongoing development of your operations strategy. These roles are shown in Figure 3.8. It categorizes four pure types of role called governors, curators, trainers and facilitators. Remember though that these are 'pure types'; in practice, you will play a role that is a combination of these pure types, usually with one type predominating.

Playing the role of 'governor'

Here we use the term 'governor' in the sense that you act as the agent of a central authority (the board or executive committee), interpreting its instructions and arbitrating over any disputes or matters of interpretation. We also use the word 'governor' in the mechanical sense to describe the mechanism that prevents an engine running out of control and damaging itself. Don't

Figure 3.8   What role do you play in putting operations strategy together?

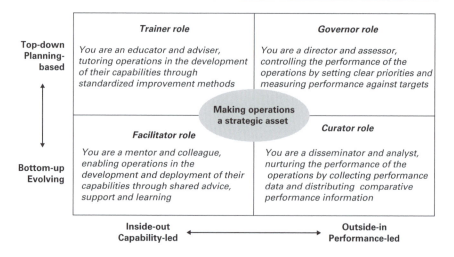

try to adopt this role unless you are willing to be the dominant power player in the process. It is your vision of what the individual parts of the operations should be doing that dominates. This type of role involves interpreting strategy in terms of market performance, setting clear goals for each part of your operation, judging their performance and, if performance is not to target, finding out the reason why. Adopting this role requires you to have a set of predetermined responses to 'fix' operations that do not perform to requirements.

Playing the role of 'curator'

You can be concerned primarily with performance against market requirements without being top-down. You may adopt a role that takes a more 'evolving' view by acting as the repository of performance data and ideas on operations practice for the operation as a whole. The term 'curator' captures this idea. Curators collect information and examples so that everyone can learn through examining them. You will be concerned with collecting performance information, examples of best practice, and so on. You will also be concerned with disseminating this information so that managers in different parts of the operation can benchmark themselves against their colleagues and, where appropriate, adopt best practice from elsewhere.

The term 'curator' can be taken to mean more than a collector: it can also imply someone who nurtures and cares for the exhibits. So when you act as a curator you should also analyse and explain the performance data and examples of operations practice you collect. In this way you educate and encourage debate on operations practice. In fact, by playing the curator role you implicitly accept more of a two-way relationship between yourself and the various parts of your operations; only in this way can you be aware of what practice is evolving. Similarly, by publishing comparative performance data, you will, to some extent, encourage communication between the individual parts of your operations.

Playing the role of 'trainer'

Acting as a 'trainer' shifts your role from a focus on performance against market requirements to the development of operations-based capabilities. In this role your mind-set is still top-down, so once again you are the dominant player in the process and it is your vision that shapes what the individual parts of the operation should be doing. As a 'trainer' you should go to some effort to develop clear objectives, usually derived, top-down, from overall company strategy, as well as devising effective methods of developing the skills required to meet them. Because the specific needs of individual parts of your operation may differ, you may need to devise improvement methodologies that can be customized to meet each specific need; but only to some extent. Your approach should be coherent with a relatively common and centralized view of operations development. Even if individual parts of your operation do initiate contact with you, they do so in the role of clients seeking advice from 'consultants' who bring a standardized approach. As an internal consultant, however, you can accumulate considerable experience and knowledge.

Playing the role of 'facilitator'

In some ways this final role is the most difficult to adopt effectively. As a 'facilitator' you are again concerned with the development of operations capabilities but you do so by acting as a promoter and agent of change rather than a directive instructor. Your role is to advise, support and generally aid the development and deployment of capabilities through a process of mentoring operations staff. In fact, you share responsibility with operations staff in forming a community of operations practice. The development of the relationships between you and operations staff is crucial in encouraging shared learning. The significance placed on these relationships becomes, in effect, the prime mechanism for control of the strategy development process. The facilitator role is entirely dependent on regular, strong and two-way communication between yourself and the community of operations staff. Implicit in this type of role is the acceptance that you are in it for the long term.

Your role should be a blend of all four types

Of course, our real behaviour during the process of putting operations strategies together will be a mixture of all of these roles, each of which has its strengths and weaknesses. More importantly, each is more or less appropriate for different conditions. This means that, although we will always adopt a blend of the four roles, there are times and circumstances when we need to let one role and its associated behaviour dominate. If you want to know which role should dominate, look at its strengths and weaknesses. A 'performance-led' approach is better at having short-term impact than the longer-term focus of a capabilities-led approach, which is why, if your operation is in trouble, you will often focus on short-term performance targets. At least that will help you to survive. A capabilities-led approach, however, will build up your operation's know-how and experience that will form the foundation for your future success.

Whether you should adopt a top-down planning-based, or a bottom-up evolving approach depends on the experience and maturity of your operations. A bottom-up, evolving, approach can bring you benefits, but it's not easy.

Figure 3.9 Your role should adapt as the emphasis moves from short to long term and as the operation gains experience/maturity

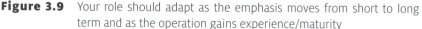

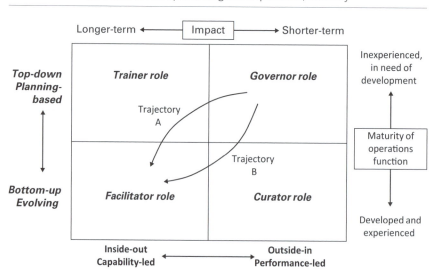

Don't assume trying to tap into the day-to-day experiences of your people will automatically bring immediate benefits: it won't, unless you have the right mechanisms, and more importantly staff skills. An experienced and 'mature' operation ('mature' in the sense that its people and procedures have fully absorbed the idea of a capability-based operations culture, as outlined in the previous chapter) can exploit an evolving approach, but not a less developed one. A less developed operation will need the guidance of a more planning-based approach.

Figure 3.9 shows this idea. It also shows two trajectories taken by two operations. Both needed to react relatively fast in modifying their operations strategy, so the senior managers in both started the process by adopting a prescriptive 'governor' role. However, one operation had been performing poorly for years, without effective operations leadership or development. Its new leadership needed to gradually increase its 'trainer' role before it could start to expect its people to cope with the communities of practice necessary for the longer-term 'facilitator' role (trajectory A). The other operation needed to change its strategy, not because of past operations failures, but because the nature of its competition changed. Its relatively mature operations people and systems were capable of moving from 'governor' to 'curator' and eventually to 'facilitator' roles.

Clarify the logical links between the four elements of an operations strategy

The four elements of an operations strategy can also form the basis for making sure that the logic underlying your strategy is aligned. Looking at the links between the four elements will pose the right questions, and expose the contradictions and paradoxes that need to be overcome within the operations strategy. The challenge is twofold. First, each element must be thoroughly thought through to make sure that it is coherent. The second, and probably more difficult, challenge is to make sense of how the four perspectives fit together.

Nothing is better for exploring how the four elements fit together (or not) than an 'operations strategy map'. This is a technique that articulates and clarifies the cause–effect relationships in a business's operations strategy. The set of cause–effect relationships identifies not only *what* needs to be done to move a company or function forward, but also *why* it should be done. There are several versions of strategy mapping;[4] the version described here rearranges the four elements into a Y-shaped structure that exposes the potential tensions between the needs and interests of the business and those of its customers.[5] The technique is based on the idea that, of the four elements, the two that most businesses are initially concerned with are the top-down (what the business wants) and the inside-out (what customers want). Each of these strategic requirements is met, and any conflicts between them resolved, by the inside-out element (what is the strategic contribution of the operation's resources and processes?), which in turn is supported by the bottom-up element (what do we have to learn to do better?)

An example is the best way to demonstrate how operations strategy mapping works; see Figure 3.10. This illustrates the attempts of the aggregate and ready-mix division of a construction materials group to sort out its operations strategy for it European Major Projects market. The top two boxes in the diagram contain the key objectives that the business as a whole expects its operations strategy to achieve (the top left-hand box) and the aspects of performance that customers in this market want (top right-hand box). Of course, there are more objectives than shown here, both for the business and their customers, but these are the ones at the top of the agenda as far as the company's operations strategy is concerned. The middle box is a summary of the major 'work streams' that the operation is working on to contribute to the strategic needs of both the business and its customers. More importantly, the diagram also shows how the various operations development work streams should contribute to business and customer objectives. That is what the arrows indicate. Each arrow is, in effect, an assumption in this operation's strategy. The 'map' indicates, for example, that this strategy is assuming that if the sources of secondary aggregate are expanded, then it will have a positive impact on growing product volumes, developing a lead in the business's reputation for sustainability, and help to develop a network of long-term alliances. The bottom box represents what the business is going to have to be better at if it is to succeed in satisfactorily completing the work streams in the middle box, again with the arrows indicating the main cause–effect relationships.

Figure 3.10 is evidently a simplification of a far more detailed and nuanced strategy, but even drawing up a simplified diagram such as this does have some very significant advantages:

- It makes a logical connection between the four elements that must be present in an operations strategy if it is to genuinely make operations a strategic asset.

- It is both explicit and transparent. How many strategy documents have you read that are full of obscure and/or ambiguous language that means little? This is a picture – it's difficult to misunderstand.

Figure 3.10 Operations strategy map (simplified) for an aggregate and ready-mix group in the European Major Projects market

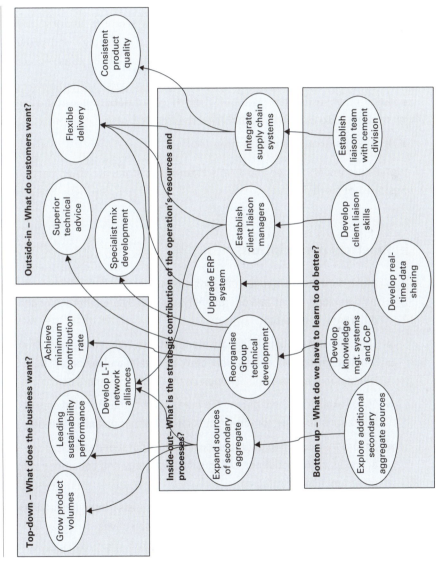

- It stresses not only what an operations strategy should be doing; it emphasizes the question of 'Why are we doing this? What specific objectives are we prioritizing?'

- It does not just identify the work streams contained within the operations strategy, but also what the operation must learn to be better at if the strategy works as we intend.

- Although the technique does not 'devise' a strategy, it does show the logical links between the various elements of a strategy and provides a discipline that encourages the clear articulation of the cause–effect relationships within the strategy.

- Like many strategic techniques, the process of debating and drawing the strategy map can be as valuable as the finished result.

- It is also a great communication tool.

Note: customers can be the firm's external customers, other parts of the business, or both.

Practical prescriptions

- Make sure that everyone in the business understands the difference between operations and operational – they really are different, and the difference is important.

- Critically and continually debate the questions, 'What is the operations function giving the business that can't be obtained elsewhere?' And, 'What can the operations function do that our competitors can't?'

- Make explicit (without getting too bureaucratic) the four elements of operations strategy: top-down, outside-in, bottom-up and inside-out.

- Ensure that everyone understands how the operations strategy achieves correspondence with business strategy and coherence with other functional strategies.

- Draw up unambiguous links between the business's intended market position(s) and the operations performance objectives.

- Critically examine the procedures and mechanisms that you have in place to learn from day-to-day experience. How many innovations in your operation emerged from 'shop floor' experience?

- Identify the capabilities of your operations (at its simplest level – the things that you are really good at doing).

- How strategically valuable they are. Do they add value by helping to exploit opportunities or avoid threats?

- How rare they are. Are they scarce, exclusive to you, or otherwise difficult for competitors to acquire?

- How inimitable they are. Are they prohibitively costly for competitors to imitate, buy or find a substitute for?

- How well are you organized to exploit the capabilities? Is your operation capable of recognizing, developing and exploiting their competitive potential?

- Critically assess the appropriate combination of roles that you need to adopt as you develop your operations strategy. Do you have an idea of how your emphasis on the different roles (governor, curator, trainer and facilitator) might change as your strategy develops?

- Draw your operations strategy as an 'operations strategy map' as illustrated in Figure 3.10. Each arrow in the map is an assumption that you have built into your strategy. Examine each arrow. How confident are you that they do represent a realistic cause–effect relationship?

Notes

1 This example is based on public sources including: Ferdows, K, Machuca, J and Lewis, M (2002) *Zara, Case Clearing House*; Jarrow, L (2013) Inditex: Spain's fashion powerhouse you've probably never heard of, *The Observer*, 15 December; Hansen S (2012) How Zara grew into the world's largest fashion retailer, *New York Times*, 9 November; Leroux, M and Griffiths, K (2013) Zara owner to open nine stores a week as it takes on world, *The Times*, 14 March

2 Sources include: Francis, I and Kashani, K (2006) *Xiameter, The past and future of disruptive innovation*, IMD case study, IMD-5-0702

3 Concept based on Barney, J B (1995) Looking Inside for Competitive Advantage. *Academy of Management Executive*, **9** (4), pp 49–61

4 Strategy mapping is usually based on the work of Kaplan and Norton – Kaplan, R and Norton, D (2004) *Strategy Maps*, Harvard Business School Press, Cambridge, MA. They used the technique to operationalize their Balanced Score Card approach to performance management

5 A full explanation of this approach is available at www.ops-works.com

Set your performance framework

04

You can't make operations work better if you don't know how well you are doing, so just pick the right Key Performance Indicators (KPIs) and measure them periodically. It's simple, right? No, of course not. If it were, there would not be so much debate, controversy and confusion about how best to do it. So it really is worth thinking in some depth about how you should judge how good, bad or indifferent your operations are. It should be one of the first things your team should address (see Figure 4.1). In this chapter we outline the performance framework, which gives you a practical basis for thinking about operations performance, from the high level that looks at how your business fits into society broadly, to the operational level.

What is 'operations performance'?

'Performance' means how good (or bad) your operation is at achieving its objectives; how good you are at doing what you are supposed to be doing. It is not a simple concept, and it is multi-faceted in the sense that a single measure can never fully communicate the success, or otherwise, of something as complex as most operations. It's a mistake to try and reduce performance to a single measure. Don't be tempted. Accept that several measures will always be needed to convey any kind of realistic indication.

Why is assessing operations performance indispensable? Just try reversing the question. Think about the things that you *cannot* do if you do not have some idea of how good, bad or indifferent you are. You have no basis for improvement, prioritization, resource allocation or exploiting whatever capabilities or operations resources you possess. The big problem for operations managers is that operations work at a disaggregated level. You cannot evaluate the performance of the operations function in the same way as you

Figure 4.1   This chapter looks at how to set your performance framework

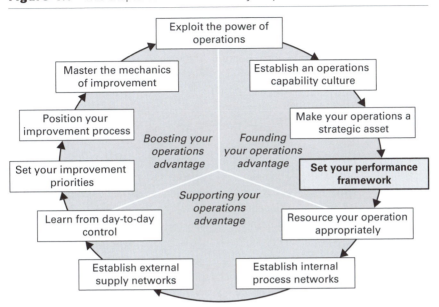

do for the whole business. CFOs have a responsibility to deal in aggregated measures such as return on capital employed, (ROCE), earnings before interest, tax, depreciation and amortization (EBITDA), liquidity, free cash flow, and so on; and of course they are important. But operations managers have a different responsibility, which is to look behind the financial indicators of performance to answer the question of 'why' financial measures are as they are. So, for operations, performance is an issue of dealing with how good you are, not just in terms of money, but also in terms of time, output, utilization, quality, flexibility, capability, satisfaction, and potential – things you can't add together. This is one reason why operations performance needs to be judged at different levels.

Three levels of performance

Operations performance can be measured at different levels, from the impact it has at the broad, long-term, societal and environmental level, to the more operational-level concerns over how day-to-day efficiency is changing, or how it serves its individual customers. For all practical purposes, you need to be assessing performance at three levels:

1 The high-level, broad, societal level: how sustainable (in both a business and environmental sense) your operation is.

Table 4.1   The three levels of operations performance

Level	Objective	Typical measures	Scope	Timescale	Degree of discretion
Societal	Operations sustainability	Triple bottom line (planet, people, profit)	The whole business	Long-term (several years)	Mandatory for the whole business
Strategic	Operations has a positive strategic impact	Costs Revenue Return on capital Risk Capability building	The businesses operations/ operations function	Medium-term (quarters/ months)	Different degrees of emphasis for each part of the business
Operational	Process performance contributes to strategic objectives	Quality Speed Dependability Flexibility Cost-efficiency	Each individual process within operations	Short-term (months/ weeks/ days)	Different processes likely to have different priorities

2 The strategic level: how your operation can contribute to your business's overall strategy.

3 The operational level: looking at the state of your 'performance objectives' in individual parts of the operation.

Although these three levels need treating separately, they are clearly related. Responsible performance at the societal level depends on business sustainability as well as environmental sustainability. Business sustainability has to be built on the long-term strategic success of the business, and strategic success is more likely if operational performance makes a positive contribution. The rest of this chapter provides you with a framework that sets out what aspects of these three levels should be present in all operations' performance metrics – summarized in Table 4.1.

Judge your operations performance at a societal level

Some claim that operations managers have a tendency to be too 'head-down' and focused only on their local day-to-day performance. It is a criticism that still has some validity in some businesses, but less than it once did. Most operations managers accept that they can no longer afford to neglect broader 'societal' performance. For operations not to formally incorporate such issues in its performance assessments is at best short-sighted and at worst unethical.

The common term that tries to embrace the idea of performance at this level is the 'triple bottom line' (TBL, or 3BL),[1] also known as 'people, planet and profit'. It is a straightforward idea: organizations (and by extension their operations function) should measure themselves not just on the traditional economic return, but also on the impact their operations have on society (communities, customers, employees, etc) and their ecological impact on the environment. The key issue is 'sustainability'. A sustainable business is one that creates an acceptable profit for its owners, but minimizes the damage to the environment and enhances the existence of the people with whom it has contact. The idea is not just that there is a connection between businesses and the wider environment – that is self-evident. Rather it is that businesses should accept that they bear some responsibility for their wider impact and balance these external consequences of their actions with the more direct internal consequences, such as profit.

The problem facing you is not just whether to adopt such measures as the triple bottom line; that's between you and your management team, your conscience, and your view of reputational risk. Rather it is what measures you can use to make it work. This means identifying which of your decisions, taken explicitly or implicitly, will have an impact on societal and environmental performance. To some extent it will depend on the type of operation you manage. For example, garment retailers will have to focus on the ethical behaviour of their suppliers (difficult at a distance, but necessary), cement and aggregate firms on their energy usage (high) and environmental impact (potentially very significant), and so on. The example, 'Sustainability performance assessment at Novozymes' shows how one business approaches this level of performance.

CASE STUDY   Sustainability performance assessment at Novozymes[2]

It's not surprising perhaps that a company like Novozymes, whose products help other firms to operate more sustainably, should itself be more than competent at measuring its operation's environmental and social performance. The Danish-based company produces enzymes, microorganisms and biopharmaceutical ingredients that help its customers to 'make more from less, while saving energy and generating less waste'.

When reporting on its own performance it balances financial returns for its shareholders with the impact it has on environmental and social change. As well as tracking conventional financial performance, its environmental performance is monitored in two ways. The first is the impact of its products and services on customers' performance using peer-reviewed Life Cycle Assessment (LCA) studies. The second is the assessment of its own operation's consumption of natural resources and its impact on mitigating the negative environmental impact of its production processes. Improving energy efficiency at its global production sites and the amount of waste and by-products that are sent for landfill or incineration has the double effect of reducing the cost of waste treatment and minimizing the company's environmental footprint. As a result, the Dow Jones Sustainability Index has ranked Novozymes among the top 3 per cent of companies in its sector.

Social performance is tracked through employee satisfaction and development, diversity and equal opportunities, occupational health and safety, compliance with human rights and labour standards, corporate citizenship efforts and business integrity. Novozymes also sets long-term performance targets that are integrated into incentive schemes throughout the organization. Long-term financial performance is measured conventionally, but in addition it has a number of 'impact targets'. The company says that its aim is, within five years, to:

- Reach 6 billion people, especially in emerging markets, with its products that enhance sustainability.

- Educate by providing knowledge of the potential of biology to 1 million people.

- Catalyse five global partnerships for change through high-impact partnerships with public and private organizations.

- Deliver 10 innovations that change the lives of people and fulfil sustainability goals.

- Save the world 100 million tons of carbon dioxide a year through its products.

- Enable its employees to develop their skills.

Judge your operations performance at the strategic level

As we keep stressing, although many of your activities as an operations manager are operational in nature, not all are, and even the operational activities can have a strategic impact. Therefore, any evaluation of the performance of your operations function should include the impact it has on your organization's strategic success. This means evaluating five categories of performance (see Figure 4.2):

1 your effective cost base;

2 your ability to attract revenue through service;

3 your return on the capital invested in the operation;

4 the risks that your operation is subjecting the business to; and

5 how well your operation is building capabilities for the future.

It will not be easy. All are important, but strategic measures of performance pose significant challenges.

Operations performance should include its effect on cost

It seems almost too obvious to state, but almost all the activities that operations managers regularly perform will have a very significant impact on the cost of producing products and services. Cost performance is almost always critical for any operation. For many of us it is *the* most important performance measure. Yet measuring cost performance is far from simple. Operations are complex; they usually have several operating areas, differing products or services that often pass through the same operating areas and share the same staff. It all make assigning true costs difficult. To add to the difficulty, fluctuations in volume and mix can swing costs into unknown territory. Changes in output volumes incur many, often small and sometimes discretionary, fixed cost breaks. Nor are variable costs always constant for a given unit of volume. This is why operations managers routinely see traditional cost-of-goods-sold accounting as a very blunt instrument.

Even where cost accounting makes efforts to become more revealing, it can neglect the needs of operations managers. What they want is cost information that addresses their overall cost drivers: volume, variety, variation and visibility (see Chapter 2). However – and it's a big 'however' – there are questions that operations managers ought to be putting to their accounting colleagues that make measuring cost performance a considerably more valuable exercise. These questions should include the following:

- Can you give figures that allow us to distinguish between the cost of bought-in materials and services on the one hand, and how efficiently we convert those into finished products and services on the other? They represent different challenges and require different approaches.

Figure 4.2 Operations can contribute to strategic success through keeping costs low, securing revenue, reducing risk, using capital efficiently, and building the capabilities for future innovation

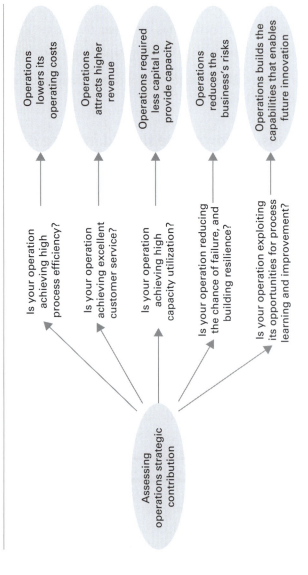

- Within an expected operating range, how does the operation's volume of activity affect costs? In particular, where do the real fixed cost breaks occur?

- How does product and service variety affect cost? What is the marginal cost effect of an incremental increase or decrease in variety?

- What costs are incurred by underutilizing capacity? (Note here that under-utilized capacity may not be a bad thing in itself. There are plenty of instances where pursuit of high capacity utilization can be counterproductive.)

- What are the cost implications (bad and good) of responding fast, faster or immediately to customer demand?

These questions should not imply that all operations managers do, or should, prefer high volume and low variety, variation and visibility. But being able to debate the cost of not pursuing such classical low-cost strategies is a valuable contribution all operations managers should be able to make.

CASE STUDY What is your 'technology limited' cost?

One way of exploring the effect of some of the important cost drivers on an operation's total cost performance is to imagine its 'technology limited cost'. This is the (admittedly hypothetical) cost performance of the operation if the major drivers of cost are eliminated. For example, ask, 'What would our cost per unit of product or service be if, using the same technology, equipment and staff as now, we produced:

- only our highest volume product/service;

- at a constant volume that equalled our maximum capacity;

- ignoring any variation in demand;

- without the necessity for maintenance (I know, but work with me here); and so on with these impossible conditions?'

OK, it's totally unrealistic. That's not the point. The idea is to get an estimate of the lower bound of cost with existing resources. If the technology limited cost is close to existing costs, then the market conditions under which you are operating are not significantly affecting costs. More likely, this hypothetical cost will be very much better than your real costs, in which case, which of these unrealistic conditions is saving the most cost? It can give you a starting point for debating what really is impacting your costs.

Operations performance should include its effect on revenue

Seeing your operations purely, or even primarily, in terms of cost, is a huge mistake. Operations activities can also have an enormous effect on revenue. Products and services that are of high quality, produced in an error-free manner, delivered fast and on time, where the operation has the flexibility to adapt to customers' needs, will generate more revenue than those with lower levels of quality, delivery and flexibility. More than that, operations with these abilities are best placed to take advantage of market opportunities when they arise. The main point here, and one that is surprisingly forgotten by some operations managers, is that operations performance has an impact not just on the second line of the P&L (cost), but on the top one (revenue) as well. As a wise manager once said, 'Profit is a small number made up of the difference between two big numbers.' It doesn't take much increase in revenue and reduction in cost to make a huge difference to profitability. Operations should be judged on both.

The problem in measuring revenue is one of attribution. How do you know the extent to which operations' activities have had any impact on revenue? It is not directly measurable as such. Products and services may be selling either despite the operation's quality, responsiveness, dependability and flexibility, or because of it. Yet the connection between operations and its effect on revenue is clearly too important to ignore and should be assessed. Part of this assessment needs to be how well the operation supports the market-facing parts of the business in exploiting existing revenue-earning opportunities. This does not mean automatically trying to do anything that they ask regardless of consequences; it does mean being able to understand and spell out the consequences of exploiting revenue opportunities.

Don't stop there. You can make your operations more proactive than this. You can deliberately develop those aspects of its performance that hold the most potential for seizing revenue opportunities. So you should also be judged on the extent to which you prioritize the improvements that fit in with future marketing plans. One of the key questions that operations should continually be asking (of themselves and of Marketing) is: 'What marginal improvement in operations performance would lead to the greatest increase in revenue – is it higher quality? Faster response? Keeping delivery promises? Greater flexibility?' This provides a basis for operations to prioritize improvement. Of course contributing to this type of discussion is very much helped by a prior understanding of what revenue opportunities might arise in the future. Operations resources tend to be more difficult and take longer to shift than Marketing's view of the market, which is why it is always sensible for operations managers to keep up with how their marketing colleagues see markets developing and how they might respond.

Operations performance should include .its effect on return on capital

Operations select and manage capital resources. It seems obvious then that judging operations performance at a strategic level should include how you use capital resources. Producing more output with the same capital resources, or producing the same output with fewer resources, affects the business's return on investment, so needs to be formally assessed. Look at the ratio analysis in Figure 4.3; it is crude but it makes the point.[3] The simple return on investment ratio profit over total investment is broken down into 'profit/output' and 'output/total investment'. This first ratio (in effect average profit) can be further broken down into 'average revenue' minus 'average cost'. Operations indirectly affects the former through its ability to deliver superior levels of competitive performance. It affects the latter through the more productive use of it resources. And these two measures have been seen as the great operations balancing act – keeping revenue high through standards of service and competitive price, while keeping costs low.

What about the other part of the ratio – 'output/total investment'? This ratio represents the output being produced for the investment being put into the operation. It is shown in Figure 4.3 broken down into three ratios, 'output/capacity', 'capacity/fixed investment' and 'fixed investment/total investment'. Take these in turn. First 'output/capacity' is the utilization of the operation. This is determined largely by the operation's ability to adjust its capacity to match demand. Operations with a high degree of volume flexibility will be able to keep effective capacity at a level which is close to the demands placed on the operation. Next 'capacity/fixed investment', or what is sometimes called 'the productivity of fixed investment'. This is governed by the skill of the operation's technologists, and how skilfully they procure capital equipment. An operation that achieves the required capacity levels without needing large amounts of capital expenditure will have a better ratio than the operation that has thrown money at the problem. Finally 'fixed investment/total investment', is a ratio very much affected by the working capital requirements of the business. As far as the operations function is concerned, this usually means the level of inventories held.

Figure 4.3 Decomposing the ratio profit/total assets

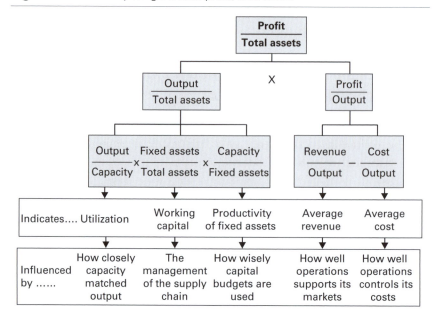

The point here is that your operations function can influence return on investment in more ways than keeping operational costs down; though this is important. It is also vital to tackle the other influences – volume flexibility, sharp imaginative and economical design of the process, and tight inventory management.

Operations performance should include its effect on risk

In assessing how your operations affects risk, we face similar problems to measuring its impact on revenue – but more so. Yet, again, there is clearly a connection. Well-designed and run operations should be less likely to fail; if they do fail, well-run operations should be able to recover faster and with less disruption (technically, this is called 'resilience'). However, it is worth pointing out that not only is the connection between operations and risk difficult to compute, contrary to the belief of many, risk is not always a 'bad thing'. Operations should not always be obsessed with minimizing risk. Instead, their objective should be to be better at taking risks than their competitors. Risk aversion can be costly and can make a business uncompetitive.

An operations advantage means having a better insight into the risks you are taking. This means being able to forecast your operating environment and understand the consequences of any failure occurring; and then make appropriate operating decisions based on this. Risk is relative. It might appear that you are taking more risks than others in your sector, yet you might be doing so with a full understanding of what you are doing. For example, one electricity-generating company developed a knowledge of the failure rates of its turbines, which was better than its turbine supplier actually had. Because of this it was able to get months' more operating time than its competitors from these assets before planning a maintenance outage. It reduced its operating cost significantly.

In assessing your risk performance, perhaps you should not only be concerned with 'avoiding mistakes' and 'maintaining operational controls' (although these can never be neglected). These are the ways to manage those risks that are already known about. Rather, you should also be building your knowledge of the risks that, as yet, are not known to exist. Perhaps you should be asking yourself these questions:

- What more do we now know about the risks we are potentially subject to?

- How good are we at either preventing them or coping with them?

- How clear are we about the extent to which we need to become really good at forecasting potential failure?

- Should we be deploying resources to try and prevent failure, or do we accept the potential for failure and get really good at fixing it when it occurs?

Operations performance should include its effect on building capabilities

The way you manage your operations affects their ability to build the capabilities on which future innovation is based. It is a vital part of your operation's contribution to strategy, so it is worth trying to make some kind of assessment of how good you are at it. Once more, it is not an easy thing to do, and it can't be measured directly as such, but (again) that is no excuse for ignoring it.

It's surprising just how rarely operations do conduct a proper audit of their capabilities and the resources on which they are based. OK, you will have allocated a monetary value to your physical (non-human) assets. You may even have included some kind of 'goodwill' element. But a full evaluation of how well each part of your resource base contributes to long- or even medium-term competitiveness? Probably not. If you do, you're one of the few.

Your operation's resources are not simply passive financial elements; they have a learning potential and a role that needs to be thoroughly appraised. Of course, your appraisal will have to start with a simple listing of your operation's resources, but this alone is rather like describing an automobile by listing its component parts. To understand how your operation (or your automobile) works you need to examine the interaction between its resources: how different resources, technology, operating sites, distribution networks, etc are positioned relative to each other; what skills your staff have, how they are organized into units, and so on. These arrangements of resources form the backdrop, and the limits, for how the processes of your operation have been designed. If you want to continue the automobile analogy, these processes are the mechanisms that power, steer and control the auto's performance, how it performs on the road, its style, its feel and its 'personality'.

What about the driver? The most technically advanced auto (or operation) is wasted on a novice driver. Yet even a novice, if he or she has the potential and a learning attitude, will, given time, eventually be able to excel. It is the same with your operation's resources and processes. The ability to learn moves your operation beyond its obvious tangible assets. Any audit of a company's capabilities needs to include the most important of its intangible resources – the ability to learn. As Bill Gates, who guided Microsoft in its most successful years, pointed out, 'Our primary assets, which are our software and software development skills, do not show up in the balance sheet at all.' (In Chapter 8 we will look in more detail at how the intangible resources and capabilities of your operations can be grown.)

Judge your operations performance at the operational level

Societal-level performance through the idea of the triple bottom line sets the backdrop for assessing the operation's contribution to the business's general strategic objectives which, in turn, forms the backdrop to assessing operations performance at a day-to-day level. This level requires the more tightly defined set of 'operations performance objectives' that we touched on in the previous chapter. There are five of them and they apply to all types of operation. Four are components of revenue – quality, speed, dependability and flexibility; the other is (again) cost-efficiency, but this time applied at the operational level. Each of them needs to be understood and defined in the context of your particular operation; the following points will help.

Quality

No one really disagrees with quality. Quality is virtuous, we all believe in it. This is not surprising. Quality leads to far more than individual virtue. It is the foundation of most other aspects of operational-level performance. However, 'quality' is a multi-faceted idea, and several different meanings and definitions can be (and are regularly) used. One important distinction is between 'specification quality' and 'conformance quality'. Quality can also be defined as 'fit for purpose'. That is, an operation's products or services do what they are supposed to do. It is a useful strategic definition, and the basis of the legal definition of quality in some jurisdictions, but it is not very helpful at an operational level. This is because 'fit for purpose' incorporates both specification and conformance quality, which are best treated separately.

Specification quality simply means how well the *intended* condition of a product or service meets the needs of customers. Generally, several aspects of specification are needed to properly define it and, of course, what these are will depend on the type of product or service you are producing. The job of individual operations managers will be to decide which particular features to include in their definition of specification quality. (A good rule of thumb is to use the features that have the biggest impact on customers, or cost, or both.) On a day-to-day level, specification quality may not be a major concern for many operations managers because it is largely a function of the design of the product or service. *Conformance quality* is of far more concern. It is an operation's ability to produce goods and services to their defined specification, reliably and consistently.

Quality as the gap between expectation and perception

One particularly useful way of thinking about quality is as the gap between customers' expectations and their perceptions. It is an approach that was originally used to describe service quality, but it works very well for diagnosing quality issues for either products or services.[4] The premise is simple: if your customers' perception of a product or service is better than expected, they will be satisfied and quality is perceived to be high. By contrast, if their perception of a product or service is worse than their expectations then they will be dissatisfied and quality will be judged to be poor. If the product or service matches expectations, then the perceived quality of the product or service is seen as acceptable.

Figure 4.4 A gap model of quality based on your customer's perceptions and expectations

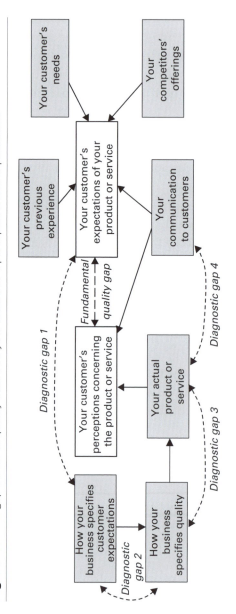

It is both a strength and a weakness of this approach that it relies on 'subjective' ideas of customer perception and expectation. It emphasizes the reality that the quality of a particular product or service is whatever customers perceive it to be. However, individual customers' expectations can be very different. Past experiences, individual knowledge and history will all shape your customers' expectations. Nor are your customers' perceptions absolute. They can (probably will) change, they may be based on misperceptions (which is still your responsibility to correct), and they could be being used as a negotiating ploy, so you have to use this approach carefully. Yet it does place the customer at the centre of how quality is judged – almost always a good thing. Just as powerful, by basing quality on the gap between perceptions and expectations, it allows us to explore why any gap might exist. Figure 4.4 shows some of these factors shaping expectations and perceptions and the potential gaps between them.[5]

If you use this 'gap model' of quality it allows you to diagnose the 'fundamental' quality gap (between customers' perceptions and their expectations) in terms of 'diagnostic gaps' elsewhere. There are four of these:

Diagnostic gap 1: *The 'customer's expectation – organization's specification' gap*. Perceived quality could be poor because there is a mismatch between your own internal specification of quality and that expected by the customer. In other words, your understanding of your customers is flawed at best, or plain wrong at worst.

Diagnostic gap 2: *The 'organization's specification – quality specification' gap*. Perceived quality could be poor because there is a mismatch between what you intend the product or service to be like (its specification) and the way this specification has been translated into a workable set of operational measures that you can use to control quality.

Diagnostic gap 3: *The quality specification – actual quality gap*. Perceived quality could be poor because there is a mismatch between the actual quality of the service or product that you produce and its internal quality specification. This is the conventional and widely used 'conformance to specification' definition of quality.

Diagnostic gap 4: *The actual quality – communication gap*. Perceived quality could also be poor because there is a gap between the external messages that you (or your Marketing people) give, either intended or not, and the actual quality delivered to the customer. It could be called the 'marketing – operations gap', and may be down to operations failures, marketing hype, or both.

It is obvious how you can use this gap model to take a broad view of why quality problems may be occurring. It is wise, periodically, to undertake a critical questioning of each gap to search for potential root causes of quality problems – note the 'periodically'. Such questioning cannot be a routine procedure for every can of beans emerging from a canning plant, or customer passing through a Metro system. In that case the questioning of the gaps would be only occasional. However, if you have lower-volume, higher-variety operations such as supplying customized capital goods, construction or consultancy, it can provide a logical framework for post-delivery analysis.

Speed

Time is more than money; time is value. It both saves cost to your operation and gives benefit to your customers. Moving information and materials through your operation faster makes for a leaner and more productive operation. It also brings customer request and your response closer together, giving greater satisfaction to your customers and less complexity for your operation. Increased responsiveness is an investment both in customer satisfaction and in reducing your cost base.

At its most simple, speed indicates the elapsed time between a process being triggered and its completion. This may relate to an external event, for example from the time between customer request and delivery. Or it may be internal; for example the time for material or information to move through a process. Naturally, internal and external speed are related. Part of the external elapsed time to respond to customers may be the internal core processing time, but it should also include any time needed to clarify a customer's exact needs, design products or services if they are customized and the time to deliver, transport and/or install the product or service. Figure 4.5 illustrates some of the significant 'process' times that show the steps in customer response, and demonstrate what it means for an IT systems supplier.

The issue for most operations is how to define the speed of delivery. Limiting it to the elapsed time taken by your core process (usually the element you can most directly control) is inadequate. From your customers' view the total process could start when they become aware that they may want or need the product or service and ends when they are completely satisfied with it 'in use'. It could even be argued that, given the need continually to engage the customer in other revenue-generating activities such as maintenance or improvement, the process never ends.

Figure 4.5 Example – some significant times for the delivery of an IT system

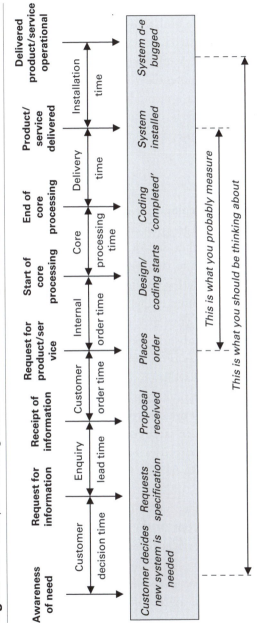

Not all of these stages and events will necessarily apply for all parts of your operation, but the general idea is clear – all elements of your total response time should be included in any assessment of your operation's response performance. Just as important, what determines the elapsed time of each stage needs to be both understood and critically examined. So, for example in the case of the IT system in Figure 4.5, customer decision time will be influenced by how effectively this supplier has communicated the ways in which it could potentially serve its customer, how well it can help the customer make a decision, and how well it helps the customer to specify its requirements. Enquiry lead-time is a function of the speed of the business's internal proposal preparation processes, and so on.

Dependability

Dependability means keeping your delivery promises – honouring the delivery time you have given to your customer, whether it was made explicitly or implicitly. It is the other half of total delivery performance, along with delivery speed; in fact the two performance objectives are often linked. Theoretically, it is simple for you to achieve high dependability merely by quoting long delivery times, in which case you are using the extra time as an insurance against your lack of dependability inside your operation. However, if you try to absorb poor dependability inside long lead-times, you can finish up being poor at both. There are two reasons for this. First (and as an example of Parkinson's Law) delivery times tend to expand to fill the time available. Second, long delivery times are often a result of slow internal response, high work-in-progress, and large amounts of non-value-added time. All of these can cause confusion, complexity and lack of control, which are often the root causes of poor dependability in the first place. Good dependability can often be helped by fast throughput, rather than hindered by it.

However, speed and dependability are fundamentally different types of objective. Speed is up-front in the competitive process. It is quoted, and defined as part of the specification for an order. It can be as much a part of a product or service offering as its technical specification. Customers may make some attempt to specify dependability – by the use of penalty clauses for late delivery for example, but all too often it remains a 'hindsight' performance objective. It becomes important only when a history of performance – good or bad – is established. To quote the well-worn sales saying, 'Without a fast delivery promise you don't get a chance to prove how dependable you are – you just don't get the order.'

In principle, dependability is a straightforward concept:

dependability = due delivery time – actual delivery time

'On time' means the equation equals zero. But what is the meaning of 'due time'? The time originally requested by your customer or the time quoted by your operation? Also, delivery times can be changed, sometimes by customers but more often by your operation. If your customer wants a new delivery time, should that be used to calculate delivery performance (generally, yes)? Or if your operation has to reschedule delivery, should the changed delivery time be used (generally, no)? It is not uncommon in some circumstances to find four or five arguable due times for each order, nor is the actual delivery time without its complications. When, for example, should one count the product or service as having been delivered? When it is ready for delivery? When the customer receives it? When it is working? Or when everyone involved is fully comfortable with it?

Come clean with customers – delivery integrity is as important as dependability

Managing your customers' expectations can be as important as your actual performance. A bad sign is when the first indication of a late delivery is Sales receiving an irate phone call from your customer. Given sufficient notice of a potential late delivery it may be possible to do something that helps reduce its impact. A simple early warning system that alerts everyone to the likely problems ahead may be all that is necessary. Bowing to the inevitable late on in the delivery cycle is far more disruptive than an early admission of problems together with sensitive customer management. This idea of 'delivery integrity' as opposed to 'delivery dependability' is important. They are clearly related concepts, and good delivery integrity can go some way to compensate for poor dependability, but should be seen as an occasional recovery tactic, not 'the way we deal with a lack of punctuality'.

It all adds up – dependability (or lack of it) is cumulative

One of the problems with managing your dependability performance is that it tends to only work one way – dependability, when lost, is difficult to retrieve. This is because each stage in an operation's internal supply process can be performing reasonably in its own terms, yet when taken together, contributes to a far worse total performance for the whole process. For example, Figure 4.6 shows the customer 'decision tree' that charts the hypothetical progress of 100 customers' service from a business. (This example is based on a customized environmental control system company.) Supply performance, as seen by the core operation (the system assembly operation), is represented by the shaded part of the diagram. It has received 35 customer orders, 32 of which were 'produced' (designed, assembled and tested) on time. However, originally 100 customers requested proposals, 20 of whom found the business could not supply appropriate systems (did not have appropriate capability), 10 of whom could not be satisfied because required delivery times could not be met (insufficient capacity). This leaves 70 potential orders still in the process, 30 of whom were not satisfied with the price. Five dropped out anyway (frustrated by the process?) Of the 35 orders received, 32 were produced as promised (shipped), but 12 could not be installed as promised because of 'on-site' problems. So what seems a 91 per cent dependability for the 'core process' (35 orders, 22 shipped on-time) is in fact a 20 per cent performance from the customer's perspective.

This is just one business in what might be a far more extensive supply chain. Include the cumulative effect of similar reductions in performance for all the operations in a chain, and the probability that the end customer is adequately served could become remote. The point here is not that all

Figure 4.6   Always take a customer perspective on dependability performance – it can be surprising

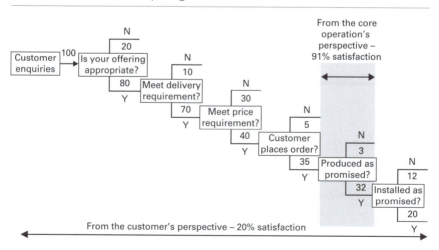

operations or supply chains have unsatisfactory supply performances (although most have considerable potential for improvement). Rather it is that the performance both of the supply chain as a whole, and its constituent operations, should be judged in terms of how end-customer needs are satisfied.

Flexibility

'Flexibility' is one of those words. We all use it, and it is generally thought to be a good thing, but it has a whole variety of meanings. One definition sees flexibility as meaning the 'ability to be bent' or, to put it in operations terms, the ability to take up different positions or do different things. Your operation is more flexible than others if it can do more things; produce a greater variety of products and services, or operate at different output levels.

Yet the range of things your operation can do is only one aspect of what we mean by flexibility. We use the same word to mean the ease with which something can move between its possible states. An operation that moves quickly, smoothly and cheaply from doing one thing to doing another is more flexible than one that can only complete the same change at greater cost and/or disruption. The cost and the time of making a change are the 'friction' elements of flexibility. In fact, for most types of flexibility, time is a good indicator of cost and disruption. So the first distinction to make is between *range flexibility* – how much the operation can be changed, and *response flexibility* – how fast it can be changed.

The next issue with 'flexibility' is what it relates to, what is being changed. For example:

- Product/service flexibility – the ability to introduce and produce novel products or services or to modify existing ones.
- Mix flexibility – the ability to change the variety of products or services being produced by the operation within a given time period.
- Volume flexibility – the ability to change the level of the operation's aggregated output.
- Delivery flexibility – the ability to change planned or assumed delivery dates.

Each of these types of total operations flexibility has its range and response components, described in Table 4.2.

Table 4.2 The range and response dimensions of the four types of operations flexibility

Total operations flexibility	Range flexibility	Response flexibility
Product/service flexibility	The range of products and services that the company has the design, purchasing and operations capability to produce.	The time necessary to develop or modify the products, or services and processes that produce them, to the point where regular production can start.
Mix flexibility	The range of products and services the company produces within a given time period.	The time necessary to adjust the mix of products and services being produced.
Volume flexibility	The absolute level of aggregated output the company can achieve for a given product or service mix.	The time taken to change the aggregated level of output.
Delivery flexibility	The extent to which delivery dates can be brought forward.	The time taken to reorganize the operation so as to re-plan for the new delivery date.

The key issue for most of us is, 'Which types of flexibility are important for us?' Different competitive conditions will imply different types of flexibility being valued. For example:

- Unpredictable markets = volume (response) flexibility, and possibly volume (range) flexibility if peak to trough demand is particularly large.

- High variety markets, or markets that value customization = mix (range) flexibility; mix (response) flexibility, and possibly product/service (response) flexibility.

- Fast moving, innovative, markets = product/service flexibility (range and response).

- Markets where your customers are subject to high levels of uncertainty = delivery (response) flexibility.

Flexibility may not come for free. It may need investment in flexible technology, surplus capacity, a wide supply base, etc. Extra cost to obtain more flexibility is not always necessary, but it can be. So, developing your flexibility means: 1) identifying the types of flexibility that best serve your market conditions, and 2) investigating the costs of providing the flexibility – it may not be worth it.

Cost-efficiency

Earlier we made the obvious point that cost is a key strategic objective; also that the most common cost drivers at the strategic level are volume, variety, variation and visibility. But cost is important at any level, although the way it is treated is different. At the operational level it is the efficiency with which materials and information are processed that becomes important. The key drivers of your cost efficiency at this level are your quality, speed, dependability and flexibility. Think about it in the following way.

Quality reduces cost

Using quality to mean conformance to specification, the effect on cost is almost always significant. Making fewer errors within the operation directly reduces reworking, waste and the need to check everything; it also means fewer surprises in the operation, more internal dependability, and so less confusion. More than this, error-free operation enhances your operation's ability to reduce throughput time, which in turn reduces your cost.

Speed (fast throughput) reduces cost

When material or information moves quickly through your operation, it spends less time in inventory, attracts fewer overheads, and makes forecasting easier, all of which have a positive effect on your costs. Fast throughput also encourages dependable delivery since small deviations from schedule can be accommodated faster.

Dependability reduces cost

Internal dependability reduces the confusion and uncertainty in your operation. If all materials and information are transferred within your operation exactly as planned, the (often considerable) overhead you have to devote to chasing up late deliveries is eliminated, as is all the effort of rescheduling to accommodate the late delivery. It also allows your throughput to be speeded up. Reversing this logic: if you are not internally dependable there is certainly no point in trying to speed up throughput.

Figure 4.7 Internal performance objectives can be mutually reinforcing and benefit external performance objectives

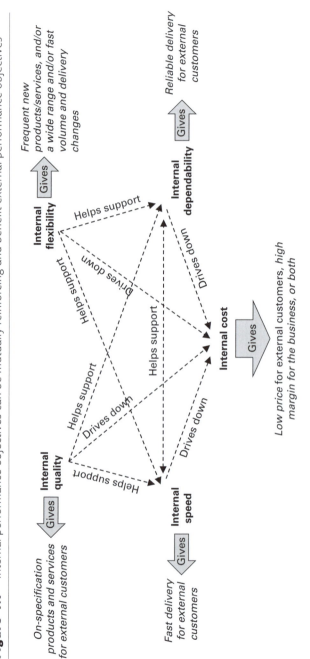

Flexibility reduces cost

Enhancing some kind of flexibility (mainly response flexibility, see earlier) can also improve your costs, both directly and indirectly: directly, by letting your operation change from doing one thing to doing another with little lost output (for example by increasing changeover flexibility); indirectly, by reducing throughput time that in turn reduces your costs. Flexibility can also increase internal dependability, for example by allowing you to use an alternative process route to bypass a breakdown, which in turn again reduces cost.

Figure 4.7 shows this general relationship between internal performance objectives. The message from it is that internally there should be no trade-off between cost-efficiency and the other performance objectives. They all support and reinforce each other, which in effect sets the general question for the operational improvement of your costs: 'How can quality, speed, dependability and flexibility improvement be made to improve cost performance?' This is a topic we shall return to.

Practical prescriptions

- Do not confine your view of operations performance to operational measures. Always assess your operations performance at different levels, ranging from societal to strategic to operational. Each level is important.

- Make a clear link between what your operation does and social and environmental performance as well as financial performance.

- Explore how changes in the volume, variety, variation and visibility of your operation affect costs. They are the strategic drivers of operations costs.

- As a benchmark, try estimating your 'technology limited cost'. It will indicate your 'cost floor' with your current technology and organization.

- Make a clear link between your operation's activities and their effect on revenue. It won't always be easy, but make some estimate of how quality, speed of response, dependability and flexibility impact on revenue.

- Again, spell out how your operations activities and decisions affect return on assets. Use the ratio analysis of Figure 4.3 as a starting point.

- Make a formal assessment of how well your operations function understands how its activities affect risk. This should go beyond simple failure prevention and include how good your operation is at building its knowledge of the risks that, as yet, are not known to exist.

- Conduct an audit of how well your operations function builds capabilities and the resources on which they are based.

- Use the 'gap model' of quality as a diagnostic tool to evaluate where quality failures may be occurring.

- Evaluate response time to your customers, including all elapsed times from the time customers become aware of their need for your products or services, to the point where they are fully satisfied.

- Measure dependability from your customers' viewpoint rather than that of each individual link in the internal (and external, if appropriate) supply chain.

- Flexibility can mean many different things. Make sure that you have identified and defined what types of flexibility are important to you. Also remember to distinguish between 'range' and 'response' flexibility.

- At an operational level, develop an understanding of what impacts the cost-efficiency of your processes. In particular, make sure that everyone appreciates the effect improvements in your internal quality, speed, dependability and flexibility can have on cost-efficiency.

Notes

1   The phrase 'the triple bottom line' was first used in 1994 by John Elkington, the founder of the British consultancy, SustainAbility. Read Elkington, J (2007) *Cannibals with Forks: The triple bottom line*, Wiley, New York

2   Source: Novozymes Annual Report, 2015

3   This analysis was originally put forward (as far as I can find out) by Eilon, S, Gold, B and Soesan, J (1976) *Applied Productivity Analysis for Industry*, Pergamon Press, Oxford

4   An idea originally proposed in Zeithaml, Parasuraman and Berry (1990) *Delivering Quality Service; Balancing customer perceptions and expectations*, Free Press, New York

5   Again based on Zeithaml, Parasuraman and Berry's work

Resource your operation appropriately

05

Resourcing your operation 'simply' means deciding how many resources you should have. It's a fundamental question: 'How big should you be?' Put more formally: 'How many resources do you need to provide the capacity that you require?' Getting the resourcing decision wrong is almost always serious, sometimes terminal. Getting it right is vital in achieving an operations advantage. Too much capacity underutilizes resources and drives your costs up. Too little capacity limits your ability to serve customers and therefore earn revenues. It is important because the risks inherent in getting capacity wrong lie both in having an inappropriate level of resources and in mismanaging the process of changing capacity over time. We will look at both these issues in this chapter. It is also the first chapter to deal directly with what is needed to support your operations advantage; see Figure 5.1.

What is involved in resourcing?

'How much capacity do you need' seems a relatively simple question, but there are a number of ways that you can look at it, and a number of questions that need answering:

1 How should you decide on the resourcing levels that you need in the short, medium and long term and, more importantly, how do you integrate these decisions?

2 On what assumptions are you basing your resourcing needs? What demand forecasts are you using? What assumptions are you using about your ability to deal with demand?

3 Do you really want to meet demand? Can you afford the capacity you need to meet demand? Can you realistically meet demand in the required timescale?

4 How should you flex your capacity (if at all) as demand fluctuates?

Figure 5.1 This chapter looks at how to resource your operation appropriately

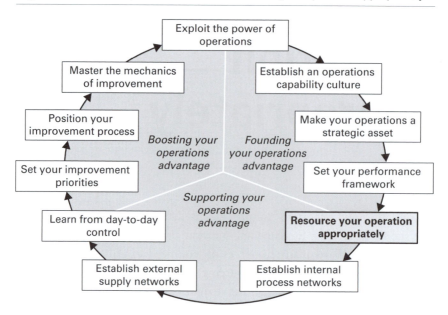

5 What are the consequences of not fully utilizing your capacity? (It's not necessarily a bad thing.)

Deciding on resourcing levels in the short, medium and long term (and integrating these decisions)

The number and mix of resources that you have will affect your capacity. Capacity is your operation's potential for producing goods or delivering services over a period of time. Deciding on capacity takes place in all operations minute-by-minute, day-by-day, month-on-month and year-on-year. Every time you move someone from one part of the operation to another, you are adjusting capacity within your operation. Every change to shift patterns, every adjustment of working hours, impacts on your effective capacity. These decisions may not be strategic, but they do impact directly on the long-term physical scale of the operation. They also take place within the constraints of the physical limits of the operation, the ability of its suppliers to supply, the availability of staff, and so on. In other words, although capacity decisions are taken for different timescales and spanning different areas of the operation, each level of capacity decision is made with the constraints of a higher level. Figure 5.2 summarizes some decisions taken at each level.

Figure 5.2 Capacity planning should be integrated across levels because each level constrains what can be done in the level below

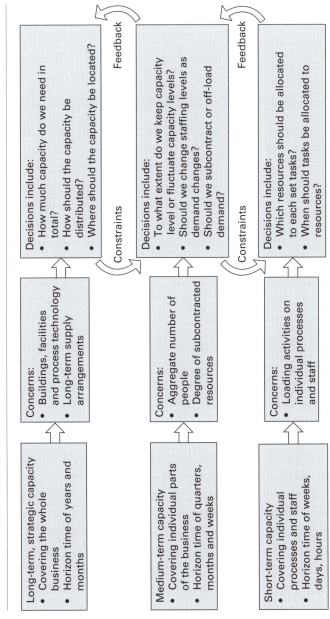

However, it is worth noting that what Figure 5.2 shows as three levels of capacity decision making are, to some extent, arbitrary. There will always be some overlap between the levels, and the actual timescales of the three levels will vary between industries. The important point here is that capacity planning should be integrated across levels because each level constrains what can be done in the level below, which is why some kind of hierarchical approach is particularly useful.

Respect the hierarchy of planning and control

Resourcing, like all operations planning and control decisions, can be complicated and fraught with a whole host of uncertainties. Added to this, the cumulative lead-times for sourcing outside supplies and for production itself are usually longer than customers are prepared to wait. This is why 'hierarchical approaches' are necessary. They try to bring some order to the complexity by dividing up all the interrelated planning and control decisions into sub-problems that match your organization's structure and hierarchy. They also allow a degree of stability in the planning process so that relatively complex operations can be protected against too many short-term changes. At the same time, they can give some independence to planners at different levels. Doing this requires three types of integration:

1 Integration of decision making at different levels – long, medium and short term.

2 Integration of planning and control between the various parts of the organization.

3 Integration between different time periods.

The key test of how well your process integrates these aspects of planning and control can be judged in two ways: 1) how well the constraints imposed by decisions made at the higher level of planning, the wider span of the organization, or the longer timescale, are transmitted to lower, narrower, or shorter levels; and 2) how well the execution of detailed decisions at the lower level can provide the necessary feedback so that the quality of higher-level decision making can be judged. Do not be too limited in how you interpret the principles behind hierarchical planning and control. Different organizations can perfectly legitimately interpret this general structure in different ways, using different terms, incorporating different decisions, and having different numbers of levels. What is important is consistency between whatever levels are chosen, and that each hierarchical level agrees a reasonably common set of decision rules and methods, planning horizons, levels of detail of information and forecasts. Without these, integration between levels can be difficult to the point of dysfunction. So before attempting hierarchical planning and control you need to address several questions:[1]

- How many planning levels do you need?

- What decisions should constrain what other decisions and how tightly?

- Is there a danger that your hierarchical approach will reduce the speed of decision making by requiring continual upward referral?

- How much autonomy and local control should you devolve to lower levels or to distributed operations facilities?

- Is it likely that stability will be achieved only by excessive rigidity, at the expense of speed and responsiveness?

- Are you sure that all your data is accurate, timely and in common formats?

- Are all your team committed to the significant degree of managerial discipline that is required to guarantee effective transition between the various planning levels?

What assumptions are you using to plan your resourcing needs?

There are two sets of assumptions that you need to make when deciding on resourcing. Both are important, but both can be difficult. The first assumption is demand forecasts – how much demand your operation will have to cope with; in other words, how heavily will your resources be loaded? The second is how much of that load will your resources will be able to handle; in other words, what is its capacity? This comparison between loading and capacity is the central issue in any kind of (long-, medium- or short-term) resourcing. (It is also an essential element in process design, as we shall see in the next chapter.)

Demand forecasts are necessary – just don't believe them

It is always worth remembering two points about forecasting: 1) without some kind of forecast of future conditions you cannot be expected to plan your resourcing needs effectively, and 2) forecasts are almost always wrong.

Some things we can forecast with accuracy (yes, the sun will rise tomorrow), but most things we cannot. Yet forecasts are more than just necessary: they are fundamental to resourcing decisions. Unless you can switch on capacity instantly, you need to plan ahead, and planning requires at least some idea of what demand, and therefore loading, your operation will have to handle. We need forecasts, even when we have reservations about them. The economist Tim Harford is realistic about them: 'The truth is that forecasts are like Pringles – nobody thinks that there's any great virtue in them but, offered the fleeting pleasure of consuming them, we find it hard to resist.'[2]

We all know that forecasts will be wrong. Hopefully only by a bit, but sometimes they are so far out that your plans look (at best) unwise. We do not know *precisely* how many orders we will receive or how many customers will walk through the door tomorrow, next month, or next year. As the economist John Kenneth Galbraith said, 'the only function of economic forecasting is to make astrology look respectable'. Without going as far as the ancients, who believed that all forecasts were an affront to the gods, it is as well to be sceptical. Yet there are some precautions that you can take.

1 Insist on probabilistic forecasts

The future is uncertain. So why do we pretend that a single number representing the 'best estimate' is appropriate? Maybe it is because we like to think that our forecasting colleagues are the experts who have decoded the mystery of how markets work. But the world does not 'run on rails', and operations managers should not accept any forecast that implies that it does. We should not be interested in a single point forecast. That is the one value of demand that is almost guaranteed not to occur. Point estimates give no information on how much uncertainty is wrapped up in the forecast. What we need is a probabilistic estimate – a good idea of the range of demand that might occur. Range of possible demand is helpful because tied up with our estimate of future demand is the corresponding decision of how much capacity we should plan for. The uncertainty that is implied by a probabilistic estimate may act as a brake on us foolishly investing in capacity to meet a hypothetical level of demand.

You will react differently to a forecast that estimated next quarter's demand at 1000 units ± 10 units than you would to an estimate of 1000 ± 500 units. Exactly how you should react to lower and higher estimates will depend on the economics of your operation. It could be that, should the lower level of demand actually occur, the financial consequences would be unacceptable. Similarly, other consequences of over- and under-capacity should also be considered. For example, planning resources that give capacity at the higher estimate of demand may give your operation the flexibility to respond to short-term surges, particularly valuable when satisfying short-term demand can have long-term implications.

The message here is that there are significant advantages in probabilistic forecasts when planning resourcing levels. They do require more thought, both from forecasters and operations managers who use the information, and it is more difficult to shift blame to forecasters when things go wrong, but using them is a far more 'grown up' response to planning in an uncertain world. Moreover there is some evidence that most of us make better decisions when presented with probabilistic forecasts.[3]

2 Look for the assumption behind the forecasts

Forecasters forecast, and operations managers manage operations. Shall the two meet? Yes, if you want to avoid the potentially drastic consequences of your resourcing plan being undermined by inaccurate forecasts. All operations managers should spend a little time understanding the assumptions behind forecasts – and there always are assumptions. Often they are simple human biases. The most common one is assuming that things will broadly stay the same: when sales are growing, expecting them to keep on growing; when falling, to keep on falling. The cause of such biases is an over-reliance on looking at the past to predict the future. Of course, past market behaviour is important, but it is only one factor in forecasting the future.

Forecasters will usually combine two different approaches. One is indeed data-based, grounded on how markets have behaved in the past. The other is model-based, formed by how they believe markets will behave, given their assumptions about the market. Most models are based on identifying the key drivers that impact demand. However, even sophisticated forecasting models are just that – models. They are only simplifications of, and approximations to, a complex and possibly fast-changing reality. This is why it is worth interrogating their assumptions. The most obvious things to check out are the following:

- The total market – growing? Shrinking? Why? What is driving customer behaviour?

- Your market share – what are competitors doing? Are they launching new offerings? What is their sales strategy?

- Your sales and marketing efforts – what is happening with your sales force? Are you changing pricing policy? Are you changing promotional efforts?

- Your offerings – are you launching any new offerings? What might that do to the confidence you have in your forecasts?

- Your strategic targets – has there been any pressure to adjust forecasts to 'support' targets? Are you deliberately avoiding 'unpalatable news'? (A forecast should never be a target; all it will do is undermine faith in the forecast.)

3 Check on 'true demand'

It is a mistake to always assume that the demand that your operation is asked to fulfil is the 'true' demand for your offerings. Demand can 'get lost' in the sales fulfilment process. It as well to make sure that 'forecast errors' are not, in fact, problems that your own internal systems have created. If you use statistical forecasting models, you will need to check that 'demand' is the same as 'orders placed', which is fully reflected in 'shipments to customers'. Reasons why this may not be the case include the following:[4]

- An order that cannot be filled immediately may be turned down by your sales order processing, or (more likely) cancelled by the customer, meaning that the order may not show up as demand.

- An unfilled order may be rolled ahead into a future time bucket, meaning that true demand is overstated in future time buckets. It may even mean that the order appears in both the original and the future time bucket.

- If a shortage is anticipated, customers (or even your salespeople) may adjust (usually exaggerate) their orders to take a larger share of any allocation.

- If customers suspect a shortage or delivery disruption, they may withhold their orders, change the orders to a different product, or place their orders with another supplier. So how now to judge 'true' demand? Even if customers truly did want your offerings, their demand will not show in your records because no order was placed. Or maybe worse, if customers ordered an alternative offering this will overestimate its true demand.

- Perhaps the worst case is that, if there are persistent supply shortages and customers go elsewhere, then all information on their demand is lost.

There could be other reasons why true demand is hidden from you. The answer is always to dig behind simple 'order' or 'shipment' data to get some idea of what demand could be.

Capacity forecasts are also necessary – but treat them with caution

Demand forecasting is difficult but necessary. It is exactly the same with estimating the relationship between your resources and the capacity that they can provide. For relatively small and self-contained operations that produce standardized physical offerings, the link between resources and capacity can be reasonably straightforward. A basic machine-paced assembly line that produces a product every 30 seconds will have a capacity of 960 products per eight-hour shift, though even this estimate of capacity will need adjusting for occasional glitches in the technology or supply of parts. A larger, more interdependent operation producing a wider variety of products will present more challenges. Bottlenecks shift around, individual processes may not always mesh together and potential output will depend on the mix of products being produced. Ask almost any operations manager what his or her capacity is and the answer will almost always be, 'it depends'.

When it comes to service operations it is even more difficult. Output can be intangible, the effectiveness of the service produced dependent on the perceptions of individual customers, and productivity is harder to measure. How, for example, do you accurately measure the potential output of a call centre? Would you judge a 15-minute haircut better or worse than a 30-minute one? When it comes to anything that involves creativity and complex judgement, the link between resources and capacity becomes very tenuous indeed. What is a reasonable number of creatives in an advertising agency? What output should you expect from an R&D engineer? A common question from operations managers in all but the simplest operations is: 'How many people should I have?'

As a first step, it is worthwhile looking at how individual resources and the way you organize them affect capacity. Go through the following list and try to identify the resources that are limiting your capacity:

- *Facilities* – How much of a constraint are your buildings? That is office space, factory size, warehouse volume, consulting rooms, whatever physical space is needed to produce your offerings. Also, their effective capacity might be their location and layout.

- *People* – Do the tasks that are required by people's jobs match their skills? Do they have the ability to switch tasks when required? Are they time-flexible through extra working hours or changed shift patterns? To what extent do motivation, absenteeism and labour turnover constrain capacity?

- *Product/service mix* – Standardized offerings, even complex ones, are relatively predictable; not so when one produces a wide variety of offerings. By how much will moving resources from one activity to another reduce your capacity?

- *Technology reliability* – Process technology may have a capacity that can be measured relatively easily. What may be more difficult to estimate is the effect its reliability has on effective capacity. How much allowance is reasonable for downtime, either unexpected or planned maintenance?

- *Output specification* – Can the specification of your offerings (usually services) be flexed to provide extra effective capacity? For example, customers are (more or less) comfortable with the idea that packages may take longer to arrive at peak times like Christmas.

- *Scheduling* – Within your operation, do scheduling problems between processes result in waiting or competition for resources?

- *Supply* – Can internal changes to resource capacity be matched by external parts of the supply chain?

- *Inventory* – Are restrictions on inventory levels limiting the timing or the extent to which your capacity can be flexed?

CASE STUDY Karolinska hospital improves resource utilization

In healthcare, resourcing issues can literally mean the difference between life and death. When the Karolinska hospital in Sweden faced a resourcing crisis it prompted an investigation into how well its expensive and scarce resources were being utilized. What it found was that its operating theatre surgeons and other staff were being utilized for little more than 50 per cent of their time, largely because of how patients were being scheduled through its resources. The hospital realized that it would have to change how its processes operated if resource utilization was to be improved. When the bottleneck resource was discovered to be the operating theatres themselves, the hospital looked at ways in which it could reduce the time the patients needed to spend in the theatre.

It created a separate patient preparation area that allowed activities to be carried out on patients in parallel rather than in sequence with the surgery. It also discovered that some delays were caused because anaesthetists were being called away to other parts of the hospital. So, instead of operating independently, anaesthetists were formally allocated to the operating theatre team and a pre-operative clinic was created to evaluate patients prior to surgery.

Tackling these process issues, largely around throughput, the hospital found that more operations could be carried out using the same resources. More than this, it became possible to create a much more reliable schedule because the time between diagnosis and surgery had been cut dramatically.

Get a fix on your surge capacity

It is a mistake to try and fix an absolute relationship between resources and the capacity they provide. There is obviously a relationship, but it can be a loose one. In most businesses the same set of resources can be capable of providing different levels of capacity depending on how long they are expected to do it for. We may be able to gain an increased level of output by asking our people to work longer or differently than normal. We can delay routine maintenance, push staff holidays into another period, or pull in favours from suppliers – but not indefinitely. Most of our operations will have some level of 'surge capacity' that can be maintained for a relatively short time. We probably would not want to do this for long, and it may lose its effectiveness if we try to do it too often. However, it is worth trying to work out what our surge capacity might be, how we would arrange it, and how long we could keep it up for. Then, should we need to, we would be better placed to 'switch on' the extra capacity without too much delay or confusion.

Capacity leakage and OEE

Capacity 'leaks' from an operation. The theoretical capacity of an operation is rarely achieved in practice. One popular method of assessing this reduction in capacity is overall equipment effectiveness (OEE). Do not be put off by the name. As it suggests, it was originally devised as a method for assessing capacity efficiency in heavy equipment-based operations. However, it's general principles are universal and can be applied in any type of operation. The OEE calculation thinks in terms of operating time and what causes it to be 'wasted' or 'lost'. In particular, it focuses on those losses that are (or should be) avoidable; these are shown in Figure 5.3. As with the name of this approach, it's best not to get too hung up about the names used in the figure. Different authorities use different names.

The essential idea is to distinguish between the losses that are unavoidable as far as the operation itself is concerned, such as demand not warranting

Figure 5.3 Where capacity 'leaks' – the OEE approach

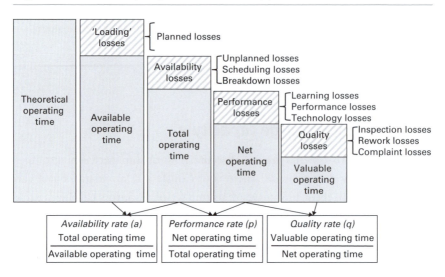

making capacity available (loading losses), and avoidable losses. Avoidable losses are categorized as:

- Availability losses – for example, time lost through changeovers, when equipment or people are being prepared for the next activity, scheduling gaps, and breakdown failures or absences.

- Performance losses – for example, when temporary staff are not working at a full rate, when an IT system is running slowly.

- Quality losses – for example, the time lost through inspection delays, rework or handling customer queries/complaints.

If the time lost for each of these categories can be measured, as they can in equipment-dominated operations (such as cement plants), an OEE calculation can be used to compare the performance of operations. In this case:

$$\text{OEE} = a \times p \times q$$

where a is the availability rate of the operation; p is the performance rate of the operation, and q is the quality rate of the operation.

Don't just use past performance to estimate future resourcing needs

This is what most of us do. If last quarter our 10 helpdesk technicians coped reasonably well and next quarter's demand is expected to be 10 per cent higher, then one extra technician should give about the same level of service. It's a quick and easy approach, but it's kind of lazy. Better to attempt to unpick, at least approximately, how resources affect capacity. Look at the example, 'How many service engineers?' In this case the operations manager made some attempt to bring a degree of quantification to the process of linking resources to capacity. Admittedly it was a rough 'first pass' attempt, but it did give two important benefits. It set a simple benchmark, which almost certainly would have to be adjusted in the light of experience, but nevertheless gave some consistency. Just as important, because he approached the process in a collaborative way, it opened up the debate on how the design job could be standardized.

CASE STUDY How many design engineers?

This time last year Lee had been worried about the demands that were going to be placed on his design unit in the upcoming year: 'So many things were changing. We were launching a new range of products that would enable our customers to take advantage of some of the latest technology allowing them to improve their energy efficiency significantly. We had just taken over a smaller but very dynamic competitor. Finally, we were expecting an increase in demand overall because of the increased market interest in more sophisticated building management systems.'

Lee was the operations director of a successful heating, ventilation and air-conditioning (HVAC) company. But success had not been without its problems. One was how they should plan for the increased load on his design engineers: 'We now had 15 design engineers, 11 who had always been with us, and four from the company that we acquired. The acquired company operated in more or less the same way as we did, but they seemed to do it in a far more efficient way as far as their design function was concerned. Our original engineers coped with around $1.5 million of business each last year, but our new people seemed to have been dealing with in excess of $2 million each. It isn't that the systems being designed were more expensive, or that they had better technology. As far as I could tell, they were just more productive.

'The first thing that we did was to break down a typical design assignment into its constituent elements. This took some doing because not every design assignment is the same. Nevertheless, we eventually agreed on a standardized approach that could be used for any kind of assignment. The next task was to try and estimate the time that would be necessary for each element. That posed a problem because the time necessary could vary quite significantly.

Nevertheless, we eventually agreed both an average time and the upper and lower limits of possible times for each element. We took some time over this and did it collaboratively with all the engineers. We did not want them to feel as though we were imposing a too-rigid set of standards on them.'

What came out of this exercise was not only an agreed set of standards but also the revelation that the acquired company actually used a different approach to its design that involved each engineer undertaking several projects simultaneously. This led to improvements in the unit's design practice generally.

What kind of demand variation are you responding to?

Demand varies. Sometimes it varies in a fairly predictable manner, sometimes not. Sometimes it takes you by surprise. In either circumstance, you are faced with the decision of how to flex your resourcing levels (if at all) to respond to the changed demand. In fact, how you respond should depend on the balance between your predictable and unpredictable variation in demand. The most benign situation is where demand is both stable and predictable. You can then focus on making sure that resourcing levels really do match demand appropriately. If demand changes are largely predictable, resourcing adjustments can be planned in advance. The aim should be to take advantage of the predictability to make the changes as efficiently as possible. Where variation in demand is highly unpredictable, if your operation is to react to it at all (an option is not to), it must do so quickly, otherwise the change in resourcing will have little effect on your operation's capacity. If you are unlucky enough to have both highly variable and highly unpredictable demand, your unenviable task is to try to adjust resourcing as fast and as efficiently as possible.

Figure 5.4 shows how the aims and tasks of resourcing vary depending on the balance between predictable and unpredictable variation. It also indicates how the whole issue of flexing resources can be made easier. As one would expect, it is a matter of enhancing market knowledge: not just getting better forecasts (although they help) but rather a deeper understanding of how demand could possibly be managed to reduce variation. The key question is, 'What more do we need to know about our customers that would allow us to shift demand to our mutual advantage?'

Figure 5.4 The aim of managing resourcing levels depends on the mixture of predictable and unpredictable demand

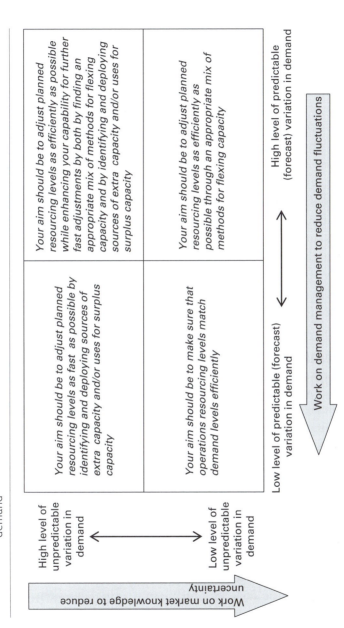

High level of unpredictable variation in demand

Your aim should be to adjust planned resourcing levels as fast as possible by identifying and deploying sources of extra capacity and/or uses for surplus capacity

Your aim should be to adjust planned resourcing levels as efficiently as possible while enhancing your capability for further fast adjustments by both by finding an appropriate mix of methods for flexing capacity and by identifying and deploying sources of extra capacity and/or uses for surplus capacity

Your aim should be to make sure that operations resourcing levels match demand levels efficiently

Your aim should be to adjust planned resourcing levels as efficiently as possible through an appropriate mix of methods for flexing capacity

Low level of unpredictable variation in demand

Work on market knowledge to reduce uncertainty

Low level of predictable (forecast) variation in demand

High level of predictable (forecast) variation in demand

Work on demand management to reduce demand fluctuations

Do you really want to meet demand fluctuations?

Don't read the previous discussion as implying that you always must respond to demand fluctuations. It can be a perfectly sensible option to keep your resourcing levels constant and face the consequences of mismatched demand and capacity. There are obviously costs associated with doing this. If demand fluctuations are absorbed through underutilizing your resources, there will be a unit cost penalty. If you cannot meet demand immediately because of under-capacity your revenue (short and/or long term) will suffer. These disadvantages may be small compared to the costs of flexing resources quickly enough to meet demand. It is always worth asking the two questions: can you afford the resources you need to meet demand, and can you realistically do it in the required timescale?

Of course, if your offerings are standardized, physical and not particularly perishable, you have another option – make to stock. When your capacity exceeds current demand products can be stocked in anticipation of later sales. Even so, there are the normal costs of carrying inventory (working capital, storage, obsolescence, damage, etc) and the higher the level of inventory, the higher the costs will be. Expensive maybe, but worthwhile considering if the costs of inventory are low compared with changing output levels.

Remember that demand can be managed (to some extent)

Resourcing is not the exclusive problem of your operations function. It is only half of the 'supply–demand' equation. The market-facing activities of your colleagues can influence the resourcing decision. Almost all markets can be controlled to some extent. The issue is whether it is in the long-term interests of the business to do so. Do not engage in potentially expensive and difficult resourcing manoeuvres until demand management options have been explored.

The objective of demand management is to change the pattern of demand to bring it closer to your available resourcing capacity. This is generally done by either stimulating demand in off-peak times or constraining peak demand. It can be done in a number of ways. For example, pricing may be an obvious option. There is nothing new about using price to impact demand. Both energy prices and motorway tolls, for example, are used in some markets to match supply and demand. It may not always be popular with customers, and it can damage longer-term trust, but developments such as the Uber (taxi app) 'surge pricing' model may make this approach more acceptable for B2C operations.[5]

CASE STUDY The Bauli Group and its panettone production[6]

The demand for panettone is seasonal. The dome-shaped confection became a national symbol of the Italian Christmas and now has spread throughout the world. The largest panettone manufacturer is the Bauli group, one of the foremost manufacturers of confectionery in Europe. Its output of panettone accounts for 38 per cent of Italian sales. Its size, say the company, is an advantage: *'High investment in research and technology allows us to manage natural fermentation and guarantee a uniform quality that artisanal bakeries find hard to achieve.'*

Although Bauli diversified into year-round products like croissants and biscuits, seasonal cakes account for over 50 per cent of its turnover. Focusing on seasonal products does give the company a resourcing problem. It tackles this partly by hiring large numbers of temporary seasonal workers. At peak times there can be 1,200 seasonal workers in the factory, more than its permanent staff of around 800. It also starts to build up inventories before demand begins to increase for the Christmas peak. Production of panettone lasts about four months, starting in September. *'Attention to ingredients and the use of new technologies in production give a shelf-life of five months without preservatives,'* says Michele Bauli, deputy chairman. Other seasonal (but not Christmas-related) products are being promoted such as the *colomba*, a dove-shaped Easter treat, which utilizes resources during the spring.

How to meet demand fluctuations

If you do want to flex your resources to meet demand (what is technically known as a 'chase demand' strategy) the main issue is which method of flexing to use. Each will incur costs and an important element of deciding which method to use should be a full understanding of what, and how much, these costs are. It's surprising just how many operations managers do not have access to this information. It is worth pushing your accounting colleagues to give you an idea of the costs involved in flexing resources Other factors need to be included in the decision on what methods to use, the most significant of which tend to be the effect of resource fluctuations on quality levels, and the timescales involved. Table 5.1 summarizes some of the major methods and their consequences. It is obviously not an exhaustive list, nor are all the consequences listed, but it should be a guide to the issues that need to be investigated when devising an appropriate mix of methods.

Table 5.1   Some of the major methods of flexing resources and their consequences

Method of flexing resources	Potential costs	Timescale	Potential effect on quality
Overtime/ longer working hours	Overtime payment normally necessary (unless basic salary is high, eg financial services), can reduce productivity over long periods	Relatively quick and convenient	Excessive hours can adversely affect quality
Annualized hours	Can reduce the costs associated with overtime	Depends on agreement, but limited if demand highly unpredictable	Only affected if excessive hours in short term
Staff scheduling	May be some shift premium required	Can be difficult to change shift patterns in the short term	Should not be affected
Varying the size of the workforce ('hiring and firing')	Can reduce basic labour costs, but learning and recruitment costs can be significant. 'Zero hour' schemes could involve reputational risk/cost	Can be more effective at reducing rather than increasing capacity	Would you be interested in quality if you were likely to be laid off at short notice?
Temporary agency staff	Usually expensive compared to permanent employees.	Can be useful in adjusting capacity to meet predictable demand fluctuations	Some quality risks. May need extra training/ monitoring
Multi-skilling staff	Extra training investment in skills training needed. May cause some internal disruption	Fast method of reacting to short-term demand fluctuations	Can be some quality risks if changes too frequent
Short-term sub-contracting/ outsourcing	Costs depend on market conditions and outsourcer's volumes	Not usually easy in the short term unless an ongoing agreement is in place	May not be as motivated to give same service, or quality. Risk of knowledge leakage?

The list in Table 5.1 also shows the sheer range of options available for using your resources to flex capacity. There are many alternative mixes of these methods that could be tried at any point in time. Exactly which mix you choose should depend on (as the table implies) relative costs, timescale and potential effect on quality. It 'should' depend on these things, but in fact many businesses never fully explore the full range of options they have access to. They will stick to one or two methods rather than investigate alternatives.

How you flex capacity is (partly) governed by the long- and short-term outlook

The timescale over which demand is being forecast is important. One of the main influences on the choice of method of resourcing flexibility is the interplay between short-term demand and how you see demand playing out in the longer term. For example, if your expected short-term demand is higher than expected long-term demand, do you plan to provide resources to meet the short-term peak or plan to satisfy only longer-term sustainable levels of demand? Conversely, if your short-term demand is relatively low compared to your longer-term demand, should you plan your resources for the short or long term? Look at Figure 5.5. It shows how the options for flexing resourcing levels are very much constrained by long- and short-term demand.

Forecast the future or respond to the present

Underlying the whole of the resourcing task are two opposing approaches. One stresses the importance of getting as accurate a forecast as possible. The argument goes like this:

> It's important for forecasts to be as accurate as possible. We cannot plan operations resourcing levels otherwise. Without good forecasts we finish up either with too many resources (thereby increasing costs), or too few (thereby losing revenue and dissatisfying customers).

The counter argument is very different:

> Demand will always be uncertain, that is the nature of demand. Get used to it. The only way to satisfy customers is to make the operation sufficiently responsive so it can cope with demand, almost irrespective of what it is.

These points of view are not mutually exclusive, and both have some merit. Both are extreme positions. In practice, all operations must find some balance between having better forecasts and being able to cope without perfect forecasts. Trying to get forecasts right has particular value where your operation

Figure 5.5 How you flex resourcing levels depends partly on the long- and short-term outlook for volumes

	Forecast long-term demand is lower than current resourcing level	Forecast long-term demand is same as current resourcing level	Forecast long-term demand is higher than current resourcing level
Short-term demand likely to be higher than current resourcing level	Temporarily increase resourcing, eg • Increase working hours • Hire temporary staff	Temporarily increase resourcing, eg • Increase working hours • Hire temporary staff	(Semi) permanently increase resourcing, eg • Hire staff • Enter new supply agreements
Short-term demand likely to be same as current resourcing level	Plan to reduce resourcing (semi) permanently, eg • Freeze recruitment • Modify supply agreements.	Maintain resourcing at current level.	Plan to increase resourcing above current level, eg • Hire staff • Enter new supply agreements
Short-term demand likely to be lower than current resourcing level	Reduce resourcing (semi) permanently, eg • Reduce staffing levels • Reduce supply agreements.	Temporarily reduce resourcing, eg • Reduce staff working hours • Modify supply agreements.	Reduce resourcing temporarily, eg • Reduce staff working hours, but plant to recruit • Modify supply agreements.

finds it difficult or impossible to react to unexpected demand fluctuations in the short term, particularly if customers are not willing to wait. Some other types of operation that work in intrinsically uncertain markets may develop fast and flexible processes to compensate for the difficulty in obtaining accurate forecasts. Look again at the example of Zara in Chapter 3. It shows how fashion garment manufacturers try to overcome the uncertainty in their market by shortening their response time to new fashion ideas (catwalk-to-rack time) and the time taken to replenish stocks in the stores (replenishment time).

What are the consequences of underutilization?

It is tempting to assume that the ultimate objective of resourcing is always to make sure that your operation's capacity, more or less, matches demand. Not so. In fact, high levels of capacity utilization can be more of a problem than a benefit. Certainly, fully utilizing your resources does tend to reduce your costs (because the fixed cost element is covered by higher volume), but the effect on service levels can be negative. The reason for this is the variability that is a natural characteristic of any operation.

Even in a closely defined highly automated operation, not every process takes exactly the same time, every time, to do the same tasks, and not all tasks times are predictable: they can have different and/or irregular needs. Deliveries can arrive late (or early), process technology can temporarily malfunction, and items may need to be recycled for reprocessing or for further information. Most significantly, demand varies in an unpredictable manner. There are any number of reasons why variability occurs in all operations. It is this variability that affects how operations perform, and it is important to understand its effect on capacity utilization.

Start by considering what an operation with no variability would be like. All demand is perfectly predictable. All deliveries are always on time, in full. Everything works in exactly the same way all the time. (I know it's unrealistic, but work with me here.) As the level of demand increases, the utilization of the operation's resources increases until the demand equals its maximum capacity, that is 100 per cent utilization (point X on Figure 5.6). Even better, no customers will have had to wait because there are sufficient resources to cope with the demand. However, any further increase in demand beyond the capacity of the operation will simply cause orders to build up (theoretically, for ever). So the relationship between resource utilization and customers' waiting, when there is no variability, is described by the dotted line in Figure 5.6.

Life (or managing resourcing) is never that simple. The reality is that things vary: supplier deliveries, machine downtime, task times, reprocessing – nothing is totally 100 per cent predictable. This means that any operation will have both customers waiting and underutilization of its resources at the same time. The relationship between resource utilization and customer waiting will be something similar to the curved lines shown in Figure 5.6. Relatively little variability in the operation will give a curve close to the dotted line (which represents zero variability); greater variability will result in a curve further away from the dotted line.

The operations management triangle

The implications of these curves are hugely important for the resourcing decision. They mean that, for a specific amount of variability, the only way to guarantee very low customer waiting times is to suffer low resource

Figure 5.6 The relationship between resource utilization and customer waiting time

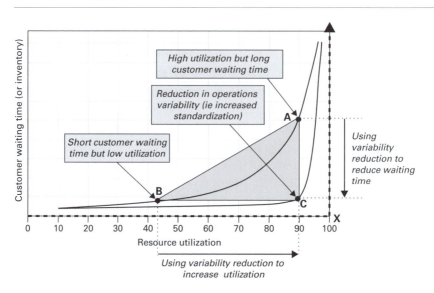

utilization. Conversely, the only way to achieve high utilization is to accept that customers will have to wait (or you will have to maintain high inventories if your output is capable of being stored). In other words, there is a trade-off between resource utilization and waiting time (or inventory). This is for a specific level of variability; one way of reducing the trade-off is to reduce the amount of variability in the operation. To put it another way: increase the degree of standardization in the operation. This is a phenomenon that has important implications for the design of operations (or processes, or whole supply chains for that matter). In effect it presents three options for resourcing, as shown in Figure 5.6. Either:

- accept long average waiting times and achieve high utilization (waiting times are long because there are in-process queues, but that is why no part of the operation is waiting for work – point A);

- accept low utilization and achieve short average waiting times (waiting times are short because low resource utilization means that there are few, if any, bottlenecks in the operation – point B); or

- reduce the variability in the operation by standardizing what is done in the operation and how it is done, achieving both higher utilization and shorter waiting times – point C.

This idea is sometimes called the 'operations management triangle'. It exposes an important choice. You must decide which is more important: fast throughput time (which means low inventory) or high utilization of your resources. The only way to have both of these simultaneously is to reduce variability in your processes (that is, increase standardization), which may itself require strategic decisions such as limiting the degree of customization of your offerings, or imposing stricter limits on how offerings can be delivered to customers, and so on. It also demonstrates an important point concerned with the day-to-day management of operations – the only way to absolutely guarantee a 100 per cent utilization of your resources is to accept an infinite amount of work in progress and/or waiting time.

The operations management triangle also shows the power of standardization to overcome the trade-off between resource utilization and waiting time. It is one of the most powerful arguments for standardization. So, while accepting that not everything can (or should) be standardized, it has a major impact on resource effectiveness. As shown in Figure 5.6, you must decide how to use the benefits of standardization. Do you want to increase resource utilization while keeping customer waiting time low? Alternatively, do you want to use it to reduce waiting times for customers while keeping resource utilization high?

The risks of operating close to 100 per cent utilization

There is another important implication of the operations management triangle: the closer you operate to 100 per cent utilization, the more vulnerable you are to small disruptions causing a seizure in the flow through your operation. Take the example of London Heathrow, one of the busiest international hubs in the world. It suffers frequent delays. On an average day, 60 per cent of arrivals (that's over 55,000 customers) spend time in one of Heathrow's four 'holding stacks'. Delays range from four to 10 minutes, rising to 20 minutes in the late morning peak, when between 32 and 40 jets typically circle over London.[7] The costs of these delays include £119,000 of wasted fuel per day, 600 tonnes of additional CO_2 emissions, and the frustration of many customers losing valuable work and leisure time. The problem? Capacity utilization of around 98 per cent. 'When you have one of the most utilized pieces of infrastructure in the world, then one of the results is that you have airborne holding,' says Jon Proudlove, managing director of the National Air Traffic Service (NATS) at Heathrow. With such high utilization of its resources, the impact of any disturbance (such as poor weather) has an immediate impact on aeroplane processing speeds.

Practical prescriptions

- Put effort into fully understanding the consequences of having to many or too few resources, in particular the costs of having too many resources and the impact on service and revenue of having too few.

- Do not make long-, medium- and short-term resourcing decisions in isolation. They are interrelated and should be taken together. Such planning should be done formally (or semi-formally), potentially through a hierarchical planning process.

- Always examine the assumptions on which you are basing your demand and resourcing forecasts.

- Demand forecasts are never right – get used to it. And never blame bad forecasts unless you have done all you can to help your forecasting colleagues. In particular, insist on probabilistic forecasts, examine all assumptions behind the forecasts, and check that the demand you are experiencing is 'true demand'.

- Examine what determines the relationship between the resources you have and the capacity they provide. In other words, how do factors such as your facilities, people, product/service mix and specification, technology, internal scheduling systems, supply arrangements and inventory, affect your capacity?

- Try and get some idea of your 'surge capacity' – what capacity your resources could achieve for a limited time, how you would arrange it, and how long you could keep it up for.

- Try using the underlying principles of 'overall equipment effectiveness' (OEE) to assess your capacity 'leakage'.

- Distinguish between predictable and unpredictable demand variation. Each type requires different objectives – predictable variation should be done as efficiently as possible, unpredictable variation should be done as fast as possible.

- Do not assume that you always have to meet demand. There may be 'market-facing' options (eg pricing) that should be explored. Sometimes meeting demand just isn't worth it.

- There are many different methods of flexing resource capacity to follow demand fluctuations, and even more permutations of these methods. It is important to explore the relevance of all these methods, not just what you have done in the past.

- Look at the differences between long- and shorter-term outlook for demand. Examine how capacity flexing methods might be constrained by any differences.

- There should be a continuing debate about the balance between trying to forecast demand so you can plan to meet it, and developing your operation so that it can respond to whatever demand turns out to be.

- Do not assume that underutilizing your capacity is always to be avoided. Use the idea of the 'operations management triangle' to decide whether you want to stress high resource utilization, fast customer service, or greater standardization.

Notes

1 Based on the work of Professor Bart MacCarthy of Nottingham University

2 Tim Harford (2016) Why predictions are a lot like Pringles, *Financial Times*, 8 January

3 Savelli, S and Joslyn, S (2013). The advantages of predictive interval forecasts for non-expert users and the impact of visualizations, *Applied Cognitive Psychology*, **27**, 527–41

4 Gilliland, M (2010) Defining 'demand' for demand forecasting, *Foresight: The International Journal of Applied Forecasting*, Summer

5 *The Economist* (2016) Jacking up prices may not be the only way to balance supply and demand for taxis, 14 May

6 Sources include: *The Economist* (2009) A piece of cake: Panettone season arrives, 10 December; Bauli website, http://www.bauligroup.it/en/

7 Sources include: Equants (2012) London Heathrow airport – economic and social impact, Ecquants.com/2012_LHR.aspx; Heathrow Airport Holdings Company (2014) Heathrow Airport Holdings Company Information, retrieved 12 October

Establish internal processes networks

If you were asked to choose the one idea in management practice that was most misused (and abused), you could do worse than choose the idea of 'process'. It seems to bring out the worst in all of us. Partly this is because a lot of processes are, frankly, dumb; partly it is because we misunderstand what is meant by 'process'. So let's start with a simple definition. Processes are 'how you do stuff'. If you do stuff, you are part of a process. If you manage people who do stuff, you manage processes. Processes are how you perform activities. A process is simply a framework, around which you can think about who should do what, and when.

Even if your 'process' is to sit in a darkened room with a glass of wine and wait for inspiration to strike, it's still a process. You have thought about, and described, how to do it. Processes are not necessarily formal, highly constrained or detailed – though they might be. Some processes really do need to be meticulously defined, with every activity tightly controlled and double-checked. The darkened room approach doesn't work for airline pilots performing their pre-flight checks, for instance. That kind of process must be both detailed and defined; but not all processes need be. That's the point: processes need to be designed to fit with what they are supposed to achieve.

Your operations are process networks

How individual processes are designed, and how they are linked together to form networks, is important to you. Processes are the building blocks of your operation. They link together to form an 'internal process network' through which material, information, or people are 'processed'. As no chain is stronger than its weakest link, the output from a process is limited by the effectiveness of its worst stage. No operation is better than its weakest

Figure 6.1 This chapter looks at how to establish internal process networks

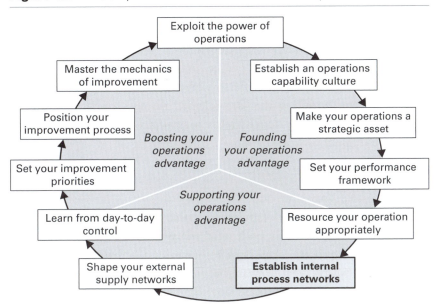

process. Configuring internal process networks involves designing each process and integrating individual processes to form an effective network. The root causes of business failure are often the result of the failures of everyday operational processes. More positively, long-term success can be built on getting these process networks right.

Why the problem with 'process'?

There are two wildly contrasting views about process management, both of which give processes a bad press. You might have heard both of them argued with force and passion, although not always with rigour. The first is that everyone is part of a process whether you like it or not. So, if we are all part of a process, we should be able to apply a standardized set of disciplines and rules that can make us both more effective and more efficient. The objective is to find the one best way to do anything and to enshrine it in an unvarying set of actions that will ensure the same result every time, all the time. The virtue of 'process', in this view, is its discipline. It imposes control through uniformity.

The other view is very different. It holds that effective management must always rely on empathy, creativity and intuition. You can't, according to this school, reduce everything to a process. People are almost always involved in processes, and people can't be treated like cogs in a machine. The problem with the 'process perspective', they say, is that it looks on everything as a machine-like set of mindless routine activities. In reality, everything comes back to people, and effective management must always rely on the quality of leadership given to those people – the vision, imagination and intuition that are released through empathetic leadership. Closely defining any activity into the straitjacket of 'process' kills the essential humanity of working life.

Two cultures?

The problem with these two (admittedly rather stereotyped) perspectives is that they are simultaneously both right and wrong. Go back to the original meaning of 'process' – a set of resources and activities that produce value. That is exactly what is meant by 'process', no more and no less. Sure, everyone really is part of a process, but nothing is necessarily implied about de-skilling anyone's job, or always doing things in the same way. No assumptions are being made about eternally conforming to the same sequence of activities. There are no implicit requirements to closely specify every little activity, nor about rigidly sticking to this specification irrespective of the circumstances. Of course all these things may be a good idea, but not for every process in all circumstances.

That's the point. Not all processes are the same (or, more accurately, *should not* be the same). The way we shape and run processes should depend on what we want them to do; what value they should be delivering and what kind of activities are deployed to deliver the value. Processes certainly should not diminish the role of empathy, creativity and above all, leadership. The argument, sometimes characterized as 'people versus process', is based on a false distinction. People are the most important element in (most) processes, and 'process' is simply how we do things.

Yet anyone who tries to improve their processes will have to negotiate these two attitudes. We are caught in an ongoing conflict between those who love the order and discipline that processes bring, and those who instinctively react against such formality and regulation. In many ways it's an old conflict and it's been going on forever: Roundheads versus Cavaliers, scientists versus artists, 'suits' versus 'creatives', the methodical versus the flamboyant. To be successful, all businesses need to bridge this gap between what are effectively the two cultures of process management.

Process forensics

The cynicism surrounding 'process' exists because processes can so often go wrong, or appear pointless, or simply get in the way of getting work done. Put it another way: the process is 'broken'. Broken processes don't do what they are supposed to do. We have all been the victims of them. Your bank fails to stop a direct debit. Some idiot in human resources fails to authorize your new assistant's salary. A supplier delivers wrong parts. There are missed errors in your sales brochure. Broken processes are everywhere, they are frustrating, they are wasteful and they stop you focusing on what's really important. Broken processes mean that simply 'keeping the show on the road' dominates your life. The errors may be minor and the frustration relatively small compared with the really big challenges in life, but they add up to a constant, debilitating irritation. Broken processes destroy the stability that should be the foundation of improvement. They represent a waste of time and effort that you will finish up paying for one way or another.

It doesn't have to be like this. Processes can be repaired. To do this, we must, first, be able to detect when processes are not fit for their purpose and, second, have the skills to redesign them until they are.

Spotting broken processes

A broken process is one that fails to deliver what's expected of it, or consumes too many resources, or takes too many risks, or fails to adapt to changing circumstances, or is so irritating that people ignore or avoid it. This last point is one clue for finding broken processes: it's where there is a gap between what people are supposed to do (according to the process) and what actually happens. The people that operate processes will know exactly which processes are broken. That leads to the obvious advice on identifying broken processes – ask your staff. Obvious maybe, but frequently ignored. It's the same with customers. They know (or can give a clue to) the processes that are failing to deliver. Again, it is often the people that operate on the customer-facing front line who can best identify the processes that are letting customers down.

It's worth giving a word of warning here though. Not all the criticisms that you will hear about your processes are justified. Processes win few popularity contests. So identifying your broken processes can involve some judgement. An important question is, 'Broken for whom?' Many processes may be fine as far as some people are concerned, but irritate the hell out of others. This means that one has to distinguish between reasonable criticisms and those that are less valid.

Are your processes broken?

There are some perfectly legitimate criticisms of a process that are the result of bad/inappropriate design. Do you recognize any of these?

- This process treats all my decisions/items as the same, when in reality they have different requirements.
- This process is too rigid and it can't be adapted to suit different needs.
- This process has excessive 'recycling' with information or items having to be returned to previous stages.
- This process doesn't reflect business or customer needs.
- This process is 'too detailed'. It's 'over-engineered'.
- This process doesn't have sufficient capacity at some stages.
- This process is too repetitive.

All these criticisms are the result of either the inappropriate resourcing of the process or the poor configuration of the process's individual activities. Either way, they can be addressed through better process design.

Some criticisms are less to do with how a process is designed and more concerned with how it is managed on an ongoing basis. For example:

- This process simply promotes 'box ticking'. You just 'go through the motions'.
- This process doesn't learn from success or failure, it just goes on and on.
- This process dilutes any responsibility for taking decisions or ensuring good quality.
- This process encourages people to simply 'hide behind the process' – 'I did what the process told me to,' or 'The computer says no.'
- This process demotivates you; it grinds you down.

In fact all these criticisms have the same root cause: the process is seen as being unconnected with the nature of the job itself. There may be nothing wrong with the process as such; rather whoever is responsible for managing it has allowed it to reinforce negative behaviours, the origins of which probably lie far deeper than process design.

Some criticisms are kind of valid but could be seen as the price you pay for the benefits that a formal process can bring. For example:

- This process has a 'friction cost' – it takes up time to go through each stage.
- This process forces me to do things in a certain way.
- This process has made me change how I do things.

Well, yes, that's the nature of introducing any kind of formality into a process. However, one does have to careful that the 'friction cost' is worth it, that all parts of the imposed method are really necessary, and that the 'changed method' is better than the previous one.

Not all processes are the same

A process may seem 'broken' when, in reality, it is just designed in a way that is inappropriate for the task in hand. This is why it is important to distinguish between different types of process. One size (or type) does not fit all in process design. It is a mistake to take the same approach to designing them, irrespective of their purpose. so some way for you to distinguish between different types of process is vital.

Back in Chapter 2 we introduced the idea of using a number of dimensions to distinguish between different types of operation. The 'Four Vs analysis' used the volume, variety, variation and visibility characteristics to differentiate between your operations. We can use it again to distinguish between processes. In fact, it is the first two of these characteristics, volume and variety, that have the strongest effect on processes design. Also, volume and variety are related. Low-volume processes usually have a high variety of products, services or decisions to deal with, and high-volume processes usually have a far narrower variety. It's not a hard and fast rule, but it generally holds true.

Figure 6.2   Examples of processes in two businesses that have different volume–variety positions

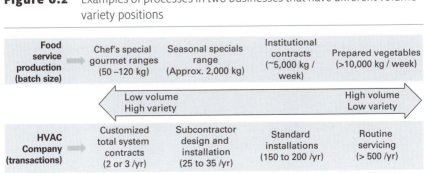

Processes can be *positioned* on a scale from those with low volume and high variety, through to those with high volume and low variety. The volume–variety position of a process will affect almost every aspect of its design. Processes with different volume–variety positions will need to be configured in different ways, and will need different types of resources. Figure 6.2 shows examples of processes from two businesses producing different offerings that have different volume–variety positions.

Of course there are other characteristics that will influence how your processes need to be designed. Some processes require expert knowledge and the ability to interpret specialist opinion, while others are relatively straightforward and can be performed by almost anyone. Some processes are essentially creative, requiring innovative outcomes, whereas others are there to prevent any deviation from strict conformance to specifications. Yet most characteristics more or less fit with the volume–variety characteristic. Knowledge-based, creative processes tend to have low volumes and (by definition) high variety. Low-skill, high conformance processes tend to be high volume and (again, almost by definition) low variety. So, notwithstanding any slight approximations, the volume–variety position of a process is still the best indicator of how it should be designed.

Process networks

In Chapter 1 we used the idea of 'networks' to show how your operation can be described as being both made up of, and part of, networks. Your supply network is an arrangement of whole operations, which are themselves networks of processes, which are arrangements of individual resources. This is of more than theoretical interest. It is fundamental to making all your networks, including process networks, work better together. Figure 6.3

Figure 6.3 Processes network and internal 'process chains'

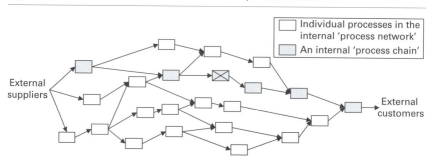

shows a (simplified) process network for one business. It has many processes that transfer (in this case) parts and information between each other. Through this network there are many 'process chains', one of which is highlighted. A process chain is one thread of processes within the network. So, if you look after one of these processes, say the one identified with a cross, what are the benefits of seeing yourself as part of a process chain?

Do your processes have a clear 'line of sight'?

One obvious advantage is that understanding your place in your internal process chain gives you a clear 'line of sight' forward through to your customer groups, so that the people working in each process have a better chance of seeing how they contribute to the final value-added for the business's customers and, importantly, how they can help the intermediate processes that lie between them and the customer, to add value. It also gives you a clear 'line of sight' backwards through to your suppliers. Making it easier to understand how previous processes help you to add value will, in turn, help you to help them. So for each of your processes, key questions are:

- Where are you positioned in your internal process chain?
- What are the processes in your line of sight forwards to external customers?
- What can you do to help your internal customers (and your internal customers' customers) to add value?
- What are the processes in your line of sight backwards to external suppliers?
- What can you do to help your internal suppliers (and your internal suppliers' suppliers) help you to add value?
- What/where are any 'hand-over' problems as things are passed between processes in the chain?
- Which of the processes in your line of sight (forwards and backwards) are the most critical?
- What are you doing to help these critical processes in the process chain?

Conversely, not understanding how process chains interact can reduce the effectiveness of the whole operation, and increase the risk of disruption spreading. Look at the example, 'Not the company's finest hour' for an example of how process chains can become conduits for chaos when things go wrong.

CASE STUDY 'Not the company's finest hour'[1]

If you were flying British Airways (BA) through Heathrow airport when its much-heralded Terminal 5 opened, you may remember the chaos. It works fine now, but the opening was a disaster, what BA's boss Willie Walsh said, with magnificent understatement, 'was not the company's finest hour'. The chaos made news around the world and was seen by many as one of the most public failures of basic operations management in the modern history of aviation. Two hundred flights in and out of T5 were cancelled in its first three days. Some customers were still without their luggage after three weeks. It needed an extra 400 volunteer staff and courier companies to wade through the backlog of late baggage.

So what went wrong? It was not one thing, but several interrelated problems. That's the point – they were interrelated because the problems spread along the T5 internal process chain. Press reports initially blamed glitches with the baggage handling system. And indeed the baggage handling system did experience problems that had not been exposed in testing, but BAA, the airport operator, doubted that the main problem was the baggage system itself. The system had worked until it became clogged with bags that were overwhelming BA's handlers loading them onto the aircraft. Partly this may have been because staff were not sufficiently familiar with the new system and its operating processes, but handling staff had also suffered delays getting to their new (and unfamiliar) work areas, negotiating (new) security checks and finding (again, new) car parking spaces. Also, once staff were airside they had problems logging-in. The cumulative effect of these problems meant that the airline was unable to get ground handling staff to the correct locations for loading and unloading bags from the aircraft, so baggage could not be loaded onto aircraft fast enough, baggage backed up, clogging the baggage handling system, which in turn meant closing baggage check-in and baggage drops, leading eventually to baggage check-in being halted.

Shortly after the opening, British Airways announced that two of its most senior executives, its director of operations and its director of customer services, would leave the company.

What about service-level agreements?

Some businesses try to bring a degree of formality to process relationships by using service-level agreements (SLAs) and operating-level agreements (OLAs). Their track record is not always great. Even if they have been useful when initially setting up the terms of a relationship, they often either gather dust, are ignored, or become battlegrounds for inter-departmental disputes. Any SLA that stays unchanged over time is not doing its job. For SLAs to work effectively, they must be treated as working documents that establish the details of ongoing relationships *in the light of experience.* Used properly they can become a repository of the knowledge that both sides have gathered through working together.

The process of process design

Generally, processes are not designed; they are redesigned. Usually the task being examined is pre-existing, so some sort of 'process' will be being used, even if it is informal. Most process design involves taking some task and improving how it is being done. Fortunately, there are some well-tried steps for doing this. In other words, there is a process for process design. The steps of this process are illustrated in Figure 6.4.

Step 1. Get design objectives straight

Don't even attempt to start designing or redesigning a process until you have a reasonable grasp of what you want it to be good at. Different process objectives will result in different process designs. For example, if your process will be judged primarily on its ability to respond quickly to customer requests, it would need to be designed for fast throughput. This means no unnecessary hold-ups in the flow of items through the process (bottlenecks). If there is inventory, it is best held close to the source of demand so it can be dealt with quickly, and resources will need to be sufficiently flexible so that minor disturbances do not disrupt the flow.

Figure 6.4 The process of process design

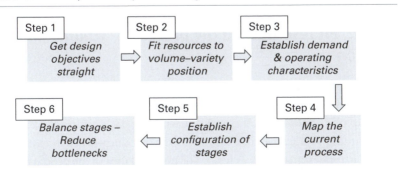

Table 6.1 Some implications for process design of various process objectives

Major process objective	Implications for your process design
Specification quality	Robust, high-capability process technology High skill levels 'Spare' capacity/allowed time
Conformance quality	Built-in check points Tightly specified activities Reliable process technology
Fast response	Balanced loading/capacity ratios Inventory loaded at the demand end of the process Flexible resources
Dependable delivery	Reliable process technology Parallel processing 'Spare' capacity/allowed time
Mix flexibility	General purpose technology Multi-skilling Low division of total task time
Volume flexibility	Surplus capacity Multi-skilling Parallel processing
Cost efficiency	Divided tasks Fast throughput Balanced loading/capacity ratios

Of course there will need to be other design principles at play, depending on the circumstances. The point is that these principles will be different if the process objective is different. Table 6.1 illustrates just some of the implications that follow on from different process objectives. It is not an exhaustive list, but it illustrates the differences.

Step 2. Fit resources to the processes' volume–variety position

Almost all resources used by a process are influenced by its volume–variety position; in particular the technology it uses, the way it defines the role and activities of its people and the physical arrangement of its resources. All can be illustrated in a framework known as the 'product–process' matrix (even though it applies to services as well). The essential idea of the product–process matrix is to show how the resources and configuration of a process are strongly influenced by its volume–variety position. Figure 6.5 illustrates the product–process matrix. It shows what is known as the 'natural diagonal' that associates technology, job design and flow, with the volume–variety position of a process. Briefly, as volume increases and variety reduces:

- Technology tends to move from relatively manual, general purpose, individual and flexible, to automated, dedicated, integrated and inflexible.

- People's jobs tend to move from relatively broad, undefined, with decision-making discretion, to narrow, closely defined, with less decision-making discretion.

- The flow through the process tends to move from being relatively intermittent, with possibly many different routes, to smooth, continuous and following one predictable path.

Again, there will be exceptions, but the idea does represent an intuitive common sense. If your process builds 10 customized communication satellites each year, you will use process technologies, value particular skills and organize work in a very different way than if your process makes tens of thousands of near-identical mobile phones every year.

The diagonal in Figure 6.5 represents the most appropriate process design for any volume–variety position. Processes lying on the natural diagonal of the matrix will normally have lower operating costs than ones with the same volume–variety position that lie off the diagonal. Processes that are off the natural diagonal to the right would normally be associated with lower volumes and higher variety, so they will be more flexible than they need to be. They are not taking advantage of the ability to standardize. Conversely, processes that are on the left of the diagonal are in a position that would normally be right for a higher volume, lower variety position. These processes will be over-standardized and too rigid for their volume–variety position.

One note of caution here. Although this is logically coherent, it is a conceptual model rather than something that can be numerically scaled. Nevertheless, a good first test is to check if your processes are on the natural diagonal. One often finds processes where, for example, the volume–variety position of the process may have changed without any corresponding change in its design.

Shifting positions on the product–process matrix

Figure 6.6 illustrates two examples of operations that had to modify their processes as their volume–variety position changed.

Figure 6.5 The product–process matrix

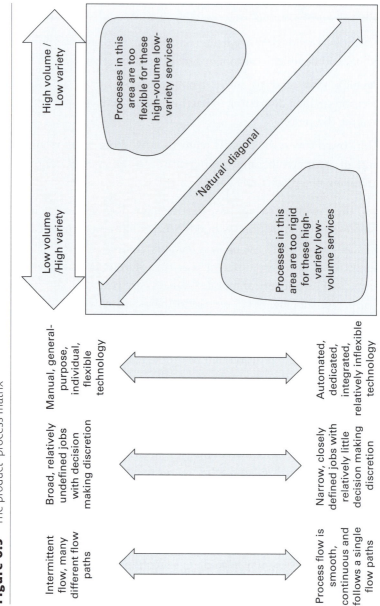

Low volume
/High variety

High volume /
Low variety

'Natural' diagonal

Processes in this
area are too
flexible for these
high-volume low-
variety services

Processes in this
area are too rigid
for these high-
variety low-
volume services

Intermittent
flow, many
different flow
paths

Process flow is
smooth,
continuous and
follows a single
flow paths

Broad, relatively
undefined jobs
with decision
making discretion

Narrow, closely
defined jobs with
relatively little
decision making
discretion

Manual, general-
purpose,
individual,
flexible
technology

Automated,
dedicated,
integrated,
relatively inflexible
technology

Figure 6.6 The product–process matrix: two examples of changing conditions

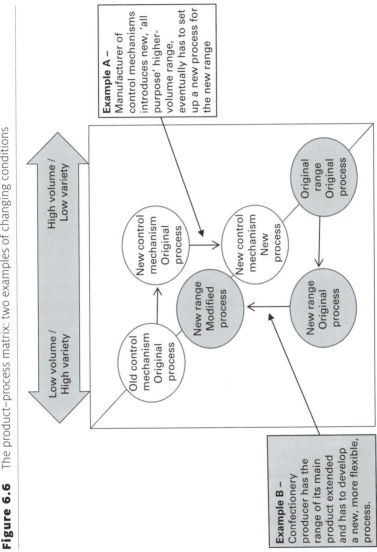

Example A – Manufacturer of control mechanisms introduces new, 'all purpose' higher-volume range, eventually has to set up a new process for the new range

Low volume / High variety

High volume / Low variety

Old control mechanism Original process

New control mechanism Original process

New range Modified process

New control mechanism New process

Original range Original process

New range Original process

Example B – Confectionery producer has the range of its main product extended and has to develop a new, more flexible, process.

Example A is a manufacturer of electro-mechanical control mechanisms for a variety of OEMs (original equipment manufacturers). The original manufacturing process used simple bench assembly with individual employees using general-purpose tooling, and making batches of between one and 20 products to customer order. When the company introduced its own self-designed product intended for a less specialized, higher-volume market, it tried initially to make the new product using the same process as its original range. This proved unpopular with its existing workforce, who disliked the repetition involved in producing batches of up to 250 of the new product at a time. It also proved an inefficient way to produce the products, with costs some 20 per cent higher than originally forecast. The organization soon decided to set up a dedicated line-style process for the new product (helped by its higher than forecast sales) with newly recruited, lower-skilled staff and some limited specialist technology.

Example B is a site of a global confectionery manufacturer, originally dedicated to producing one branded product in single and multi-pack versions. After the global marketing organization decided to launch a major brand extension, the plant was made responsible for producing an extended range of the same basic product, in various flavours and sizes. Given that the original process had been developed for a single flavour and size, it struggled to produce the extended range, even though, technically, it had sufficient capacity. The operations team at the plant had to develop fast changeover procedures and technology that allowed the process to overcome its original inflexibility.

CASE STUDY Space4's housing processes[2]

Looking at a process's volume–variety position is a useful starting point, but it is always worth testing out assumptions. For example, house building is traditionally towards the low-volume, high-variety end of the volume–variety scale, which is why its processes are generally on-site and flexible – but not always.

Space4 is a division of Persimmon, the UK's largest house builder. In what some believe could be the future of house building, it uses a process that is more like the way you would expect an automobile to be made. Its production line, whose 90 operators (many of whom have automobile assembly experience) is capable of producing the timber-framed panels that form the shell of the new homes at a rate of a house every hour. There is a direct link between the computer-aided design (CAD) systems that design the houses and the manufacturing processes that make them, reducing the time between design and manufacture. Because of their previous automobile assembly experience, staff are used to the just-in-time high-efficiency culture of modern mass production.

Completed panels are dispatched to building sites across the UK. When they arrive, the exterior of a new home can be assembled in a single day. Furthermore, the automated production process uses a type of high-precision technology that means there are fewer mistakes in the construction process on site. This means that the approval process from the local regulatory authority also takes less time.

Step 3. Establish demand and operating characteristics

This is the stage where it gets just a little technical. Not too much so, nothing that an eight-year-old kid couldn't cope with. If you are tempted to skip this stage because it has 'sums' in it – please don't. A surprising number of managers seem to shy away from any kind of quantification, even of the simplest kind. If you do this in process design you really are making a serious mistake. There are only one or two simple calculations, and they are very necessary.

The first calculation is to work out how many items your process should be capable of producing. This is best indicated by the 'output interval' that the process is designed to achieve.[3] The 'output interval' of a process is the time between completed items emerging from it. It is a vital factor in process design and should be one of the first things to be calculated. It sets the pace or 'drum beat' of the process. However the process is designed it must be able to meet this figure, and it is easy to calculate by considering the likely demand for the products or services over a period and the amount of production time available in that period.

For example, if (say) a process needs to check the calibration of 1,600 items per week and the time available to process the applications is 40 hours per week, the process must be capable of performing the calibration check once every 1.5 minutes, or 90 times per hour.

$$\text{The 'output interval' for the process} = \frac{\text{The time available}}{\text{The number of items to be processed}}$$

$$= \frac{40}{1600} = 0.025 \text{ hours}$$

$$= 1.5 \text{ minutes}$$

The next simple calculation is how much capacity you need in the process to meet the output interval. To calculate this, you need a further piece of information – the 'work content' of the process task (how long it takes). The larger the 'work content' of the process task and the smaller the required output interval, the more capacity will be necessary.

For the calibration check, the total work content of all the activities that make up the total task is (say), on average, 6 minutes. So, a process with one person could check an item every 6 minutes. That is, one person would achieve an output interval of 6 minutes. Two people would achieve an output interval of 6/2 = 3 minutes, and so on. So the general relationship between the number of people in the process (its capacity in this simple case) and the output interval of the process is:

$$\frac{\text{The work content of the process task}}{\text{The number of people in the process}} = \text{The output interval}$$

$$\text{The number of people in the process} = \frac{\text{The work content of the process task}}{\text{The output interval}}$$

$$\text{In this case, The number of people in the process} = \frac{6}{1.5} = 4 \text{ people}$$

So, the capacity that this process needs if it is to meet demand is four people.

Little's Law

The mathematical relationship that connects output interval to work in process and the average time it takes for an item to go through the process (throughput time) is called Little's Law.[4] It is simple, but very useful, and it works for any stable process. Little's Law is:

Throughput time = Work in progress × Output interval

or:

Work in progress = Throughput time × (1/Output interval)

Put another way:

Work in progress = Throughput time × Throughput rate

For example, a test and repair process has an output interval of 12 minutes, and a quick check reveals that there are 4 items within the process being worked on, or waiting to be worked on. How long, on average, will items take to get through the process? Using Little's Law:

Throughput time = work in progress × output interval, which here is: 12 × 4 = 48 minutes

The fear of all sums

One final plea for embracing these simple calculations before leaving them behind. They are not difficult and they give important information. Ignorance of the 'true' figures is not an excuse. Don't worry too much if you are estimating values such as 'work content' or how many items need to be processed in whatever time is available. All these figures will be estimates anyway. Using average figures, or even reasonably informed guesses, is far better than not attempting these calculations at all. At the worst, using 'guestimate' figures will give approximations of a process's characteristics. These calculations are the answers to very relevant questions. Remember that approximate answers to the right questions are more useful than precise answers to irrelevant questions.

Step 4. Map the current process

If you ask three people to draw what happens in a process, you are likely to get three different answers. This is why drawing (or 'mapping') a process is an essential step in improving it. A process map is simply a picture of how a process works, or is supposed to work. At its most basic level, process mapping involves describing processes in terms of how their activities relate to each other. The problem is that, often, existing processes are not always well defined, or they don't reflect what is really happening; maybe they have developed over time without ever being formally recorded. But processes that are not formally defined can be interpreted in different ways, which leads to confusion and impedes improvement. This is where process mapping comes in.

Why process mapping is important

There is a temptation to avoid the effort of going through the process mapping stage. It is understandable in a way; it can involve both time and effort. It also means getting the people together who understand the process. This is why it is a big mistake to skip this activity:

- It allows a critical examination of each and every stage in your process. In particular, it encourages the key question of 'Does this activity really add value?'

- It is an essential starting-point for your process improvement. How can you improve something that is not fully understood?

- It is one of the best opportunities you have to bring together teams from different parts of an operation to share their perspectives on how things should be done.

- The exercise can, if properly managed, help you to create a culture of process ownership and responsibility.

- It gives everyone an overview of a complete process, often for the first time.

- Your output is a process map that is a 'picture' – easy to understand and difficult to misinterpret.

There are many (actually quite similar) techniques that can be used for process mapping. However, they all have two main features: they identify the different types of activity that take place during the process, and they show the sequence of these activities as items flow through the process. There are also various symbols that are sometimes used to represent different types of activity; by far the most convenient, and most commonly used, method is simply to use Post-It notes to indicate each activity. They are easy to move about as discussion progresses. Do not 'fix the process in stone' too soon.

Process mapping – some hints

Without getting into too much detail, there are some straightforward things to remember when mapping any process:

- Before you start, decide on the scope and level of the process map. Where does the map start and finish? At what level of detail are the activities to be described, at a very detailed level (what is known as 'low-level' mapping), or with large aggregated blocks of activities (high-level mapping)?

- Trace the progress of items (material, customers or information) at every step through the process. Record everything that impacts on the items at every stage.

- Trace how many times items pass from one part of the process to another. What could go wrong at each of these hand-offs?

- Estimate the approximate time that is likely to be taken at each step. Never miss this step out (see earlier).

- Estimate the average number of items waiting between each stage. This will obviously vary, but it gives a reasonable idea of total work in progress, which can be used to estimate total throughput time.

- Estimate the amount of real value added (either for the 'customer' of the process, or the business). If there is little value added, question why the activity is there.

- Identify any steps in the process that are causing problems for 'customers' or the business.

Processing people is different – emotional mapping

Process mapping is different when the 'items' being processed are customers (internal or external). Processes with a high level of customer 'visibility' (see Chapter 2) cannot be designed in the same way as processes that deal with inanimate 'items'. People are not just processed, they *experience* the process, and are subject to emotions, not all of which are necessarily rational. Because customer experience affects satisfaction, it also has the potential to produce customer loyalty, influence expectations and create emotional bonds with customers. Designing these people processes requires the systematic consideration of how customers may react to the experiences they are exposed to, including the sights, sounds, smells, atmosphere and general 'feeling' of the process. One of the most common methods of mapping such processes is to consider 'touch-points' – the points of contact between a process and customers. These are, 'everything the consumer uses to verify their service's effectiveness'.[5] There might be many touch-points in a process, each contributing to the accumulation of all the experiences that shape customers' feelings.

Designing people processes should involve making sure that all the messages coming from the interactions at each stage of the process are not

Figure 6.7   Customer experience map of an insurance medical check-up

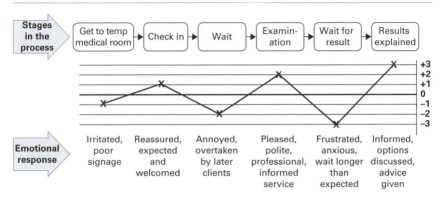

wrong or misleading. 'Emotional mapping' can indicate the type of emotions engendered in the customer's mind as they experienced the process. Figure 6.7 is a simplified version of how this might work for a scheduled visit to a temporary clinic for an examination for medical insurance. In this case a simple scoring system has been used, ranging from +3 (very) positive to −3 (very negative). At each stage, the reasons for the score are briefly noted.

Step 5. Establish the configuration of stages

One of the fundamental process design decisions is how much you should divide up the total process task. Take a simple example. Suppose a task that, in total, takes around 40 minutes to complete is required to be processed at a rate of 6 per hour (that is, an output interval of 10 minutes). Four people will be needed to achieve this output rate (40 minutes/10 minutes, remember), but how should these four people be arranged? One option is to divide the total task between the four people so that the first person does the first 10 minutes' worth of work; the second person does the second 10 minutes, and so on until a completed item emerges, every 10 minutes, at the end of the process. This is the top configuration shown in Figure 6.8. An alternative

Figure 6.8   Process configuration, from sequential to parallel

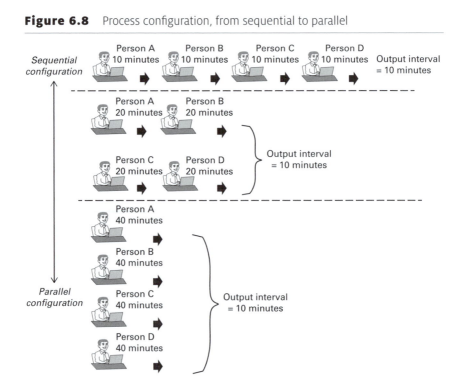

is to arrange the four people in two parallel configurations of two stages, each person having 20 minutes of work. Between them, the two parallel arrangements will again produce a combined output interval of 10 minutes. Finally, each person could, in parallel, complete one item every 40 minutes; again with a combined output interval of 10 minutes.

So, generally there are alternative configurations, from long and sequential through to shorter and parallel. Or, one could adopt a combination of series and parallel configurations. The advantages of *sequential configurations* include:

- A more controlled flow of items through the process that is relatively easy to manage.
- Simple materials handling – especially if the items being processed are heavy, large or difficult to move.
- Lower capital requirements if specialist pieces of equipment are needed only at the stage where they are needed (on short fat arrangements every stage would need one).
- Efficiencies can be exploited if divided tasks reduce the proportion of non-productive work, such as picking up tools and materials.

The advantages of *parallel configurations* include:

- Higher mix flexibility because, if the process needs to produce several types of product or service, each stage can specialize in different types.
- Higher volume flexibility – as volume varies, parallel stages can simply be closed down or started up as required.
- Higher robustness – if one stage breaks down or ceases operation in some way, the other parallel stages are unaffected; a long thin arrangement would cease operating completely.
- The work is less monotonous; the people in the short fat arrangement are repeating their tasks less often.

Step 6. Balance stages – reduce bottlenecks

Bottlenecks are when the capacity of your process as a whole is limited by the capacity of one part or stage in the process. They are the curse of processes. They hold up the flow of items, they limit the capability of the process and they can upset whoever has to cope with the localized overloading. Because the output rate of the whole process is limited by the longest allocation of activity times to an individual stage, the more equally work is allocated, the less time will be 'wasted' at the other stages in the process. However, it is nearly always impossible to achieve an absolutely perfect equal allocation of work, so some degree of imbalance will always occur. The objective is to minimize it.

Bottlenecks are also dynamic. Some are essentially short term. They are caused by transitory difficulties such as when key staff are temporarily absent, or process technology malfunctions. These bottlenecks will eventually be cleared up, only to be replaced by other short-term bottlenecks elsewhere. It's a game of whack-a-mole and, as in the real game, the faster these short-term bottlenecks can be eliminated, the more effective the process can be. More importantly, the more effectively the root cause of these short-term bottlenecks is tackled, the less disruptive they are, and the easier it is to focus on the more serious longer-term bottlenecks. They are the ones that are caused by the loading on one part of the process being fundamentally greater than its capacity to cope with it.

Finding bottlenecks

There are two approaches to finding bottlenecks. Look where they *should* be, and look where they *appear* to be. Sometimes (just sometimes) these are the same.

Where bottlenecks *should* be is where the loading on a part of the process is greater than its capacity. Loading can be estimated by multiplying the average number of items processed over a period of time by the average time taken to process each item. So, for example, if one stage in a process has to work on 250 items each day and if the average time that each item takes at that stage is 2.3 minutes, the loading on that stage will be 575 minutes' worth of work. If that part of the process is working for 8 hours (480 minutes) a day, that stage will be overloaded by 575/480 = 20 per cent. Of course, that stage may not show as such a significant bottleneck if the people working there increase their work rate in an attempt to cope, but it would need treating nevertheless.

That is why it is also wise to look for where bottlenecks *appear* to be. When a process works on physical items, as in manufacturing, identifying bottlenecks is usually relatively easy. One can see items piling up immediately before a bottleneck stage. In information processing, it can be more difficult. Sometimes excessive inboxes, backlogged work, long waiting times, or even paper accumulating in an in-tray, are the equivalent. Similarly, high stress levels amongst staff, frequent absences, a reluctance to devote time to other work and so on, can be a result of overloading. Be careful though. Excessive inventory before a stage could be the result of the previous stage being under-loaded. This is not as ridiculous as it sounds. If one part of a process has the potential to produce more output than is required by the rest of the process, it can give the appearance that the subsequent stage is a bottleneck.

Curing bottlenecks

Essentially there are two ways of 'unblocking' a bottleneck. Either improve the effective capacity of the bottleneck stage, or reduce the loading on the stage. At its simplest, improving the capacity of the bottleneck could mean putting more resource into that stage, but this is not necessarily the best long-term solution. For one thing it is an incentive to become overloaded. More importantly, it misses the opportunity to learn from why overloading is happening. What has changed? Are the process activities no longer fit for purpose, or are they not being followed? This leads to the other way of tackling bottlenecks, which is to reduce the loading on the stage by increasing efficiency at the bottleneck. This can be done using standard improvement methods and approaches (see Chapters 10 and 11). Or to put it another way, if you want to know where to start your improvement activities, starting with bottleneck activities is a sensible initial step.

Who should do process design?

This is the last, but in some ways the most important, issue. Who should do all this process design? The answer is straightforward and unambiguous – you should, or at least you should be very actively involved. Again it is worth stressing that process design is much more than a mere technical activity. It is important because it determines the actual performance of your processes, and the performance of all your process networks makes up the performance of your total operation. Any operations manager surely must carry responsibility for how his or her processes are put together. Do not even consider handing over responsibility for the design of your processes entirely to junior staff, or to internal 'experts' (although they have their role and can be usefully involved), and certainly do not hand it over entirely to external consultants. It is just too important a task to delegate or to outsource. After all, you will be held accountable if it all goes wrong. Of course, there is a major difference between being engaged with, taking responsibility for, and understanding process design, and getting bogged down in the minutiae. Especially for activities in the mid- to low-volume range, process design is often a matter of imposing a sensible structure on the activity without constraining individual judgement, initiative or creativity.

Practical prescriptions

- Take a broad approach to what you mean by 'process'. Don't let anyone equate it necessarily with tightly defined, machine-like, mindless, routine activities. A 'process' is simply a framework, with and around which you can think about how jobs should be done.

- Look for the 'broken processes' in your operation. They are the ones that fail to deliver what's expected of them.

- Think about processes on a volume–variety scale. Identify the highest volume-lowest variety processes and the lowest volume-highest variety processes in your operation, and position all the others between these two extremes.

- At the start of any process redesign or improvement, make sure that everyone agrees on the relative importance of the process's performance objectives.

- Use the product–process matrix to check that processes have resources to match their volume–variety requirements. Think through the implications of any move off the 'natural diagonal'.

- For 'people processing' has the process's effect on people's emotional responses been considered?

- Do not even think about skipping the basic (and simple) calculations that establish the demand and operating characteristics of any process. These should include its output interval, the (theoretical) number of people required, and the throughput time (using Little's Law).

- Map all of your important processes. Check that process maps represent a shared understanding of how the process should work. If a process involves customers, check that their emotional responses to the process are understood.

- Think through the most appropriate configuration of stages of each process, from pure sequential to pure parallel.

- Check that the process is balanced, with no significant permanent bottlenecks. If not, can the bottleneck stages be redesigned to achieve better balance?

- Get your hands dirty in the process of process design. Don't leave it all to junior or specialist staff.

Notes

1 Sources include: Hines, N (2008) Heathrow T5 disruption to continue over weekend, *Times Online*, 28 March; Done, K (2008) Long haul to restore BA's reputation, *Financial Times*, 28 March; Done, K (2008) BA to cancel hundreds more flights from T5, *Financial Times*, 30 March; Robertson, D (2008) Why Heathrow's T5 disaster provides a lesson for Dubai's T3, *The Times*, 29 November

2 Sources include: Davey, J (2010) Today we built a house every hour, *The Sunday Times*, 31 January; Persimmon company website; Brown, G (2010) Space4 growth gives boost to former car sector workers, *Birmingham Post*, 27 August

3 What we here call the 'output interval' goes by a number of names. In Europe it is often called 'cycle time', which in the US has a different meaning. So beware, and check how these terms are being used

4 Little's Law is best explained in Hopp, W J and Spearman, M L (2001) *Factory Physics*, 2nd edn, McGraw-Hill, New York

5 Shostack, L (1984) Designing services that deliver, *Harvard Business Review*, **62** (1), pp 133–9

Shape your external supply networks

No operations manager's responsibility should stop at the boundary of his or her operation. It extends out to the relationships you have with your customers and customers' customers, your suppliers and suppliers' suppliers, your regulator (if you have one), industry bodies (likewise) and even your competitors; in fact all the other players in your extended supply network. Networks are the linkages between operations. They are the 'plumbing' that connects your business to the other players in your supply network, and when plumbing goes wrong, you notice. The idea of managing networks effectively is absolutely central to developing an operations advantage. Once you have configured your internal process networks, as discussed in the previous chapter, your focus should move on to shaping external networks, more commonly called supply networks; see Figure 7.1.

As we pointed out in Chapter 1, one implication of visualizing supply networks, or operations, or processes, as networks is the emphasis that it puts on the relationships between the elements in the network. If you want to fully understand your supply network, you need to know the capabilities of each operation in the network and the effectiveness of the relationships between them. Do people in each part of the network have a clear line of sight from their part of the network to the end customer? Where are the bottlenecks inhibiting flow? What are the weak elements of the network?

OK, you may say, surely other parts of the business are responsible for these relationships. Marketing and sales strike deals with customers. Procurement contracts with suppliers. Well, yes they may conduct the negotiations and do the deals, but it is operations that provides the channels through which they work. It is the people who run the operational 'mechanics' of how the day-to-day relationships work that define how the relationships actually work.

Figure 7.1   This chapter looks at how to shape your external supply networks

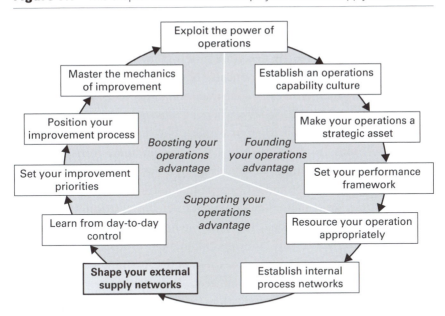

What is involved in 'shaping your external supply network'?

Broadly this chapter is concerned with how you should think about, configure and run your supply network. It is a big subject and one that could (and indeed does) fill many books. Here we focus on those aspects of supply networks that are particularly relevant to the idea of an operations advantage. This involves answering several especially important questions:

- What do you want to do yourself (in-house) and what do you want to buy-in/outsource?

- Which potential suppliers of bought-in goods and services do you want to use?

- What kind of relationship should you be developing with your suppliers?

- How should you fit with the rest of your supply network on an ongoing basis?

- What risks should you be on the lookout for while managing your supply network?

What do you want to do yourself (in-house) and what do you want to buy-in/outsource?

No business does absolutely everything itself. They buy in a whole range of services, materials and components. No business does nothing: even the so-called 'virtual' businesses contribute some sort of value through the coordination they provide. So somewhere in between doing everything and nothing is where you will want to be. The question is, 'Where exactly?' Where you choose to draw the line that divides in-house from out-house activities defines how much of your supply network you want to own. Where should that line be and how might that line be changing?

At one time large aluminium companies not only vertically integrated mining, refining and smelting, but also extended their operations to the production of 'downstream' fabricated aluminium products such as sheet and plate, extruded products, wire, cable and tubes, and foil. However, changes in markets, technology and geopolitics increasingly fragmented once 'Velcro-linked' stages of production. Computer businesses would make their own microchips as well as writing the operating system and applications for the computers they mass-produced and sold. Now chips can be designed by one company, made by another and assembled by subcontractors for whoever owns the brand. Certainly, specialists will do applications development, probably as part of a complex 'ecosystem' of firms in what has become a dynamic but fragmented industry.

Yet vertical integration is of far more than historical interest. There are plenty of examples from current (and successful) businesses. Starbucks buys and roasts all its own coffee and then sells it through its own stores. Zara owns and integrates much of its supply chain to achieve fast delivery (see Chapter 3). The chocolate company Ferrero bought the Turkish operation that processes the hazelnuts that go into its Nutella spread. Silicon Valley tech company Tesla owns the world's largest battery plant and sells its cars directly to customers. Vertical integration is far from dead; in fact it could be making a comeback. Some see the much-reported trend towards 're-shoring' work away from low-cost regions as more than a temporary phenomenon.

Drawing the in/out-house line is important, complex, and defines everything you do (and don't do)

Deciding what you do or don't do in-house is usually called the 'scope' of your operation's activities. It is important because so much else depends upon it. Until you know what is to be done in-house you have no clear idea about how you need to design processes, plan your resources, manage your suppliers' activities, manage risk and approach improvement. In fact, how you do all the key tasks can give you an operations advantage. So do not start making investment, supplier selection, process redesign, until you have some idea of how the scope of the operation is likely to develop in the future.

It is also a decision where there is a cost to changing your mind. Sometimes it is a very big cost. You do not want to be constantly changing what you do or do not do. Once you have decided on your scope it can be difficult to undo and, even if you could reverse the decision, continually switching between in- and out-house undermines morale and inhibits the development of potentially valuable capabilities.

There is no single answer

Do not think that there is one 'best' set of decisions that will define the 'optimum' scope of your businesses. Different firms in the same industry, and competing in the same markets, often have very different views of the scope they should adopt. In the fast fashion industry for example, two of the leading brands have quite different views of the scope of their operations. H&M subcontracts all its manufacturing, while Zara has (by the standards of the industry) remarkably vertically integrated design, production and distribution. Yet both operate successfully. Or look at the example on the contrasting strategies of ARM and Intel described here. Their very different approaches to the scope of their operations have totally defined how each company does business in essentially similar markets.

CASE STUDY ARM versus Intel[1]

In 2016 SoftBank, the Japanese multinational telecommunications corporation made a £24 billion bid for ARM Holdings. It was taken by analysts to be a vote of confidence in the way ARM had structured its operations. The company's chip designs were to be found in almost 99 per cent of mobile devices in the world. It is essentially a chip designer, developing intellectual property. It then licenses its processor designs to manufacturers such as Samsung, who in turn rely on subcontracting 'chip foundry' companies to do the actual manufacturing.

ARM's supply network strategy was a direct result of its early lack of cash. It did not have the money to invest in in its own manufacturing facilities (or to take the risk of subcontracting manufacturing), so it focused on licensing its 'reference designs'. Reference designs are the 'technical blueprint' of a microprocessor that third parties can modify as required. ARM's partners can take its designs and integrate them into their own products. Over the years a whole 'ecosystem' of instruments has emerged to help developers build applications around the ARM designs.

The Intel Corporation is different. It is around 50 times bigger than ARM in revenue terms and dominates the PC and server markets. It is vertically integrated, both designing and manufacturing its own chips. Its integrated supply network monitors and controls all stages of production, from design right through to manufacturing. It invests in hugely expensive plants: it can cost around $5 billion to build a new chip-making operation. For Intel, having the latest manufacturing technology is important. It can mean faster, smaller and cheaper chips with lower power consumption. Other companies in the industry (including ARM licensees) have to make do with shared manufacturing and mainstream technology.

It's difficult to imagine two more different companies than ARM and Intel. They have fundamentally different approaches to the structure and scope of their operations. Yet both, in their own way, demonstrate that, as far as operations scope is concerned, there is no 'one best model'.

Two ways you can look at the in/out-house decision – strategic and operational; you need both

There are two ways of looking at the in/out-house decision, two schools of thought, two traditions and two ways of approaching the problem. Both are important, and both need addressing. The first is the top-down 'strategic' approach that considers the firm's position in its supply network (usually referred to as the 'vertical integration' decision). It is a decision that requires you to tackle some fundamental questions. 'What do you want to be?' 'How do you see the future of your industry?' 'What risks do you feel comfortable taking?' As such it is clearly a far broader decision than could be taken by the operations function alone. Yet, as ever, operations should have a major contribution to make.

Deciding your operations scope cannot always be a purely strategic decision. Many smaller, more operational, decisions are routinely taken that will define the scope of your operation. Every time an individual activity or part is bought in from a supplier, an operation's scope is being defined. Every purchase decision implies a reluctance to 'do it yourself'. In fact, many businesses define the scope of their operations implicitly by making a series of 'purchase or not', 'in-house or subcontract' decisions. Yet it is a mistake to make do-or-buy decisions exclusively on an individual part-by-part or activity-by-activity basis. Think instead of the aggregation of all the do-or-buy decisions that shape the total operations network.

Figure 7.2   The operations scope decision must include both strategic and operational analysis

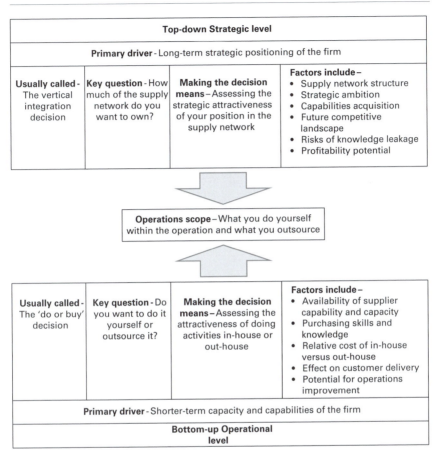

Figure 7.2 shows the differences between the strategic and operational approaches to the decision. Do not think that strategic and operational are options: they are not. You have to approach the decision from both directions if you want any degree of coherence. There is little value in devising a forward-looking strategy for your supply network positioning if your operations and their purchasing staff are not making individual do-or-buy decisions that move towards it. Nor is there much value in making decisions based purely on short-term cost criteria, blind to any long-term positioning aspirations. Both are mistakes. Both sets of analysis and decision making should be integrated. Of the two errors, making individual do-or-buy decisions without strategic guidance is probably the more common, and the more damaging. For this reason, do the analysis in this order: first look at any strategic justification for inhabiting each part of the supply network;

Figure 7.3   The decision logic of outsourcing

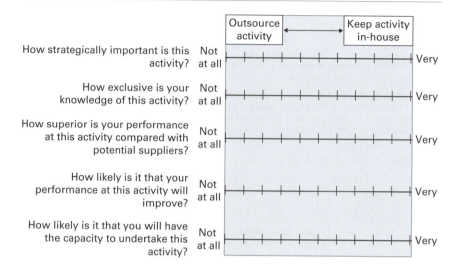

second, explore the operational consequences of individual in-house or out-house decisions. An analysis like the one shown in Figure 7.3 can be used as a first pass, although it should not substitute for more detailed evaluation.

Which potential suppliers should you use?

You are lucky if one of your potential suppliers is so clearly superior to its competitors that the decision is self-evident. More usually it is a matter of trading-off the various attributes of alternative suppliers.

It is an important decision. Every purchase decision involves putting some of your reputation into the hands of a supplier. Get it right and you could acquire (or at least, borrow) capabilities that you don't have. Get it wrong and you are exposed to potential delay, disruption and disorganization. In fact, there are two decisions wrapped up in the supplier selection task. The first is deciding on the criteria that you are going to use to evaluate potential alternative suppliers. The second is the process by which you use the criteria to choose your supplier(s).

Which criteria should you use?

As ever, it depends. It depends on the type of transaction that you want to enter into. Is it a matter of a short-term, interim contracting arrangement, or a longer-term more sustained supply relationship? Also, do you want a formal, arms-length and transactional relationship with the chosen supplier(s), or a closer relationship where your supplier is more integrated with your own operations activities? Both these questions, in effect, decide the type of criteria that you will need to look at before making a final choice. With short-term contracts, the current performance dominates. If the relationship is longer term, it is sensible to also include more forward-looking criteria. Even if a supply contract is likely to sustain over the long term, it may not necessarily warrant being integrated into your internal processes.

If the relationships with suppliers are to be integrated, then in addition to the more measurable, objective criteria such as price, quality, delivery, etc, more subjective criteria should be included. These more subjective criteria (such as the likely ease of doing business with a supplier) are not any less important, but they are more difficult to measure impartially. Again, when evaluating more integrated relationships, objective criteria are not abandoned, they are still the bedrock of evaluation, but the 'softer', more

Figure 7.4   Criteria for outsourcing

Transactional ———— **Relationship** ————▶ *integrated*

Current objective criteria
- Total cost of being supplied
- History of supplying our type of business
- Quality
- Ability to supply volume
- Responsiveness
- Dependability of supply
- Delivery flexibility
- Volume flexibility

Current subjective criteria all to the left, plus
- Ease of doing business
- Technical capability
- Willingness to engage in supplier development
- Managerial capability
- Willingness to share risk
- Ability to transfer knowledge
- Supply priority
- Risk of knowledge leakage

Interim

Forward-looking objective criteria all the above, plus...
- Pricing guarantees
- Financial stability/ sustainability
- Investment in dedicated assets
- Service and support
- Tracking and reporting procedures

Forward-looking subjective criteria all the above and to the left, plus...
- Strategic fit into supply base
- Long-term commitment to supply
- Potential for innovation
- Corporate ownership
- Vulnerability to key people departing
- Business continuity planning
- Integrity/reputational risk

Contract period

Sustained

Short-term / Long-term — Timescale of criteria

Tangible / Intangible

Nature of selection criteria

subjective criteria should be added. Figure 7.4 illustrates some typical criteria in each of these categories.

Some businesses spend too much time and effort on supplier selection; some take too little, often using inadequate and/or over-rigid sets of criteria. The latter failure is by far the most common. It is especially foolish when a long-term and integrated activity is being performed out-house (the bottom-left quadrant in Figure 7.4). Then what is being assessed is 'the current *and future* capability mentality of potential suppliers. In effect you are saying, 'You might be capable of producing this product or service but we are thinking two or three generations forward and asking ourselves, do we want to invest in this relationship for the future?'

How should you make the decision?

Most authorities recommend the use of some kind of supplier 'scoring' or assessment procedure. There are many of these. The simplest weight individual criteria then score each on a standard scale. Multiplying the weighting by individual scores and summing them for each potential supplier gives them a combined score. There are more complex and sophisticated arithmetic methods, but the mathematics involved tends to be more clever than useful. Complex evaluation methods are rarely worth it. What is far more important is the interplay between the results of whatever scoring method is used and experienced purchasing people's reaction to it. If, after turning the mathematical handle, the answer that emerges produces doubt, scepticism, or suspicion, then the way you have weighted or scored the criteria really does need examining and, if necessary, reassessing. Even if the formal procedure throws out a recommendation that fits in with your prior prejudices, it is still best to critique your scoring.

One or several? The single or multi-sourcing decision

The trend has been clear, if not totally universal – companies have moved to consolidate and rationalize their suppliers, often going as far as creating single-sourcing agreements. There are examples of where single sourcing has been very successful (see the example, 'Without commitment on both sides it couldn't have happened', later in this chapter) and it is not surprising; there are some significant advantages:

- It is easier to build strong relationships that are more durable.
- There are opportunities to work closely to solve quality or delivery problems.

- Greater dependency encourages more commitment.

- Communication is easier.

- Economies of scale for the supplier to be (potentially) passed on.

- Lower transaction costs.

These have to be balanced against two disadvantages: supply is vulnerable to disruption in the event of a supply failure, and it gives the supplier power if no alternative supply is available.

Do not imagine that if you choose to multi-source it will be exclusively for your short-term benefit. Multi-sourcing can not only be more flexible, it can also bring benefits to both supplier and purchaser in the long term. Limiting the total proportion of business with any one supplier prevents them becoming too dependent on you as a customer. You can then change volumes without pushing your supplier into bankruptcy, or over-straining their capacity.

What kind of relationship should you develop with your suppliers?

There is a spectrum of relationships that you can develop with your suppliers. At one end are strictly contractual relationships, defined by explicit (usually written, often detailed) and formal documents that specify legally binding obligations and roles of your suppliers, you, and any other parties involved in a relationship. At the other end are 'partnership' relationships. These rely less on formal contractual mechanisms. They are closer, informal, long-term and almost personal arrangements that attempt to embody the idea of a shared future between supplier and customer.

Do not view contractual and partnership relationships as being either mutually exclusive or alternative options. In most buyer–supplier relationships they coexist and are complementary. It is the balance between the two 'ingredients' that will define any relationship. However, the way you manage the two 'ingredients' does need to be aligned, irrespective of the balance between the two. A naïve faith in partnership can undermine the serious contractual negotiations that could protect both parties. Alternatively, playing hardball during negotiations over legal or financial procedures can undermine the closeness and trust that are the bedrock of partnerships.

Making contracting work

The purpose of a supply contract is to reduce uncertainty, for example by providing a well-defined description of what is and what is not acceptable within a relationship, while at the same time reducing the risk of inappropriate opportunism by either party in the future. There are many sources of (legal and quasi-legal) advice on how to structure supply contracts, from professional associations to free websites. But, at their heart, your suppliers should be meeting three conditions if you want to achieve effective control of your supply by using contracts:

1 *Your contract should be adequately codified.* If you want to avoid problems later, it needs to be drawn up in a way that specifies 'up front' measurable outcomes.

2 *Your contract should be able to be adequately monitored.* Exactly how a contract is to be monitored against the rules set out in the contract needs to be specified in the contract itself.

3 *Your contract should contain adequate safeguards.* Effective control needs to indicate what measures (and penalties) are to be to be in place to enforce the contract.

Making partnership work

In some ways, partnership relationships are attempts to achieve some of the advantages of closeness and coordination efficiencies that come from owning your 'supplier's' assets yourself (vertical integration). At the same time, it tries to capture the sharpness of service and the incentive to continually improve that can be achieved in the best free-market trading. They are an approach to how relationships in supply networks can be formed with a degree of trust that effectively substitutes for the ownership of assets. They are also one of the most potentially rewarding, yet one of the most difficult things to make work, in the whole of operations management's daunting portfolio of responsibilities.

You don't 'design' relationships; you build them over time (in life, and in supply networks). They are alliances where partners are expected to cooperate, even to the extent of sharing skills and resources, in order to realize joint benefits beyond those they could gain by acting alone. As in any partnership there are compromises and sacrifices. The idea of partnership is that you give something up in order to get something greater. You give up the option of

Figure 7.5   Some elements of partnership relationships

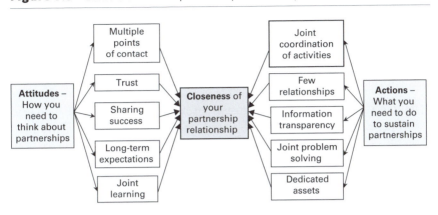

'being unfaithful' with other suppliers (or customers) so as to share the joint benefits of mutual security and improvement. Partnerships always involve some kind of sacrifice. If you think you have a partnership without giving something up – don't fool yourself – it isn't really a partnership. The degree of closeness that you can achieve in a partnership arrangement is built on two sets of things: 1) how you think about the relationship – the attitude you have towards it, and 2) what you do to sustain the partnership – the actions that you take.

Figure 7.5 illustrates some of the attitudes and actions that contribute to the closeness of a partnership arrangement; in other words, the degree of intimacy, understanding and mutual support that exists between partners. If you detect a similarity between how we talk about closeness in business relations and how the word is used in personal relations, it is quite deliberate. The degree of interpersonal intimacy you achieve relies on your attitude and the accumulation of your individual actions towards your relationships. Both are important. Intimacy relies on your belief in the other party's attitude and motivation in maintaining the relationship. Belief helps dispel any doubt that you can rely on supportive actions from your partner, while actions over time deepen and enhance the positive beliefs and attitudes concerning the relationship itself.

Attitudes – how you need to think about partnerships

- *Accept multiple points of contact* – do not always insist on one or two formally defined channels of communication. There can be many informal links between many individuals in both organizations. This may sound like an action rather than an attitude, but it is best thought of as an attitude that encourages multiple person-to-person relationships. Over time, it may lead to a close 'Velcro-connected' web of understandings being formed.

- *Trust* – if there is no risk involved in a relationship, there is not any need for trust. Without some degree of trust there is little justification for taking risks with a partner. Trust is an issue that needs to be managed explicitly. Almost all research into supplier–customer relationships highlights the importance of trust to the relationship.

- *Sharing success* – shared success means that both you and your partner recognize that you have more to gain through the success of the other than either of you have individually, or you have by exploiting the other.

- *Long-term expectations* – partnerships are for the long term, assuming that you both behave in the best interests of the other, but they are not necessarily permanent. Either party could end the partnership. In fact that is partly what keeps you both motivated to do the best for the other.

- *Joint learning* – presumably you have selected you partner on the basis that they have something to contribute beyond what you can do for yourself. An attitude of mutual learning can uncover mutually beneficial improvement opportunities.

Actions – what you need to do to sustain partnerships

- *Joint coordination of activities* – fewer individual partners should reduce the coordination effort, so the quantity, type and timing of product and service deliveries can be mutually agreed. Having said that, usually the customer side of a partnership has a greater say. Customers, after all, are closer to ultimate demand.

- *Few relationships* – partnerships do not necessarily imply single sourcing by customers, or exclusivity by suppliers. However, even if the relationships are not monogamous, they are not promiscuous. Partnerships inevitably involve a limit on the number of other partnerships, if for no other reason than a single organization cannot maintain intimacy in a large number of relationships.

- *Information transparency* – open and efficient information exchange means that you and your partner are open, honest and timely in the way you communicate. It is vital for encouraging good decision making and for preventing misunderstandings between you.

- *Joint problem solving* – no partnership will always run smoothly. (In fact, the degree of closeness would be severely limited if it did.) The way problems are addressed is central to how your partnership develops. It is only when problems arise that the opportunity exists to explore many of the issues regarding trust, shared success, long-term expectations and so on.

- *Dedicated assets* – one of the guaranteed ways of demonstrating commitment to partnership, but one of the most risky, is one partner (usually the supplier) investing in resources that will be dedicated to a single customer. It is clearly high risk and only worthwhile if you are convinced that the partnership will endure and your partner will not exploit the investment to bargain the price down.

CASE STUDY   'Without commitment on both sides it couldn't have happened'

'We always wanted a 100 per cent supply deal. We knew that it could be in both of our interests. But we didn't fully realize just how much it would be built on mutual trust. It is trust that allows you to commit resources when the success of the investment depends on another firm's cooperation.' The COO of a supplier of precision-coated photoresist film was speaking about its operation's single-source relationship with its main customer. *'We invested in a totally focused facility to supply them. Some said it was too much of a gamble, but we knew enough about our customer to know that they would not forgo the 25 per cent cost saving and better quality that a dedicated facility would give them.'*

The launch of the new dedicated facility was not without its problems, yet, with hindsight, it was overcoming these problems that helped to cement the relationship. *'Our start-up problem was potentially very serious. But we made a conscious effort to keep the customer fully informed. In fact, they were very helpful in doing anything they could to help us sort the problem. So when they had a problem handling the large rolls we were supplying, we were happy to help to solve it. Partly because we worked together on these problems, the relationship has grown stronger and stronger.'*

The supply agreement worked well, but there was one hitch. The customer's facility was over 1,000 km away. This distance caused a number of problems including some damage in transit and delays in delivery. *'During the initial single-source negotiations for our 100 per cent contract there had been some talk about co-location but I don't think anyone took it particularly seriously. But eventually the option of them moving to locate in a building attached to our plant was the preferred option. There was a lot of resistance to having a customer on the same site as us. We had never done anything like it before and we couldn't imagine working so closely with a customer. The step from imagining our customer a little closer to imagining them on the same site took some thinking about. It was a matter of getting used to the idea, taking one step at a time. But initially our main board was not happy about the idea. Providing factory space seemed a long way from our core business. We were not in the real estate business, they said.'* But they did eventually approve the idea – on condition that the door between the two companies' areas should be capable of being locked from both sides. Now, all visitors to the plant are shown the door that had to be 'capable of being locked from both sides' and asked how many times they think it has been locked. The answer is 'never'.

What relationship is best for you?

The bad news is that there is no obvious simple formula for choosing what form of supplier arrangement to develop. The good news is that you can identify some of the more important factors that should influence your decision. Remember that relationships are rarely 'pure'; they all lie on a spectrum. What seem like transactional relationships may have some partnership/collaborative features. A partnership relationship may occasionally have transactional transactions. Deciding what is right for you means answering some key questions concerning you and your competitive position, what you want to buy, and your (potential) suppliers.

You and your competitive position

1   Beware of making any kind of overarching policy decision about which kind of arrangement to adopt. It should be 'horses for courses'; different types of bought-in product or service warrant different relationships. You will always finish up with a portfolio of widely differing arrangements.

2   Supplier relationships should be aligned with your own market strategy. If you differentiate yourself by competing primarily on price, then minimizing transaction costs should influence supply. If you compete on innovation, then collaborating through partnership may be appropriate, and so on.

3   An exception to the point above is when the market for innovation-based supplies is turbulent and/or fast growing (for example, in some high-tech markets). Then, the freedom to reduce risk may be more important, either by being able to change suppliers quickly, or develop arrangements with several potential suppliers.

4 If you have particularly aggressive competitors, a close partnership (or even bringing the activity in-house) may be a good defensive move.

5 A partnership arrangement may be sensible, but unless you have an appropriate culture (set of attitudes, see earlier) then maybe a less ambitious arrangement may be more appropriate.

What you want to buy

6 Some supplies are more important to you than others, either in terms of the volume you purchase, the impact the purchase cost has on your total costs, or the impact on your ability to compete. You will almost certainly want to secure the availability of your more important supplies, possibly through partnership arrangements.

7 Some supplies can be substituted for, others cannot. How easy it is to switch from one supplied product or service to another? If switching is difficult, some method of securing supply will be important, either through multiple suppliers (possible, though unlikely) or a longer-term partnership-style agreement.

8 Are there significant operational benefits of a supplier being 'integrally connected' with your operations? For example, are there joint problems that can be tackled through close collaboration? If so, it may be worth working towards a close partnership.

Your (potential) suppliers

9 Are some suppliers so strategic to your business that they have a major impact on your competitive advantage by providing a unique product or service? If so, a close partnership may be fundamental.

10 Similarly, does one supplier significantly outperform all others? If so, partnership should be explored.

11 Trust is important in any type of relationship, but the necessary level of trust required by partnership relationships must be high. If you don't have trust (for example because of past experience), do not think that a partnership will be easy.

12 How high is the risk of supply failure? If high, then unless the cost of switching suppliers is prohibitive, either use multiple suppliers if possible, or make sure any partnership arrangement gives you priority, or safer still, bring the activity back in-house.

13 What is the cost of doing business (transaction costs) with a supplier? Low transaction costs favour transactional arrangements. High transaction costs may mean switching suppliers or jointly reducing transaction costs through a partnership.

14 If your supply base is relatively undifferentiated, providing interchangeable products or services, a transactional relationship is likely to be appropriate.

15 Is there the potential for learning from a supplier? If so, a partnership will be attractive (well, attractive to you; they might need persuading).

How should you fit with the rest of your supply network on an ongoing basis?

Your 'fit' with the rest of your supply network contributes in large part to how it will aid or hinder your operations advantage. It's like some people: they fit in well with the group, they recognize its values, they understand the roles of others and everyone understands theirs. Individual operations in a supply network are the same. Some are seen as responsible customers or suppliers. Others get stuck with a reputation for being 'difficult' – difficult to understand their strategic objectives and difficult to work with on a day-to-day level. This is rarely because the 'difficult' business is deliberately trying to be challenging. Usually it is because it is failing to understand and/or manage the supply-side and demand-side interfaces that connect it to the rest of its supply network. It is often down to misunderstandings and misinterpretation in how these interfaces are managed.

It is worth checking if the management of your interfaces with customers and suppliers, and particularly if the assumptions you are making about each other, are aligned. Ideally, there should be a seamless logic between the needs and objectives of your customers and those of your suppliers. To achieve this alignment you need to make sure that there are no gaps of understanding in three links:[2]

1 that between you and your customers;

2 the internal link between your market-facing people who deal with customers and your supplier-facing people who deal with suppliers; and

3 that between you and your suppliers.

These three links are the channels for two types of perception (and more important, misperception). Flowing upstream is the possibility that your and your customers' requirements are being misunderstood. Flowing downstream is the possibility that you, and your suppliers, are misjudging supply performance. Figure 7.6 illustrates this idea and poses the questions that can reveal gaps, both in what is required and how well those requirements are satisfied.

Figure 7.6 Some potential perception gaps in customer requirements and supplier performance

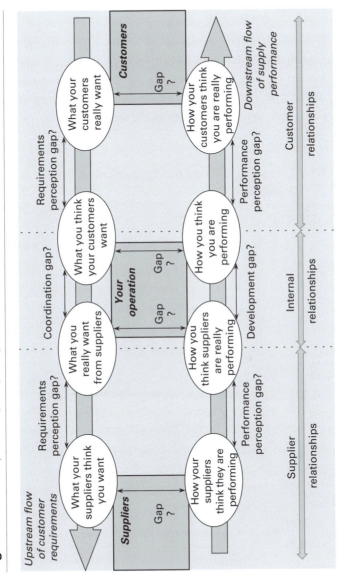

Even in well-run operations there is plenty of opportunity for perception gaps to occur, either between what is required by the next stage in the supply network, or in how supply performance is judged. It is not just the external relationships themselves that need scrutiny: they rely on how supply-side and demand-side relationships are connected internally. Even internally it is not unusual to find that market-facing and purchasing people do not coordinate (or sometimes even communicate). This means that there are four potential mismatches between and within each stage in a supply network. So if you want to look for mismatches, try mapping the various elements of what constitutes requirements and performance between you and your suppliers and customers, as is shown in Figure 7.7.

Figure 7.7   The various factors of performance can be mapped in terms of any perception gaps

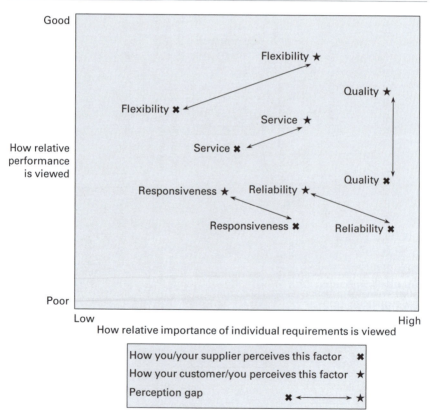

What risks should you be on the lookout for while managing your supply network?

The benefits associated with the growing use of outsourcing and the reliance on global supply networks are numerous and significant. They can bring efficiency, improved business focus, reduced capital investment, and flexibility. Inevitably though, an increased dependence on other players in the supply network also increases risk.

Supply network risk is different to other types of operations risk. One obvious difference is that the origins of the risk lie outside your boundaries and are therefore, partially, out of your control. So the usual first step in managing risk – trying to prevent operations failures – is more difficult. It's not impossible: it is always worth taking an interest in (and some responsibility for) the failures of other operations in your supply network. After all, you depend on them. However, the main focus of managing supply network risk tends to be on mitigation and recovery; in other words, reducing the negative effects of supply network failure and getting back on your feet after any failure.

Types of supply risk

Before thinking about how your supply network risks can be mitigated, the first thing to do is to review the type of risks to which you may be exposed. If you follow the high-profile stories that tell tales of supply network jeopardy, you may think that all disruption was caused by major disasters – tsunamis wiping out suppliers' factories, volcanoes disrupting air transport, terrorist attacks, dramatic technical failures. Not so. Most disruption for most companies tends to be smaller scale, less dramatic, but this does not mean that they are not irritating, distracting and costly. More significantly, announcements of supply disruptions can have an appreciable impact on financial performance, with stock market reactions resulting in declines in market capitalization of as much as 10 per cent.[3] Of course, the major disruptions that become headlines across the world are potentially more devastating in terms of their consequences and need addressing, but, whether small and frustrating, or large and dramatic, most supply network risks will impact one (or more) of the following:

- Disruption to the *volume* of supplies – a sudden cessation of supply from a local failure such as the bankruptcy of a supplier, or a more widespread event such as the 2011 Japanese tsunami and earthquake that disrupted supply worldwide.

- A break in service *availability* – like a disruption to the volume of supply but affecting 'continuous' services such as IT failures. The Royal Bank of Scotland (RBS) suffered a major outage in 2012 with millions of business and personal customers unable to access accounts or make payments.

- Errors in demand *forecasts* – when their forecast for the US market proved to be disastrously wrong, Treasury Wine Estates had to pour over £20 million of its wine down the drain because it had spent too much time in the supply chain and had become 'too old'.

- Damage to *reputation* – in 2013 horsemeat was found in processed 'beef' products sold in supermarkets around Europe. In France, supermarkets withdrew all frozen beef meals made by Findus and Comigel. Complexity in the food industry's supply chains was held partly responsible. The horsemeat sold as beef came from Romanian slaughterhouses, was sold to a Dutch food trader, then to a Cypriot trader before being supplied to the French companies.

- Unreliable *quality* – Whirlpool's decision to outsource the production of water seals for its dishwashers to a Chinese supplier saved over $2 million annually. But when the supplier changed its rubber supplier the new rubber seals leaked. It eventually cost the company millions of dollars; far more than the original savings.

- Delays to expected *delivery* – the 40-day Hong Kong port workers' strike in 2013 caused delays at production plants around Asia, encouraging ships to bypass the port in favour of rival ones elsewhere in Asia; resulting in a backlog of between 80,000 and 90,000 containers.

- *Cost* of supplies – price hikes are never welcome (to customers) and can be particularly damaging when they are unexpected. They tend to be the result of monopoly (or near-monopoly) supplier power, as in some drug supplies to national healthcare systems, or politics, for example Russian gas supplies, or currency fluctuations, as in the Swiss franc's dramatic appreciation in 2015.

- *Malicious* interventions – cyber attacks are a relatively recent, but growing, supply risk. An aggressor can find the operation in the supply network that has the weakest cyber security and, through it, get access to others in the network. For example, in 2014 a cyber-espionage group called Dragonfly was discovered targeting third-party software suppliers whose 'malware-containing' software could then be used to infiltrate their customers' systems.

CASE STUDY   Chipotle sources locally[4]

The quick service restaurant (fast food) industry competes on fast service (obviously), low cost and consistent, predictable quality. Its critics complain of industrialized bland food, ignoring local sourcing in their drive for standardization, and over-complex food supply chains where it is difficult to keep track of where supplies originate. Also, there are reputational risks inherent in using some large food processors, for example animal rights campaigners have expressed concerns over how animals are treated in large plants.

One solution is to focus on locally sourced supplies. It can even form the basis of a brand strategy – 'we use fresh local ingredients'. That was the direction taken by the US chain Chipotle Mexican Grill: 'Day after day we are committed to sourcing the very best ingredients we can find and preparing them by hand.' However, more and smaller local suppliers have their own risks. In 2015 the company was associated with outbreaks of salmonella and norovirus. Some commentators raised questions about the difficulty of controlling such a widespread network of relatively small suppliers. A few large and experienced providers supply most of the chain's competitors such as KFC or McDonald's, who often have their own quality inspectors resident in suppliers' plants. Local sourcing makes that difficult and expensive. Reportedly, since the incident, Chipotle has invested $10 million in helping its network of local suppliers meet stricter safety standards.

What can you do about it?

There is no single 'magic bullet' that will eliminate your supply network risk. Different mitigation strategies fit with different types of risk. You will almost certainly need a mix of strategies, and none of them are cost-free. How well you manage when faced with such dangers depends on the type of risk and on how well prepared you are. Also, consider that these different types of risk can be interconnected. For example, using inventory to protect yourself against disruption in supply could expose you to stock obsolescence risks. Before deciding on mitigation strategies, it is essential to estimate your exposure to different types of risk. Doing this is sometimes called 'stress testing' your supply chain.[5]

Supply chain stress testing

Stress testing, in this context, means producing a common appreciation of what type of supply network risks you are exposed to. It is, by nature, something of a speculative exercise, involving 'what if' questions rather than precise evaluations. It nevertheless should be rigorous. You need to examine each type of risk that could originate from each stage in your supply network. Just as important, you need to evaluate what your suppliers are doing to mitigate their risks, what you can do, and how you could coordinate. Scenario planning is useful in stress testing, but there is a cost. Best to focus the most time-consuming evaluations of those key parts of your supply network that could potentially cause you the most problems. Remember that supply chains tend to break at their weakest link.

Table 7.1 shows some of the strategies that you can adopt to (partially) mitigate some supply network risks. Most are a blend of:

- some kind of redundancy – for example, holding reserves of excess capability, capacity, inventory, or supply relationships;

- active intervention in parts of the supply network that are outside your boundaries – for example, limiting suppliers' capacity utilization, coordinating fast response, setting minimum labour standards; and

- insurance – for example, currency hedging.

Only one strategy totally insures against (external) supply network risk – do everything in-house. Which, of course, does not eliminate risk: it just brings it to where you can keep a closer eye on it.

Table 7.1   The costs and applicability of some supply network risk mitigation strategies

Mitigation strategy	Costs	Which type of risk
Bring in-house	Forgone scale and specialization, plus investment in capacity and capability	Almost all
Multiple suppliers	Lower-volume orders, extra transaction costs	Disruption to volume Delays to delivery Cost of supplies Unreliable quality

(Continued)

Table 7.1 *(Continued)*

Mitigation strategy	Costs	Which type of risk
Geographic spread of suppliers	Transaction/coordination costs, Transport costs	Cost of supplies (currency) Disruption to volume
Currency hedging	Risk premium	Cost of supplies (currency)
Limit supplier capacity utilization (high utilization makes them vulnerable to delay)	Lower supply volumes/ capacity underutilization	Disruption to volume Delays to delivery Unreliable quality
Supplier flexibility (to change nature and quantity of supply)	Capability, and possibly capacity, underutilization	Errors in forecasts Disruption to volume Delays to delivery
Get actively involved in managing suppliers' (and therefore your) risk	Systems, procedures, staff, effort	Almost all
Keep inventory	Working capital, storage, obsolescence	Disruption to volume Delays to delivery Errors in forecast
Redundant systems/ capacity	Capacity underutilization	A break in service availability
Fast supply chain throughput/ variety postponement	Coordination efforts, underutilization, processing costs	Errors in forecast

One final point on supply network risk. You can just accept it. All of these mitigation strategies have costs. It may be that you figure that it's not worth the cost of attempting to mitigate risk. While it may seem irresponsible to just cross your fingers and hope for the best, there may be circumstances where it's sensible.

Practical prescriptions

- Fight any tendency amongst your operations function to 'stop their thinking at the boundary'. All operations managers share the responsibility for fitting their own operations into their supply network.

- Defining the scope (the balance between in- and out-house activities) is important, complex, and defines everything you do, so do not start making investment, supplier selection, process redesign, until you have some idea of how the scope of the operation is likely to develop in the future.

- Do not think that there is one 'best' set of decisions that will define the 'optimum' scope of businesses in an industry. Different firms in the same industry, and competing in the same markets, often adopt very different network scope strategies.

- Making the in/out-house decision should involve both a strategic and an operational analysis. Operations and purchasing staff should not be making individual decisions that do not fit with your strategic view of the scope you want to attain, nor should your strategic vision be independent of the operational realities of your existing supply network.

- The criteria that you use to choose between in- and out-house supply should take into account whether you want supply to be on a short-term interim or long-term sustained basis, and whether supply is to be transactional or more integrated with your internal activities.

- By all means use a scoring or other model to evaluate alternative suppliers, but such methods are best not when they 'make the decision', but when they provide the input to a more nuanced discussion.

- Make single- or multi-sourcing decisions based largely on the lower transaction costs and potentially close cooperation of single sourcing versus the reduced risks and flexibility of multi-sourcing.

- All supply relationships involve two elements – contracting and partnership. Contracting relies on adequate codification, monitoring and safeguards. Partnership relies on developing appropriate attitudes and actions to sustain the relationship.

- Deciding what balance between contracting and partnership is right for you means critically addressing some key questions concerning you and your competitive position, what you want to buy, and your (potential) suppliers.

- Your 'fit' with the rest of your supply network depends on the validity of the assumptions that you, customers, and suppliers are making about each other's requirements and performance. It is important to examine any potential gaps in the perceptions of these assumptions between you, your suppliers and your customers.

- Trends in how supply networks are developing have brought many benefits, but have also increased supply network risk. It is important to formally identify the types of supply risk that you are exposed to and put appropriate mitigation strategies in place.

Notes

1 Sources include: Burton, G (2013) ARM vs Intel: a battle of business models, *Computing,* 29 May; Turley, J (2014) Intel vs ARM: Two titans' tangled fate, InfoWorld.com, created 27 February

2 This form of analysis was originally developed by Professor Christine Harland of Cardiff University

3 Hendricks, K and Singhal, V R (2005) The effect of supply chain disruptions on long-term shareholder value, profitability, and share price volatility, *Production and Operations Management,* **14** (1), pp 35–52

4 Sources include: Torres, N (2016) Why sourcing local food is so hard for restaurants, *Harvard Business Review,* 15 June

5 This is an idea popularized in an influential paper by Chopra, S and Sodhi, M S (2004) Managing risk to avoid supply-chain breakdown, *Sloan Management Review*, Fall, 15 October

Learn from day-to-day control

08

This step in achieving an operations advantage is based on two fundamental but essentially simple ideas. The first is that all operations need to be controlled; the second is that control provides one of the best opportunities for operations to learn, and by learning build their capabilities. Alas, it is an opportunity that is often ignored. In fact it is one of the biggest disconnects in operations – we fail to associate the routine business of controlling our resources and processes with how we learn and improve operations. Partly this is because operations control is one of those things that many of us only notice when it goes wrong – when control fails to control. It is 'background' like the thermostat that controls the heating in your room. We seem to take control for granted, and in doing so we fail to realize its true importance. Operations control and operations improvement should really be mutually supportive. This is why we position this chapter at the border of the topics that deal with how to support, and how to improve your operation; see Figure 8.1.

Control – keeping things together

So what is 'control'? Dictionaries give a number of definitions, but two themes occur in most of them. One is the idea of 'constraint' (keep your dog under control), the other is that of 'guidance' (my job is to control our purchasing strategy). More technically, control within our operations function is the way that we monitor what is happening with our resources and processes, check that they are conforming to what we want, and do something about it if they don't. In fact, both the 'definitional' themes are included in what we usually mean by control in operations. Any control system should indicate constraints, or limits, to what we want our operations to do, and it needs to guide the operation back to doing what it is supposed to do if it strays.

Start with the basic model of control, shown in Figure 8.2. At its simplest, the control of any operation can be seen as 'how we correct deviations from a previously agreed plan'. So control starts with your plan, or a broad set of objectives, or at least some idea of what should be happening (for example

Figure 8.1 This chapter looks at how to learn from day-to-day control

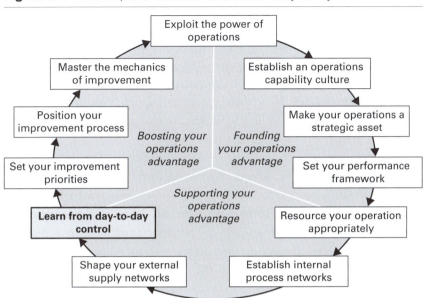

Figure 8.2 The simple model of operations control

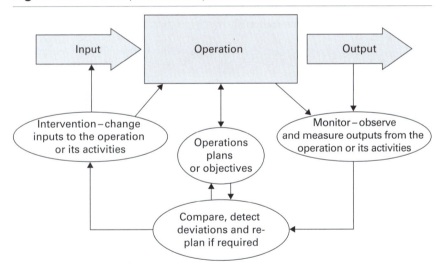

a planned output level). The output from your operation (say the output in a period), or the way it is working (say internal quality levels), has to be monitored to check that planned output or activities really are going to plan. This is formally compared with the plan (for example, output is lower than expected) and any deviation rectified through some kind of intervention in the operation, or its inputs (say, you approve more work hours). This could involve some re-planning.

Making control work for learning

The problem with this simple model of control is that it is... well, simple. It is a naïve generalization of a far messier reality. It is based on how mechanical systems such as room heaters are controlled. But of course, operations are not machines: they are complex social systems, full of uncertainty and ambiguous interactions. Nevertheless, even this simple view gives us a clue to how the activity of controlling your operations can be utilized to give you something greater than simply 'keeping control'.

The logic goes something like this. Control means monitoring your operation's output and activities and intervening in the operation's inputs or activities. Making interventions in your operation allows you to observe the effect of that intervention, so you can associate the effect the intervention has on what you did or how you did it. This association of cause with effect means that you have the opportunity to learn about what it is that makes your operation react in that way to the intervention. Repeatedly learning from these cause–effect observations allows you to build a progressively greater level of knowledge about how your operation really works, and with a high level of operations knowledge you can more accurately target what you need to monitor. This allows you to intervene in your operation more effectively, and so on. This idea is shown in Figure 8.3.

Figure 8.3 Operations control should form the basis of improvement

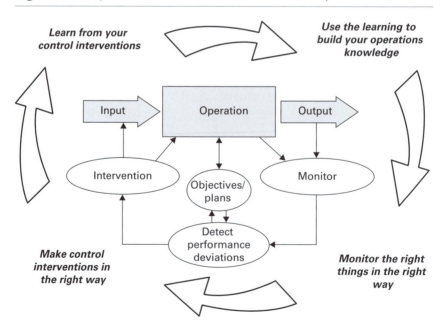

Operations control is not just operational – it's strategic

Do not dismiss operations control as being only an operational issue, not worth the attention of senior management. Read about the strategic advantages gained by the Preston Plant, in the next example. It shows how operational control can lead to strategic advantage. Getting this kind of benefit from your control processes does not come automatically. Grafting this learning cycle onto your planning activities needs to be done without disrupting the primary control task, yet fully exploits the learning potential. To do this, four questions (which form the structure of this chapter) need to be thought through:

1 Are you monitoring the right things in the right way?

2 Are you making control interventions in the right way?

3 Are you learning from your control interventions?

4 Are you using the learning to build your operations knowledge?

CASE STUDY Turning round the Preston Plant

'It was a crisis that prompted us to change how we viewed control. I was with one of our main customers and during the meeting one of their engineers handed me some of the process data that we had to supply with every batch of product, and said, "Here's your latest data. We think you're out of control and you don't know that you're out of control and we think that we are looking at this data more than you are." He was absolutely right. Production control charting was done to please the client, not for problem solving, and certainly not for any strategic reason. Data readouts were brought to production meetings, we would all look at it, but none of us were looking behind it.' (COO, Preston Plant)

The Preston Plant specialized in precision coating papers for printing, using state-of-the-art coating machines that allowed very precise coatings to be applied to bought-in rolls of paper. After coating, the coated rolls were cut into standard sizes. Although it had been supplying some well-known customers for many years, its profitability had been poor and its quality levels only just acceptable. *'Looking back, there was no real concept of control and the operation was allowed to drift. Our culture said, "If it's within specification then it's OK," and we were diligent in not shipping out-of-spec product. However, some of our customers insist on getting our process data that enabled them to see exactly what is happening right inside our operation. We were also getting all the data but none of it was being internalized.'* (COO, Preston Plant)

When the plant's management started to focus on what their control data was telling them, they realized what they had been neglecting. *'The first thing that we found was that we were shipping more product because it was passing our final quality checks. That was to be expected I guess. But within months we started to see the beginnings of more far-reaching benefits. We tried to summarize them to understand what was happening* (shown in Figure 8.4). *It was a revelation. Just look at the long-term strategic result of what is essentially a mundane operational issue – production control. Who wouldn't want secure revenue, lower costs, better new product development, good staff retention and well-established continuous improvement? The most surprising thing though was how it affected our relationship with suppliers. We eventually got to the point where we needed to integrate our control process with our paper suppliers. Imagine the satisfaction I got out of being able to say to our main paper supplier, "We think you're out of control and you don't know that you're out of control and we think that we are looking at this data more than you are." Sound familiar?'*

Figure 8.4   The strategic benefits of operations control at the Preston Plant

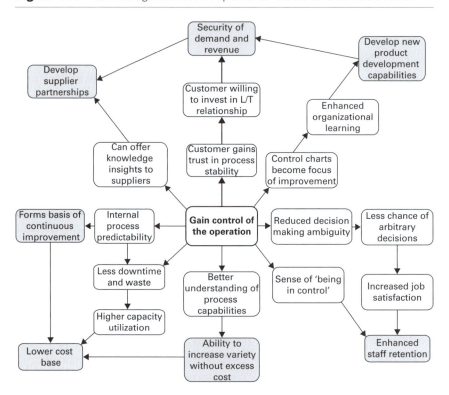

1 Monitor the right things in the right way

If you have no way of knowing what is happening in your operation there can be no future planning, no interventions – no control. Monitoring is the essential prerequisite to any kind of control. It needs to organize the regular collection and analysis of the information that comes from tracking your activities, outputs and performance. Without accurate monitoring there can be no useful detection of deviations from plan, no rational interventions to correct future actions and no learning. In short, it's important. If you are seeking advice as to what is important for regular operations control, you will be told that monitoring should focus on those aspects of performance that are particularly important to the business's competitiveness, should be done regularly, should fully document the differences between actual and planned performance, and should be done when it can have the most impact. All of which is useful advice, but for monitoring to be part of the learning cycle, more is needed.

Monitoring for learning needs a wider scope – in the simple view of control, it is the operation's output or internal activities that are monitored for deviations from plan. For learning to be encouraged, inputs may also need monitoring. After all, your inputs of bought-in goods and services will have an impact on operations performance, so if the objective of control is to learn more about how your operations behave, it needs to be monitored.

Monitoring for learning needs to tap into underlying issues – the things that you need to monitor for conventional performance reporting are not always the same as the things that you are interested in when your objective is to increase your understanding. For example, an aggregated 'on-time-in-full' (OTIF) performance measure may be a vital means of tracking your delivery performance over time, but if you want to dig deeper to understand how your interventions are affecting OTIF, you would be better monitoring more detailed delivery-by-delivery figures, out-of-stock details, avoidable delays, and the other elements that make up the OTIF figure.

Monitoring for learning needs to relate to a hypothesis – this sounds a bit 'academic', but it's common sense really. When you start the process of knowledge building, you do not usually start with a blank sheet of paper. You have some idea of how things work within your operation. This idea of 'how things work' is your hypothesis. A hypothesis is an idea or explanation for something that is based on known facts but has not yet been proved.[1] Without an initial idea of what links the interventions that you can make to change the behaviour of your operation and the actual observed changes, all you have is an observation without meaning. A hypothesis forces you to move beyond asking the question, 'Has our intervention brought the performance of our operation back under control?' to '*Why* has our intervention brought the performance of our operation back under control?'

Look at the approach taken by the contact centre manager in the example 'Sue tracks the underlying causes'. She was working within an explicit hypothesis as to that was the main driver of her 'out of control' issue and she deliberately used the intervention-monitoring (cause–effect) relationship as an opportunity to learn more about how her operation behaved.

CASE STUDY   Sue tracks the underlying causes

Sue was puzzled. Like other contact centres she had managed, the 'average call length' was one of the key measures that her telephony system tracked automatically. It was important because it was regarded as an indicator of both efficiency and service. If calls were, on average, too short, it could mean that customer queries were not being addressed thoroughly. If too long, operator productivity suffered. It was a measure that fluctuated depending on the type of calls coming in to the centre, which was to be expected. What was unusual was that average call length had been showing a steady and sustained increase for the previous month. Sue's reaction to this had surprised some of her supervisors who managed the various teams in the centre. '*Traditionally, if we thought that operators were not responding appropriately, we would increase the frequency of monitoring by our supervisors, setting the system to provide them with a team summary report every hour rather than once a day, for example. But this does not tell us much about why call length is increasing.*'

Several reasons had been put forward for the increase. One was the recent elimination of the centre's bonus scheme where a (relatively small) productivity bonus, based on calls per operator hour, was paid each month. Another was the slow migration of the centre's call-handling system from the old 'legacy' system to a more sophisticated one. During the changeover period operators could choose which set of 'prompt screens' they could use. A third suggestion was that a recently launched 'customer care' initiative had disrupted the proper balance between efficiency and customer service. Sue had firm views on how to understand what the underlying causes of the problem were. '*The biggest mistake we could make now is to change all these things at the same time. Making too many interventions is as bad as not doing enough. We have to change one thing at a time and see what effect it has. More than that, we need to dig deeper to try to see why it is, or isn't, having an effect.*'

Sue and her team decided to slow down the migration from the old to the new 'prompt screens'. At the same time they monitored how operators switched between the two systems. The results were revealing. *'We found that the longest, less efficient, customer interactions were those where there was the most ambiguity over which system would give the operators the most help. When responding to a customer query forced them into one of these ambiguous areas, there was time lost switching between systems, and sometimes back again. Without sampling operator behaviour we might have suspected this was the problem, but never known for sure. Now we not only know what to do to bring back control, we know more about how our operation actually works.'*

2 Make control interventions in the right way

The type of interventions necessary to promote learning depends heavily on the nature of the circumstances surrounding the control issue. The best way to do this is to go back to the simple model of control in Figure 8.2 and think about what assumptions lie behind your control processes. So ask yourself the following questions that are implicit in the simple model (see Figure 8.5).

Figure 8.5 What assumptions are you making about your control process?

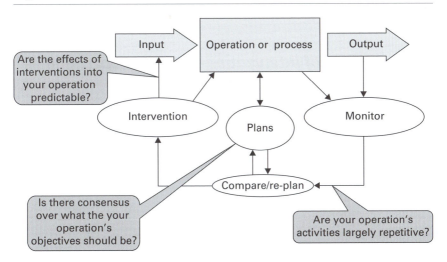

Is there consensus over what your operation's objectives should be?

Are your control objectives clear and unambiguous? Maybe so, in simple, straightforward operations, but it is not always possible (or necessarily desirable) to rigidly spell out every aspect of an operation's objectives in detail. Many operations are just too complex for that. All organizations are, to some extent, political entities where different, and often conflicting, objectives compete. Some joint venture operations, for example, are overtly political. Nor does every senior manager always agree on what the operation's objectives should be. Sometimes this is because of a high level of ambiguity. For example, listen to this operations manager in a facilities management business:

> We all agree on budgets for the moment and under current market conditions, but our market is entering a turbulent period. Customers are revising their spending plans and new competitors are entering the market. I know that my colleagues hold a range of views of how we should react. We will need time to debate our response before we can reach a consensus, if we ever can.

At other times the lack of clear objectives is because individual managers have different and conflicting interests. In social care organizations for example, some managers are charged with protecting vulnerable members of society, others with ensuring that public money is not wasted, and yet others may be required to protect the independence of professional staff. At other times objectives are ambiguous because the strategy has to cope with unpredictable changes in the environment making the original objectives redundant.

Are the effects of interventions into your operation predictable?

Another assumption in the simplified view of control is that you know (with a reasonable degree of confidence) what will happen when you make an intervention. Put another way, you can safely assume that any intervention that is intended to bring an operation back under control will indeed have that effect. This implies that the relationships between your intervention and the resulting consequence within the operation are predictable, which in turn assumes that your degree of process knowledge is high; but often this is not so.

For example, a parcel delivery service is getting complaints from its (delivery) customers that its morning notification (by text) of that day's delivery slot is coming too late for them to arrange an alternative date and time. Their solution is to send the notifications the previous evening rather than in the morning of the planned delivery. Will the extra time help customers enough to reduce complaint levels significantly? (The result was: not enough to justify bringing their scheduling window back by 12 hours.) Here the intervention did not have the assumed consequence: the operations managers who made the decision (in good faith) did not have a good enough knowledge of how the interface between their processes and their customers would behave. The cause–effect relationship was only partly understood. But don't blame them: only perfect knowledge guarantees absolute certainty about the effect of control interventions; and who has perfect knowledge?

This inability to predict the results of control interventions is made worse if the output from your operation is 'intangible' and therefore difficult to assess. For example, an oil and gas service company offers advice on the use of new exploration technology. Clients will judge the quality of this advice partly on the tangible outcomes that come from the use of the new technology, but also on the more subtle and intangible development of their relationship with the company. So at least part of the effect from any change the company makes to the way it delivers its advice will be difficult to judge, and certainly difficult to quantify.

Are your operation's activities largely repetitive?

One of the best ways to overcome any gaps in your understanding of what the consequences of control interventions would be is to keep on making interventions until the repeated cause–effect observations achieve a build-up of knowledge. So repetitive control (for example checking on a process, hourly or daily) means that the operation has the opportunity to learn how its interventions affect the process that considerably facilitates control. However, some control situations are non-repetitive, for example those involving unique (possibly customized) products or services. So because the intervention, or the deviation from plan that caused it, may not be repeated, there is little opportunity for learning. If your products or services are complex one-offs, if every output is different, you may have to accept some limits on your ability to learn from interventions.

How should you think about intervention?

The questions above have a big impact on how you need to think about intervention because the answers will guide how you should think about your control interventions. Of course you may think, 'Don't worry; the simple view of control is close enough to our conditions,' and it may well be. If your operations have fairly clear and agreed objectives, if you are reasonably happy that you can predict what will happen when you intervene in your operation, and if you manage a relatively repetitive operation, then, fine, stick to the straightforward view of control. That is what we will do for much of this chapter. But, and it is an important 'but', if parts of your operation do not conform to these assumptions, think about controlling them in a different way. Figure 8.6 illustrates how these questions can form a 'decision tree' type model that indicates how the nature of your operations control should be viewed, and how the nature of your interventions will vary.[2]

Control through negotiation – the most difficult circumstance for operations control is when objectives are ambiguous, contentious or both. For most for-profit operations this only occurs at a relatively strategic level. A series of long-term investment decisions, for example, will involve an element of risk that could be viewed very differently by individuals in the

Figure 8.6   What kind of intervention is right for your operation?

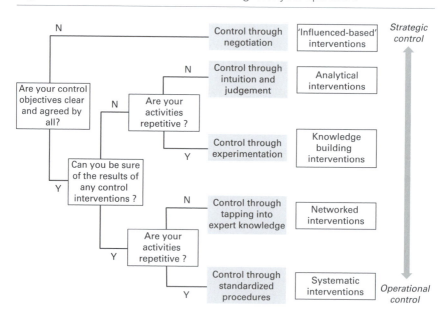

senior management team. Yet agreeing to how the investment should be planned and controlled needs an agreed position (even if some colleagues have reservations). A position needs to be negotiated that represents a compromise between conflicting views, so that, as the investment proceeds, interventions can try to keep the investment process to the agreed plan. You have to accept that interventions under these circumstances will always be 'influence-based'; in other words, they will be political in that they will always be an uneasy mixture of compromise, reconciliation and power.

Control through intuition and judgement – if your control objectives are relatively unambiguous (so you are clear what you are trying to do), but the consequences of the control interventions you may want to make are not known, you still have a problem. How do you decide how to intervene when you cannot be sure of the effect you will have? It is easier if the operation that you are controlling is reasonably repetitive: at least you can learn by trial and error until you can predict the results of your interventions. If not, then control becomes more of an art than a science. Again, it tends to be relatively strategic operations processes that fall into this category. For example, you may be setting up a strategic supply partnership where objectives are clear (joint long-term survival, an acceptable return, and so on). But the partnership is new; you are not totally familiar with their systems, or they with yours. At the operational level, people may not fully understand what has been agreed. It may even emerge that your supplier's interests are in conflict with yours. If things start deviating from the plan, you can make interventions, but because of the novelty of the situation, you cannot necessarily be sure of their effect.

It is in these circumstances that control interventions must be based on the management team using its experience and the intuition that comes from it. However, simply leaving control interventions to one's 'intuition' sounds neither safe nor particularly useful. Yet intuition, instinct and feelings are valuable attributes in any management team. They are the result, at least partly, of shared experience and an understanding of how best to organize knowledge, and decision-making skills. Intuition does not mean control interventions that are impulsive, whimsical or unreliable. Intuition is instinctive, maybe, but it can (and should) be based on a firm foundation of thorough analytical decision analysis. In these circumstances you cannot make control intervention decisions 'mechanistically', but they can be framed rationally so that connections can be made, consequences understood, and insights gained.

Control through experimentation – if your control objectives are relatively clear and/or unambiguous, but as in the previous example, the effects of any interventions you may make are not known then, if you are controlling a repetitive activity, your control task is easier. This is because you can build knowledge of how to make control interventions successfully through 'experimental' trial and error. Putting it another way, although you may not be clear about the best way to make control interventions in the early stages of control, you can learn how to do it through experience. For example, a 'quick service' restaurant franchise is opening new outlets into new markets. It may be unsure how best to manage the openings when it first enters the new market. It may even get its assumptions wrong and make a mess of the launch. But the launch is the first of several, so the control objective must be not only to make a success of each subsequent launch, but more importantly, it must learn from each intervention (launch). In fact, it is these knowledge-building skills that will ultimately determine the effectiveness of the control process when trial and error are involved.

Control through tapping into expert knowledge – if your control objectives are unambiguous, and the effects of interventions relatively well understood, but the activity is not repetitive, you have a different problem. You have not been faced with this situation before, and maybe you won't be again – but *someone* will have done it before. This is why you need to delegate control to an 'expert'; someone for whom such activities *are* repetitive because they have built their knowledge on previous experience elsewhere. For example, an operation was embarking on a programme of upgrading its ERP systems, both to enhance its internal planning processes and to progressively integrate them with its suppliers. The challenge for this operation was to upgrade its systems without disrupting its ongoing activities. To minimize the risk of things going wrong, it hired in a new CIO who had experience of managing similar situations. In effect the intervention in the control process is to explore the 'network' of available talent who can deploy their experience. For this 'expert' control to work, such experts must exist and can be 'acquired' by the firm. Even 'experts' must take account of the context in which they are applying their expertise, however, so it is also important that the 'expert' takes advantage of the control knowledge that is already present in the operation and integrates it with his or her 'expert' knowledge. In this type of control there is an emphasis on the need to 'network', both in terms of acquiring expertise and then integrating that expertise into the organization.

Control through standardized procedure – this situation looks easier. Objectives are unambiguous, the effects of interventions are known, and activities are repetitive. If your operation is like this you can control it using predetermined conventions and rules, safe in the knowledge that interventions will bring any deviations back to plan. Control is standardized and routine, and interventions are systematic. Well, at least that's the theory. There are still some challenges to successful routine control. The first is that it needs a reasonable degree of operational discipline to make sure that control procedures are systematically implemented. Without this discipline, control will be lost without your knowing about it. Worse, a spurious sense of security that systematic routine control can give could blind you to potentially damaging deviations from plan.

So along with systematic discipline, routine control should include periodic checks to make sure that its built-in assumptions are still applicable. Are objectives agreed, unambiguous and stable? What about your state of knowledge? Are you reasonably confident in your ability to predict accurately the consequences of your interventions? And repetition – are you sure that what you are monitoring really is the same thing as you were checking last time? Any divergence from the conditions necessary for routine control implies a different type of control.

3 Learn from your control interventions

Most of us learn little when we are simply told that if we do something, something else will happen, but if we actually experience the link between cause and effect, we learn in a far more fundamental way. It is the link between cause and effect that is the common element between operations control and operations learning. The interventions in the control process are the 'causes' that give rise to the 'effects' that the monitoring element of control reveals. The type of intervention that you need will depend on the nature of your control task, but control always means the interventions that hold such great learning potential. Underlying the whole concept of learning from control is a simple yet far-reaching idea – interventions, small or large, applied continuously or occasionally, can bring big benefits in terms of what can be learnt from them, and learning is a fundamental part of operations improvement. Look at the descriptions of Aggregate Industries and Werex Aerospace: two examples of learning through control.

CASE STUDY   Aggregate Industries and the London Olympics

'The London 2012 Olympics has given Aggregate Industries (AI) the opportunity to contribute to a world-class project on the global stage. But it was one of the most complex tenders, and it is one of the most challenging projects that we have ever been involved with. Some of the issues encountered have been without precedent, and demonstrate that the Olympic Delivery Authority (ODA, a public body) have used this project as an opportunity to "raise the bar" in the construction industry. Fortunately the project has been a success, and we have achieved competitive advantage through our diverse product portfolio and the wide range of logistical means available to meet customer needs.' (AI spokesperson)

The project to supply both ready-mix and aggregates was indeed complex. It also had two further aspects: first, it was substantially more 'political' than usual, involving a bewildering network of public and private organizations; second, the requirements placed an unusual degree of emphasis on the sustainability of the finished site and the construction process.

As with any large project of this type, things did not go entirely to plan. One partner contractor was forced to withdraw because of funding difficulties. The ODA became much keener on controlling costs, putting contractors under greater pressure to save money. The rail operator transporting materials began charging for late deliveries, causing confusion over invoicing which was not only time-consuming to correct, but also created the potential for a large number of invoice disputes. Eventually Aggregate Industries took responsibility for paying them directly to avoid invoice disputes. Most significantly, the planning authority initiated almost unheard-of testing specifications that were time-consuming, complex and expensive. All these deviations from plan meant that AI needed to intervene and re-plan – not always a straightforward task given that:

a There were not clear, unambiguous objectives with conflicts between public and private bodies.

b Not all individual elements of the project were well understood.

c Although some elements had been managed previously, the stakeholders here are unlikely to repeat a project of such complexity.

It approached the ODA with the unusual proposal that it should place a 'client liaison manager' within the overall coordination team. Her role was to understand the many complex relationships within the project's contractors and subcontractors. The idea proved to be particularly successful, partly because it proved an effective way of controlling large and complex projects, but also because it provided a pivot around which learning could be consolidated and shared.

CASE STUDY   Werex Aerospace

'We had been using statistical process control (SPC)[3] for years, and we thought we were pretty good at it. Our output quality was stable and well within our customers' specifications. What we didn't realize was that we were ignoring countless opportunities to be even better. The problem, although we didn't recognize it, was that process control had become a specialized function within engineering. It had become the exclusive province of experts. In fact it was only when our major customer (a large Californian aerospace firm) gave us a lower SPS (Supplier Performance Score) that we woke up. There was nothing wrong with our quality or delivery as such, they said, it was that we hadn't shown any significant quality improvement for years. Our initial reaction was indignation. "If quality is good, it's good. What's the problem?" By contrast, our customer had a "capability mentality". They said, "You might be capable of making these current products but we are thinking two or three product generations forward and asking ourselves, do we want to invest in this relationship for the future?"' (COO, Werex)

After some heart-searching, Werex concluded that they had to expand participation in their control processes if they were to exploit its potential. 'The first thing that we did was for each production team to start holding daily reviews of processing data and some "first pass" analysis of the data. This required us to invest in some SPC training, but we found that most operators were great at understanding the basic concepts, and eventually the maths behind it. Second, one day a month we brought both shifts together to look at and debate the processing data, and more significantly the implications of processing data. Some people got nervous because we were not producing anything. But for the first time you got operators from the two shifts, together with the production team, talking about operating issues. We also invited our customer's procurement engineers to attend these meetings. Remember these weren't staged meetings: it was the first *time these guys had met together and there was plenty of heated discussion, all of which our customer's representatives witnessed.'* (Engineer, Werex)

Almost immediately quality levels started to improve. More notably, the variation in quality levels started to reduce. *'When variation is low you can immediately see what effect your actions are having on the process, but also it has a positive effect on morale. People feel that things are "in control" and that it's them that exert that control.'* (Engineer, Werex)

Both of these examples illustrate how operations learning is driven by the cyclical relationship between operations control and operations knowledge; but the operations are very different. With AI contracting for the London Olympics, the type of control situation was what we earlier called 'negotiated control', with some elements of 'intuitive' and 'trial and error' control. Where AI gained an advantage was in how it maximized the learning that would come from this re-planning by placing (and funding – learning does not always come free) a 'client liaison manager' within another stakeholder's team. Werex Aerospace, by contrast, had a far more straightforward control situation, what we earlier called 'routine control'. Yet it still found that by changing how control was exercised it could both learn and improve relationships with its major customer.

Although there has not been a huge body of research exploring this link between how control is used and organizational learning, it has been demonstrated that both the design and use of control systems are significantly associated with higher levels of organizational learning.[4] However, even a well-designed control system is only a necessary but not sufficient condition for effective organizational learning. It is also important to formally manage the knowledge building that emerges from control-related learning. This is why we move on to look at how we can manage knowledge more effectively within our operations.

4 Use the learning to build your operations knowledge

Learning can evaporate. In itself learning is nothing unless it is converted into knowledge. It is where the value of learning is revealed and the acid test of whether yours is really a 'learning organization'. Central to developing operations capabilities is the concept of knowledge – process knowledge (how your individual processes operate) and operations knowledge (how the accumulation of all your processes interact together). The better our knowledge about the relationship between how we design and run processes and how they perform, the easier it is to improve them. So the key question to test the degree to which you are using control to expand your knowledge about how your operation really works is, 'What do we know now as the result of our control interventions that we didn't before?'

To help us answer this question it is useful to have a scale that can rate our operations knowledge.[5] This scale records the path of increasing operations knowledge from total ignorance of what is happening in the operation and its processes and why, through to absolutely complete knowledge where there is a perfect understanding of exactly how and why your operation is behaving as it does. Realistically, few if any operations could survive for long under conditions of total ignorance, nor will any operation ever reach the point of absolutely perfect knowledge. Between these two extremes lies the path of knowledge improvement along which all operations should be wanting to progress. Figure 8.7 illustrates this scale:

Stage 1. Total ignorance. You have no knowledge of what is really significant in your operation. Its performance appears to be totally random and unconnected with any activity or interaction that can be recognized. As far as you are concerned, pure chance seems to be the main driver of events. The good news is that the only way is up.

Figure 8.7   How control is driven by your level of operations knowledge

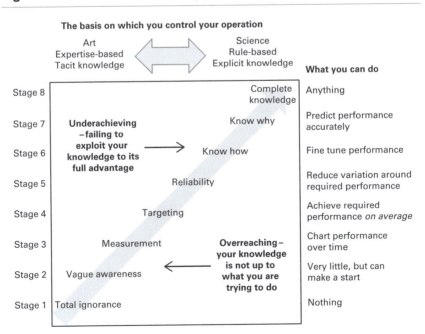

Stage 2. Vague awareness. You have an awareness that certain things may be important to your performance, but there is no formal measurement or significant understanding of how they affect performance. Managing your operation is far more of an art than a science, and controlling it relies on experience and tacit knowledge (that is, unarticulated knowledge within the individuals managing the system).

Stage 3. Measurement. You know most of the significant things that seem to affect the performance and you can even measure some of them, but you know little about how to fully control them. For the most important events that could affect your performance, you may have developed contingency plans, for example arranging emergency computing capacity in the case of system failure.

Stage 4. Targeting. You have some idea of how to affect the significant variables that impact on your performance, even if your control is not precise. This means that you can control the average level of your operation's performance even if you cannot control the variation around that average. Once your knowledge has reached this level, you can start to experiment to explore the subtleties of what affects performance.

Stage 5. Reliability. You have the knowledge to control both average performance and how it varies around the average. This allows you to formally record how your operation should be managed and controlled. It also allows you to focus on the variation in your performance and extend your knowledge level by exploring what activities reduce variability. You can standardize your responses for different operating conditions. You do not have to 'reinvent the wheel' whenever you face the same or similar issues.

Stage 6. Know how. You have a more or less complete understanding of how any intervention you make will affect your performance. You can predict exactly the consequences of any action you take. This allows you to begin to fine-tune and optimize your operation. In fact, your degree of control is such that you can run deliberate experiments that improve your understanding of what 'makes your operation tick'.

Stage 7. Know why. Your level of knowledge about your operations is now at the 'scientific' level. You have a full model of your operations that predicts behaviour over a wide range of conditions. You have a detailed understanding of the underlying causes of why your operation behaves in the way it does. If your knowledge is at this level you can control your operation 'algorithmically', with most decisions being made automatically.

Stage 8. Complete knowledge. It would be nice to have. Sadly, in practice, neither you nor anyone else will get to this stage. It would mean that the effects of every conceivable variable and condition are known and understood, even when those variables and conditions have not even been considered before.

Control should match your state of knowledge

Figure 8.7 also indicates what any operation will be able to achieve and, more important, how the basis on which you should control your operation shifts as knowledge increases. At low levels of operations knowledge, control is more an art than a science. It relies on intuition and whatever expertise and tacit knowledge your operations managers have. As your level of knowledge grows, control becomes more systematic, 'scientific' and explicit, finishing up where, under conditions of complete knowledge, the whole operation could be (theoretically) automated. This gives rise to a further question: 'What if my approach to controlling my operation does not match my state of operations knowledge?' Well, it depends on how you are mismatched.

Overreaching: if you are trying to employ sophisticated 'scientific' control when you level of operations knowledge is not sufficiently developed, you are unlikely to achieve good control or learn much from it. You need to accept your (hopefully temporary) limitations and retreat to a more intuitive, 'expertise-based' form of control.

Underachieving: if you are relying on the expertise of your operations managers to control your operations even though you have a relatively high level of operations knowledge, you are wasting an opportunity to be more efficient. Explore how you could codify your operations knowledge in such a way that you can automate at least some elements of control. If your level of knowledge is really as well developed as you think, automating control will be more efficient and probably more effective.

Growing levels of knowledge – knowledge management (KM)

Growing your level of operations knowledge can happen naturally. Your operations managers would need to be wilfully unenlightened not to pick up some clues about why your operations behave as they do. However, relying only on some kind of instinctual learning is slow, unreliable and inefficient. Better to put some effort into the deliberate management of your operations knowledge; hence the increasing interest in formal knowledge management (KM) systems. Although the idea has been in circulation since the early 1990s[6] (it is defined as 'the process of capturing, distributing, and effectively using knowledge)[7] it has remained popular. Not surprising: it is a particularly useful way of bringing together the way knowledge is recognized, recorded, evaluated, retrieved and shared.

KM has two distinct but connected components. First, it *collects* knowledge together by recording knowledge gathered, sometimes directly from a specific experience, sometimes from individual staff's more general tacit knowledge. This allows anyone with access to the knowledge base to search for, use (and reuse) the knowledge whenever, and from wherever it is required. Second, it *connects* individual staff (who have knowledge of their own) with the formal organized knowledge that has been collected, and with each other. Connecting individuals together is particularly important because it is not always possible to completely codify individual experience into organized knowledge. People need to interact in order to gain colleagues' insights that may not always be obvious when they are formalized.

If you bring together these two components of knowledge management you have the potential to prevent the underutilization of an operation's fund of knowledge. More than this, you also have the further benefit of encouraging the type of collaboration that can generate even more insights (see Figure 8.8). The idea is that individual staff with appropriate experience will share their understanding of a problem and through this discussion identify additional insights not typically stored in any explicit form.

Figure 8.8 KM systems collect knowledge and connect individuals and knowledge in order to encourage collaboration

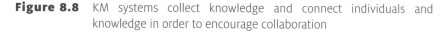

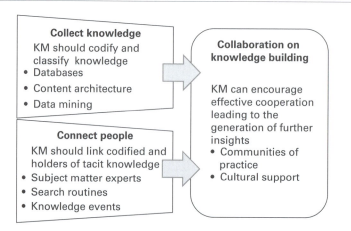

KM is not just for big firms

Almost all the published advice on knowledge management is aimed at relatively large firms. There are obvious advantages for firms with a large and geographically dispersed staff with diverse skills and they will find it relatively easy to invest in the IT systems that are designed to facilitate KM. But don't dismiss KM as an approach exclusively for the big boys. The underlying principles, and increasingly the technology that supports KM, can benefit smaller operations. Certainly whether you are big or small, you should want to preserve and develop your operations knowledge, and the basic ideas of recording and sharing knowledge are surely universal. More than that, since the advent of user-generated and social media-type web applications, the collaborative aspect of knowledge management has become increasingly accessible. Tools such as wikis, blogs and social intranet networking allow individuals or teams to facilitate collaboration, not only between internal employees, but also with external partners and customers.

Communities of practice

If you are trying KM without developing communities of practice (CoPs) you are missing a particularly important trick. Communities of practice are what make the collaboration part of KM work. A community of practice is a group of people with a common purpose who can gain useful knowledge by interacting. It is an obviously good idea, especially for operations that rely directly on a high level of expertise to compete, but some firms can underestimate the degree of effort and commitment required. Even with the use of the web-based technologies available to electronically linked communities, maintaining the effectiveness of CoPs is not cost-free. First, there are at least three key roles to be filled:[8]

1 Someone to manage and administer the flow and classification of information.

2 A moderator who can mediate between potentially conflicting information.

3 A thought leader who can interpret the rich variety of information and experiences, draw insights and understand the implications.

You need not necessarily have three separate people in these roles, but in some cases they may need to be. Second, there must be some recognition that the context is important when evaluating the experiences and knowledge reported in the KM system. What may be appropriate in one part of the firm may not work in another with different circumstances. Third, one must not be naïve about the idea of 'community'. CoP enthusiasts may assume that, if provided with sufficient time and resources, members will be happy to cooperate and in effect surrender their knowledge for the benefit of the community and the organization. Yet, in any organization there is always some degree of tension between individual and group interests. You cannot ignore issues such as resistance to change, status, conflict, struggle and power.

What you should expect from a functioning community of practice

Like any other recipient of investment, communities of practice should be reviewed to check that they are giving value. Here are some questions to ask about yours.[9] Does your CoP:

- Help to drive strategy by facilitating the smooth implementation of strategic decisions?

- Start new lines of business by exploring the application of knowledge to potential new products and services?

- Help to solve problems quickly because they link appropriate solutions with problem 'owners'?

- Transfer best practice by focusing on 'what really works' in practice?

- Develop professional skills because knowledge workers often prefer to learn from like-minded, and like-experienced, colleagues?

- Help to recruit and retain staff because CoPs help to identify professionally satisfying opportunities to practise their expertise?

CASE STUDY The Eureka Knowledge Management system at Schlumberger[10]

One of the most successful (and well known) KM systems is the Eureka system at Schlumberger, a global company whose experienced professionals '*supply the latest technology to optimize reservoir performance for customers working in the oil and gas industry*'. The founding Schlumberger brothers sowed the seeds of a knowledge culture back in the 1930s when they instituted a technical bulletin. '*That mind-set has flourished. Knowledge is respected as an important asset at Schlumberger. We've had technological solutions internally to capture knowledge since before the term "knowledge management" entered the popular business lexicon. But, while such systems are essential, the key is in how we make use of these tools. It's the sustained interaction between our people that makes the difference.'* (Susan Rosenbaum, Director of Knowledge Management) The objective of its KM system, say Schlumberger, is to *'apply everywhere what you learn anywhere'.*

Schlumberger's proprietary InTouch system is central for knowledge capture and sharing. Its database is typically the first recourse for field engineers experiencing a persistent technical problem. *'You have field and InTouch engineers interacting through the InTouch system. But you also have field engineers helping other field engineers on the bulletin boards. Field engineers can flag content on the InTouch database that they feel is outdated, to ensure it gets checked,'* says Rosenbaum. *'We're using the power of the people to keep our information up to date.'* Since it was started, the system has improved response time for resolving technical queries by 95 per cent, and by 75 per cent for deploying engineering modifications globally. *'We have a giant web of people helping people at Schlumberger,'* says Rosenbaum. *'It's become an entrenched part of the company culture.'*

Some see the success of Schlumberger's KM efforts as being founded on three principles:

1 Freedom – staff are free to join any community they want to without registration and independent of experience, education or title.

2 Leadership – each community is managed and run by a leader (or two for a large community) who is democratically elected for one year by the community's members.

3 Flexibility – communities are not fixed: they change over time with new ones emerging and others disappearing.

Practical prescriptions

- Do not neglect the opportunity to build capability through your control activities. Good control gives you more than control: it gives you the opportunity to learn more about your operations.

- Identify and check the effectiveness of the essential elements of your control system. What and how are you monitoring your activities? How are you feeding your plans into the control system? How do you compare and detect deviations from plan? How are you making interventions to bring the operation back within range of the plan?

- Critically ask yourself, 'Am I monitoring the right things in the right way?' Monitor inputs to your operations as well as outputs. Monitor the things that indicate underlying as well as obvious issues. Set your monitoring data in the context of a working hypothesis of how your operation is working.

- Critically ask yourself, 'Am I making control interventions in the right way?' Do not assume that all operations require the same type of control.

- Use the flowchart in Figure 8.6 to determine the type of control and therefore the type of interventions that apply to your situation.

- Critically ask yourself, 'Am I learning from my control interventions?'

- Look at the organizational mechanism that you have in place to examine the cause–effect relationship between how you intervene and what new knowledge is generated.

- Critically ask yourself, 'Am I using the learning to build my operations knowledge?' Examine the level of operations knowledge that you possess by using the eight-stage scale used in Figure 8.7.

- Again, using Figure 8.7, check that the basis on which you control your operation is appropriate for your level of operations knowledge.

- Use some kind of knowledge management system. It need not necessarily be based on highly sophisticated technology, but it should allow you to recognize, record, evaluate, retrieve and share knowledge.

Notes

1   Definition from the *Cambridge Dictionary*, dictionary.cambridge.org

2   Based on an original model described in Hofstede, G (1981) Management control of public and not-for-profit activities accounting, *Organizations and Society*, 6 (3), pp 193–211

3   Statistical process control (SPC) is a methodology for measuring and controlling quality during operations processes. Performance data in the form of product/service or process measurements is obtained in real time and then plotted on a graph with predetermined control limits. 'Control limits' are determined by the capability of the process, whereas 'specification limits' are determined by customers' needs

4 Reported in: Wee, S H, Foong, S Y and Tse, M S C (2014) Management control systems and organizational learning: the effects of design and use, *Accounting Research Journal*, **27** (2), pp 169–78

5 The scale used here is based on one by Bohn, R E (1994) Measuring and managing technical knowledge, *Sloan Management Review*, Fall

6 Koenig, M E D (2012) What is KM? Knowledge management explained, *Knowledge Management World*, 4 May, http://www.kmworld.com/

7 Davenport, T H (1994) Saving IT's soul: human centered information management. *Harvard Business Review*, March-April, **72** (2) pp 119–31; Duhon, B (1998) It's all in our heads, *Inform*, September, **12** (8)

8 Durham, M (2004) Three critical roles for knowledge management workspaces, in (eds) M E D Koenig and T K Srikantaiah, *Knowledge Management. Lessons learned: What works and what doesn't*, pp 23–36), Medford, NJ, Information Today, for The American Society for Information Science and Technology

9 Wenger, E C and Snyder, W M (2000) Communities of practice: the organizational frontier, *Harvard Business Review*, Jan-Feb

10 Sources include: Deltour, F, Ple, L and Sargis-Roussel, C (2013) Eureka! Developing online communities of practice to facilitate knowledge sharing at Schlumberger, CASE – Reference no. 313-122-1, The Case Centre; Schlumberger Press Release (2010) Schlumberger Cited for Knowledge Management, Schlumberger Press Office, 3 December

Setting improvement priorities

09

There is a difference between measuring your performance and deciding what you are going to do about it. In Chapter 4 we set the framework for measuring your performance. This chapter shows you how you can interpret performance measures as the first step in boosting your operations advantage. In particular, it shows you how operations improvement priorities can be derived from performance measures. Guiding *how* improvement takes place is one of the most important functions of performance measurement. It is prioritization that is the (sometimes missing) link between measuring performance and improvement. It is about how you devise a set of objectives that are capable of steering the way that operations are designed and run. Reversing the logic: if performance measurement is not helping to prioritize improvement, then either the wrong things are being measured or the measures are not being interpreted intelligently. Prioritization is a way of keeping performance measurement honest.

Importance and performance – moving towards improvement priorities

There are two schools of thought about how to treat performance measures so as to get some idea of what should be prioritized for improvement: 1) customer-focused prioritization that is centred on the needs and preferences of customers, and 2) competitor-focused prioritization that is based on the performance and activities of competitors.

Customer-focused prioritization has a particular attraction for most managers. Who would object to 'placing the customer at the centre of our thinking'? Of course, one fundamental purpose of your operations is to create products and services that meet the needs of your customers. It is reasonable to assume therefore that what customers find important, the operation should also find important. If your customers prefer low prices to

Figure 9.1 This chapter looks at how to set your improvement priorities

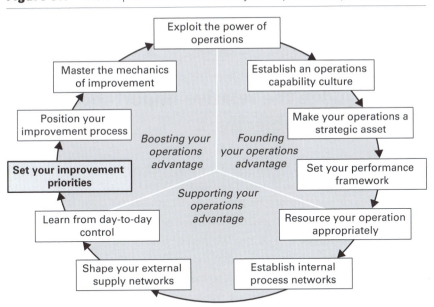

wide range, then your operation should devote more energy to reducing its costs than to increasing the flexibility that enables it to provide a range of products or services. In that sense the needs and preferences of your customers shape the relative *importance* of your operation's objectives.

Competitor-focused prioritization is different. This school of thought holds that what really matters in most reasonably free markets is your performance against competitors. From a competitive viewpoint, when your operation improves its performance, the improvement that matters most is that bit of improvement that takes it past the performance levels achieved by your competitors. It is, after all, how most of us think about our performance. Are we better than the other guys? So, the role of competitors in prioritization is in determining how we judge our achieved *performance*.

However, both what we see as important (for customers) and how we think about our performance (against competitors) form just half the story. Both importance and performance have to be brought together before any priorities for improvement can be made. Just because something is particularly important to your customers does not necessarily mean that you should immediately prioritize it. It may be that your operation is already considerably better at it than your competitors. Equally, just because your operation is not very good at something when compared with its competitors, again it does not necessarily mean that you should be immediately prioritizing it.

Customers may not particularly value this aspect of performance. Both importance *and* performance need to be viewed together to judge the prioritization of objectives, with priority given to those things that are important, but where your performance is inadequate.

How to judge the relative importance of operations objectives

Businesses that compete in different ways should want different things from their operations. If your business competes primarily on low prices and 'value for money', it should be placing its emphasis on cost, productivity and efficiency. If it competes on a high degree of customization, it should be emphasizing flexibility, and so on. We called this the outside-in element of operations strategy in Chapter 3. What matters is that there is a clear, logical and widely understood link between your market positioning and the objectives that all your operations people are working towards.

What complicates things for many of us is that the relative importance of objectives differs between different products and services created within the same operation. If your operation produces offerings for several customer groups, it will need to clarify the separate sets of competitive objectives, and therefore different priorities, for each group. For example, Figure 9.2 shows different services offered by a recycling company. Each scale on this 'polar representation' of its services represents a different objective. The closer the line of the company's services to the common origin, the less important is the objective for that service. In this case the three services illustrated show significant differences in how they compete. This will pose a dilemma for the business: should it try to use the same resources and processes for all three services or would it be better off organizing them as three parallel operations, each focusing on what its market requires? (In this case, the latter.) This 'polar analysis' does not solve that particular problem, but it does expose the differences and similarities between the performance required by a business's various products and services.

Distinguish your 'order-winners' from your 'qualifiers'

A particularly useful way of determining the relative importance, or at least the different nature, of performance factors is to distinguish between what are sometimes called 'order-winning' or 'enhancing' factors and 'qualifying' or 'hygiene' factors.

Figure 9.2 The relative importance of three services offered by a recycling business

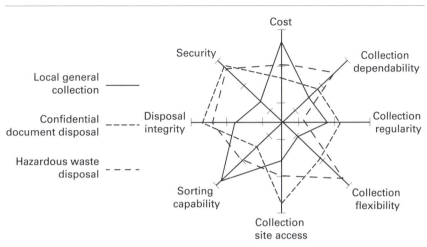

Order-winning or enhancing factors (often just called 'order-winners') are things that directly and significantly contribute to winning business. Your customers will see them as key reasons for buying your product or service. They are the most important aspects of the way a company defines its competitive position. Raising the performance of your order-winners will give your business competitive benefit, because you will attract more business or you will improve the chances of gaining more business, or gain higher margins. Reducing the performance of your order-winners will diminish your competitive benefit.

Qualifying, or hygiene factors (often called just 'qualifiers') are different. They may not be the major competitive determinants of success, but are important in another way. They are those aspects of competitiveness where your operation's performance has to be above a particular level to be seriously considered by your customers. Below this 'qualifying' level of performance many customers may not even consider buying your product or service. Above this 'qualifying' level, a purchase will be considered, but mainly in terms of the product or service's performance in its order-winners. If you improve the performance of your qualifying factors above the qualifying level it is unlikely that you will gain much, if any, competitive benefit.

The benefits of order-winners and qualifiers

Figure 9.3 shows graphical representations of order-winners and qualifiers. It is an indication of the benefits your operation gains by being good at different aspects of performance. As the performance of order-winners gets better, competitive benefit also improves. Qualifiers show a different relationship between performance and competitive benefit. Improving performance below that which competitors achieve will only start to give increased competitive benefit as performance gets near the 'qualifying level', after which it increases quickly, but probably will never much exceed 'competitive neutrality'. In other words, poor performance at a qualifier can damage competitiveness, but good performance cannot usually gain much that is positive apart from the absence of the negative. Your customers will expect these things, and are not going to applaud too loudly when they receive them. They are the givens. (In the days when landlines dominated, some used to call them 'dial tone factors' – you only notice them when they aren't there.)

Both order-winners and qualifiers can have different strengths. In Figure 9.3 the slope of the order-winner line indicates how sensitive competitive benefit is to an operation's achieved performance in the factor. With qualifiers, it is how discriminating they are. Some strong qualifiers discriminate very clearly between performance that matches that of competitors and performance that doesn't. With weaker qualifiers there is less discrimination. A word of caution here – the curves in figure 9.3 are conceptual. They are there to illustrate an idea rather than to be drawn with any degree of precision.

The example, 'Safety must always be our priority' shows how 'importance' and 'priority' are different things. In this case (if the COO is correct), both specification and conformance quality (which determine the safety of the products) are strong qualifiers. This does not mean that product safety

Figure 9.3   The competitive benefit gained from order-winners, qualifiers and delights

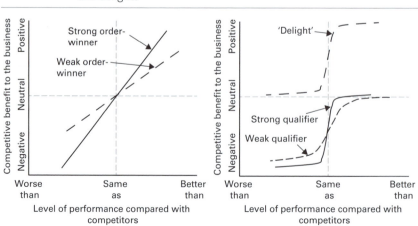

CASE STUDY 'Safety must always be our priority'

An aircraft parts manufacturer was debating how it could improve the performance of its various plants. *'Safety must always be our priority,'* said the COO. *'We must always remember our responsibility to the airlines' passengers, who after all are our end customers. We must be continually vigilant that we keep rigidly to the agreed certified product specifications. But we can't forget that we are in competition with other manufacturers. Aircraft manufacturers quite rightly insist on impeccable quality and product specification, but they also negotiate hard on price. The industry is getting far more price-competitive. Our recent sales success has been as a result of being able to offer good competitive prices. But our competitors are continuing to reduce their cost base, so in the future it will be not just keeping costs down, but also actually reducing our cost base that will be the only thing guaranteeing our survival.*

'We also will need to keep agile. The market is going through a period of uncertainty. This may mean we need to get more responsive to our customers' need to keep flexible. But safety must always be our priority.'

---

should get a lower priority than other factors. Any reduction in safety performance below an acceptable level would probably drive the company out of business, irrespective of other factors. What it does mean is that, if the operation's quality performance remains above the level required, competitiveness will depend more on the other factors. At the moment cost performance is an order-winner, and probably a strong one, but there is a hint that, if price competitiveness remains fierce, and if competitors continue to reduce their costs, competition might move to other factors such as delivery performance. In other words, factors can move between categories over time, depending on the dynamics of the market.

Include 'delights' when analysing your possible future performance

The idea of order-winners and qualifiers has been around for some years and is quite well accepted. Now some analysts add a third category, generally known as 'delights'. (Sorry, about the name, but there it is.) 'Delights' are aspects of performance that customers have not yet been made aware of, or that are so novel that no one else is aware of them, and yet they genuinely add value for the customer. Because a customer is unaware of it, the strong implication of a 'delight' is that no competitor has yet offered it to them. The competitive benefit of 'delights' is also shown on Figure 9.3.

Not having a delight (that is, very low achieved performance) will not upset customers because they didn't expect it anyway. However, as the operation starts to deliver its 'delights', the potential for customer satisfaction and therefore positive competitive benefit, kicks in. Be careful, though, about misusing this idea. Simply doing basic things right is not the same as a delight. A delight is both novel (and therefore unexpected) and genuinely adds value for customers. The idea is that the combination of added value and its unexpected nature will reinforce each other to make delights particularly attractive. Yet because they are unexpected, the competitive benefit will not become negative for the simple reason that customers are not aware of the delights.

By definition, because delights rely on their novelty, when offered in the market they will no longer be novel. Delights apply only at one point in time. It's a fair assumption that competitors will attempt to imitate them. What was once a delight, if copied successfully, will become an order-winner. In time, it may even become a qualifier, where all companies that wish to compete are expected to provide it. So, what were once delights will over time erode as competitors achieve high levels of performance in the same competitive factors.

CASE STUDY   Hotel Formule 1 makes cost a delight

'Delights' do not have to be based totally on novel products or services; they can be based on shifting some aspect of performance way beyond customers' expectations. Take the case of French hotel brand Hotel Formule 1. Back in the 1980s French hotels ranged from the most luxurious and stylish (and expensive), to cheap, often family run (and frankly, of variable quality) small establishments serving business travellers and tourists. Modern, more predictably comfortable, hotels tended to be more expensive.

Then came the super low-budget, no-frills hotel chains, most notably Formule 1 (sometimes branded as ibis Styles or ibis Budget), part of Accor Hotels. They offered conveniently located, adequately furnished, predictable accommodation, at an amazingly low price. That was the 'delight': a price that significantly undercut most of the competition. How did Accor's hotel operations manage to do it? They adopted two principles not always associated with hotel operations – standardization and an innovative use of technology. The hotels are made from state-of-the-art volumetric prefabricated units arranged in various configurations to suit the characteristics of each individual site. Each nine-square-metre room is functional, comfortable, soundproof and, most important, easy to clean and maintain. Receptions are staffed for only a specified period morning and evening. Outside these times an automatic machine sells rooms to credit card users, provides access to the hotel, dispenses a security code for the room and even prints a receipt. Showers and toilets are automatically cleaned after each use with nozzles and heating elements to spray the room. To keep things even simpler, the hotels rarely include a restaurant, as they are usually located near existing ones.

Your 'delights' won't last forever

It is this idea that your delights and order-winners will 'erode' over time that should provoke a vigorous debate for any business. The key question is, 'How sustainable are the order winners and delights on which the business depends?' Figure 9.4 illustrates a matrix that encourages this kind of analysis, in this case for a medical supply business. For many of us, there tends to be a general drift downwards (as shown by the arrows in the figure) as competitors catch up with or exceed our level of performance. For the business shown in Figure 9.4, the remote inventory management service (a delight at the time) is forecast to be copied by competitors and will erode to an order-winner. Similarly, two current order-winners (its superior range

Figure 9.4   Erosion of delights and order-winners for a medical supplies business

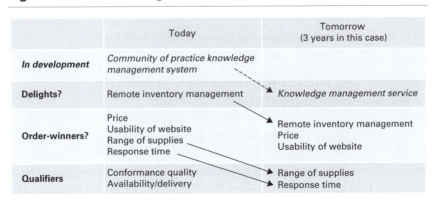

and response times) are being matched by competitors and are likely to become simply expected by customers, in other words, qualifiers. Usually the cell in the matrix that is the most problematic is that marked as 'tomorrow's delights'. This prompts the intriguing question: 'What should our operation be doing today in order to develop the capabilities that will allow us to delight our customers tomorrow?' Here, the company proposes to use its knowledge of how its supplies are used by its customers to develop a knowledge management service, which it hopes will delight its customers in the future.

How to judge your relative performance

All performance is relative. What performance is considered good against one criterion may look poor against another. For example, if you average 95 per cent on time, in full (OTIF) delivery over one month, exactly how good is that? In fact the single figure, 95 per cent, does not mean much by itself, unless you compare against something. Yet comparing it against different standards will give you differing interpretations. It could be that on a historical basis, your performance looks good. If your previous performance has been averaging 92 per cent, then 95 per cent looks good, but there again, your business may have set you an improvement goal of achieving, say, 98 per cent, which makes your last month's performance look like an underachievement.

Your business is also likely to be concerned with how you perform against competitors. If your competitors are currently averaging delivery performances of around 94 per cent, your performance now looks acceptable. However, some within your business may argue that the only 'true' performance standard should be the absolute perfection represented by 100 per cent OTIF delivery. Your actual 95 per cent now looks disappointing against this standard. Your performance here hasn't changed, it is still 95 per cent, but different standards of comparison mean different judgements.

Comparison with competitors' performance is particularly powerful

This is why standards of comparison are important. They can drastically affect how performance measures are interpreted. Different standards have different strengths. Historical standards can be motivational, always assuming that things are improving. Even a small improvement shows that things are going in the right direction. Standards based on a management-set improvement goal or target can take into account what is happening in the wider market. Competitive circumstances can change, and what is good performance in one context may not be in another. Standards based on competitors' performance are particularly powerful in assessing the strategic position of an operation (which is why we use this standard extensively later in this chapter). As the ultimate calibration, using the standard of absolute perfection, 100 per cent, absolutely no errors, is admittedly impossible to achieve, but that is not the point. Absolute standards are there to indicate just how much further improvement there is to go.

Benchmarking

You may want to consider formalizing the process of comparison with other businesses in the form of a benchmarking programme. Benchmarking is usually defined as the regular and systematic measuring of an operation's performance or processes against those of recognized best practitioners. It can be focused on one or both of two questions: what is the performance of other operations compared with yours, and how do they achieve this performance? Those 'other operations' against which comparison is to be made can be direct competitors, or non-competitors that nonetheless have similar processes. So, in this sense there are four types of benchmarking, as described in Table 9.1.

Table 9.1 Benchmarking can target performance and/or methods against competitors or non-competitors

	Performance **How good are you?**	**Methods** **How do they do it?**
Competitors	Can you really not be interested in how you compare with competitors? *Usefulness* – high *Difficulty* – medium	Can be difficult to get 'under the skin' of how competitors organize their processes. *Usefulness* – very high *Difficulty* – high
Good non-competitors	Is their performance relevant? They probably operate under different conditions, with different objectives. *Usefulness* – medium/low *Difficulty* – medium	Can be useful to get an insight into how processes could be organized and access may be easier. *Usefulness* – high *Difficulty* – medium

You will find that there is a big difference between benchmarking others' performance and benchmarking others' methods. Both pose different challenges and both serve different ends. It's difficult to imagine any business not wanting to know the answer to the first question (how does your performance compare with competitors). It is the foundation of operations improvement. The only issue is, 'Do we compete in the same way as competitors, so does it matter if our performance is better or worse than theirs?' The second question is different: 'How do they do it?' The answer to that question can be far more elusive. One can find out what technologies, or what suppliers, competitors use – but how do they organize themselves internally? That's more difficult; and how do they deploy knowledge and capabilities internally? Well that's even more difficult. This is why comparing one's operations against good non-competitors who use the same or similar processes can be so effective. Also, generally, they are more relaxed about sharing their methods.

CASE STUDY   Triumph motorcycles roar back[1]

Benchmarking can provide the stimulus that saves a well-known brand from extinction. Triumph motorcycles once built the coolest bikes in the world, but like the UK auto industry, it went into decline from the 1960s as better-designed and better-produced Japanese products captured the market. By the 1980s it had gone into receivership.

When John Bloor bought the rights to the Triumph name he did not immediately restart production. Instead he spent years rethinking how the operation should be designed and run to compete in the modern motorcycle market. With a new team of managers, he went on an in-depth study tour of Japan to analyse the production methods of the competitors that had driven the original Triumph to bankruptcy. *'We learnt a lot,'* says Nick Bloor, John's son, who now runs the company. It soon became clear to the management team that the original old factory in the West Midlands of the UK was not up to the task of producing world-class products. It was demolished and a new plant built in the UK that utilized the modern equipment and production methods learnt on the Japanese visits. Now the company's plants in the UK and Thailand produce record numbers of bikes with styling that reflects the original bike's heritage, but with standards of engineering and reliability that match the operations that it learnt from.

The whole idea of benchmarking is to provide the foundation for prioritization and improvement. It can be remarkably effective at shocking operations into accepting the need for change. There is a famous example from the early days of benchmarking when General Motors found out that in one Toyota assembly plant, operators could change-over its stamping presses between models in eight minutes, compared with GM's performance for the same task of eight hours.

Remember that benchmarking does not provide 'solutions' to be copied slavishly. Rather, it provides the stimulation, ideas and information that can lead to solutions. Benchmarking should not involve simply copying or imitating other operations. Best to think of it as a process of learning and adapting ideas in a pragmatic manner. Operations that rely on benchmarking to search for and adopt 'industry best practice' (a euphemism for copying), are always limiting themselves to currently accepted methods of operating or currently accepted limits to performance. That will lead a business only as far as others have gone. 'Best practice' is not 'best' in the sense that it cannot be bettered; it is only 'best' in the sense that it is the best one can currently find. Indeed accepting what is currently defined as 'best' may prevent operations from ever making the radical breakthrough or improvement that takes the concept of 'best' to a new and fundamentally improved level.

Internal benchmarking

Following on from the last point, not only is it an error to think that best external practice cannot be bettered. Good (perhaps even 'best') practice may already exist within your own organization. It is easy to imagine that benchmarking is all about looking externally, but it isn't. Especially in large firms, there may be good practice to be found somewhere within the organization that is not widely known about, yet has important lessons. This is what 'internal benchmarking' tries to address. It simply means the comparison of performance and/or methods within your organization. It can be the best place to start benchmarking. There is evidence that many businesses fail to exploit their own internal best practices, which often remain hidden from the rest of the organization simply because there are inadequate mechanisms for finding and spreading potential best practices.

It is obviously easier and cheaper to search internally than looking outside to other companies or other industries. So in terms of your return on the time and effort spent on benchmarking, internal benchmarking looks attractive. Ideas found through internal benchmarking may also be easier for employees to accept if the knowledge came from within. This is the clue to what internal benchmarking really is: it is the practice of knowledge sharing, analysis and dissemination throughout the business. In other words, it is about knowledge management which, as we discussed in Chapter 8, is a hugely important issue for achieving an operations advantage.

Is benchmarking worth doing?

Is benchmarking always worth it? Certainly you will want to know how your performance and methods compare with competitors, or even other parts of your business. There can be improvements in both the culture and working practices of any operation that takes such comparisons seriously. Does that really mean, though, that you want to make a huge production number out of the benchmarking process? Reading some of the advice from benchmarking specialists one would think that a business's whole strategy-making process should be based on benchmarking. It shouldn't. There is a real danger that benchmarking becomes an end in itself: an internal industry with its own super-complex procedures and specialist staff. Taking it that far is rarely worth it. Rather, think about benchmarking as a state of mind. It is an endorsement of the idea that operations managers should always be looking, outside and inside, both for ideas and for performance comparisons.

How to bring importance and performance together

Earlier, we argued that you need to bring relative importance and relative performance together in order to prioritize operations objectives. This is a process that is made far more effective if they can be quantified, not necessarily using an objective and precise scale, but at least with a scale that allows some kind of discrimination.

Using the distinction between order-winning and qualifying factors can be useful in quantifying their degrees of importance. To these two categories we can add 'less important' factors which, as their name implies, are those that are relatively unimportant compared with the others. These categories form a crude importance scale:

- very important (order-winners/enhancing factors);
- medium importance (qualifiers/hygiene factors) provided they perform better than a 'qualifying level';
- not very important (erm, less important).

Yet, to make use of this idea, you will usually need a slightly more discriminating scale. One way to do this is to take the three broad categories and divide each category into three further points representing strong, medium and weak positions. This results in a 9-point scale, where 1 is a very important order-winner and 9 something that matters very little to customers. Figure 9.5 (a) illustrates such a scale.

A similar approach can be taken to a scale that describes relative performance. Figure 9.5 (b) shows one based on judging whether achieved performance is:

- better than that of its competitors;

- the same as that of its competitors; or

- worse than that of its competitors.

In much the same way, we can derive a more discriminating 9-point performance scale.

Using the importance–performance matrix

These ratings of importance and performance can be shown on an importance–performance matrix which, as its name implies, positions each competitive factor according to its ratings on these criteria. Figure 9.6 shows an importance–performance matrix divided into zones of improvement priority. The first zone boundary is the 'lower bound of acceptability'. When a competitive factor is rated as relatively unimportant, this boundary will be low. Most businesses are prepared to tolerate performance levels that are 'in the same ball-park' as their competitors for relatively unimportant competitive factors. They only become concerned when performance levels are very clearly below those of their competitors. By contrast, with highly-rated competitive factors most businesses will be decidedly less tolerant of poor or middling levels of performance. For these, minimum levels of acceptability will be at the lower end of the 'better than competitors' class.

Below this lower bound of acceptability there is clearly a need for improvement. Above this line there is no immediate urgency for any improvement. However, not all competitive factors falling below the minimum line will be seen as having the same degree of improvement priority. The lower-right part of the matrix represents competitive factors that are both important to customers and where performance is poor compared with competitors. It is an area that represents those factors in need of urgent improvement. Remember the characteristic of qualifiers, though: a qualifier

Figure 9.5 Scales for judging, a) the relative importance, and b) performance of objectives

(a)			(b)			
Type of factor	Importance rating	Description		Performance	Performance rating	Description
Order-winning objectives	1	Provides a crucial advantage with customers			1	Consistently considerably better than our nearest competitor
	2	Provides an important advantage with most customers		Better than competitors	2	Consistently clearly better than our nearest competitor
	3	Provides a useful advantage with most customers			3	Consistently marginally better than our nearest competitor
Qualifying objectives	4	Needs to be up to good industry standard			4	Often marginally better than most competitors
	5	Needs to be around median industry standard		Same as competitors	5	About the same as most competitors
	6	Needs to be within close range of the rest of the industry			6	Often close to main competitors
Less important objectives	7	Not important but could become more so in future			7	Usually marginally worse than main competitors
	8	Very rarely rates as being important		Worse than competitors	8	Usually worse than most competitors
	9	Never comes into consideration			9	Consistently worse than most competitors

Figure 9.6   The importance–performance matrix

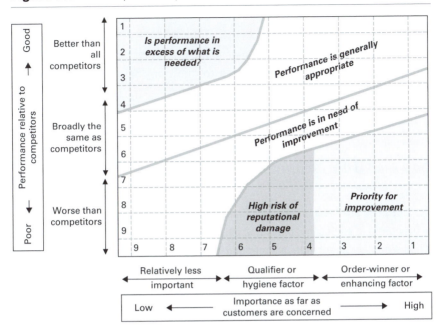

whose performance is clearly below the qualifying level represents the threat of customers actively withdrawing business. Any factors in this 'high risk' area could be even more of a threat that those in the 'urgent action' area.

Similarly, not all factors that lie above the lower bound of acceptability should be treated in the same way. Most of the matrix above the boundary represents factors that are 'appropriate'. But the top-left part of the matrix represents factors that are not particularly important to customers, yet where the operation's performance is better than that of competitors. Any factors in this zone could be regarded as 'too good'. The question must at least be asked, 'Are excessive resources being put into maintaining this level of performance?'

Segregating the matrix in this way results in five zones that imply very different priorities:

1 *The 'performance generally appropriate' zone* – competitive factors that can, in the short term, be considered satisfactory.

2 *The 'performance in need of improvement' zone* – competitive factors that must be serious candidates for improvement.

3 *The 'priority for improvement' zone* – competitive factors that must be considered as candidates for short-term improvement.

4 *The 'high risk of reputational damage' zone* – competitive factors that could represent a serious risk to the business and should be looked at as a matter of urgency.

5 *The 'is performance in excess of what is needed?' zone* – competitive factors where there may be a need to question the use of the resources devoted to achieving such a performance.

CASE STUDY Remedas Logistics

Remedas Logistics is a distributer of medical and therapeutic gases (in the form of cylinders) to clinics, hospitals and care homes. Under competitive pressure, it had recently conducted customer and competitor surveys as a preliminary to a wider operations improvement initiative. It had devised a list of the most important aspects of its distribution and collection service:

- Price – the total charge to the customer including quantity/frequency discounts.
- Quality of distribution service – the appearance of the trucks, courtesy of drivers, etc.
- Quality of products – the appearance of the delivered cylinders.
- Quality of order process – responsiveness and courtesy of the information-gaining process in the operation's call centres.
- Range of gases/cylinders.
- Enquiry lead-time – the elapsed time between customers requesting a quote for new business and the operation responding with a full specification of proposed service.
- Delivery speed – the elapsed time between customers requesting a delivery and the promised delivery time.
- Delivery slot – the 'time tolerance around' the promised delivery time.
- Delivery reliability – the proportion of deliveries actually made within the delivery slot.

The rating for each of these competitive factors, using the 1–9 scale of relative importance, and performance against competitors using the 1–9 performance scale are both shown in Figure 9.7. This allows the positions of each competitive factor to be marked on the importance–performance matrix as shown in

Figure 9.8. It indicates that some factors (delivery reliability, delivery slot, and delivery speed) lie in the appropriate zone. Others (price/cost, quality of distribution service, and enquiry lead-time) should be improved, while quality of order processing and quality of products need to be improved as a matter of urgency. One factor (range) seems to have a level of performance in excess of customers' requirements. It may be that the level of range provided by the business really is excessive, in which case reducing it could possibly save money. However, an alternative might be to maintain the level of service and attempt to persuade customers of its true value.

Figure 9.7   Importance and relative performance ratings for Remedas Logistics

	Importance scale (X = importance rating)								
	Order-winning objectives			Qualifying objectives			Less important objectives		
	1	2	3	4	5	6	7	8	9
Price/cost				X	■				
Quality of distribution service			X	■					
Quality of products			X			■			
Quality of order process		X					■		
Range		■					X		
Enquiry lead-time			X		■				
Delivery speed		■ X							
Delivery slot		■		X					
Delivery reliability	X	■							
	1	2	3	4	5	6	7	8	9
	Better than competitors			Same as competitors			Worse than competitors		
	Performance scale (■ = performance rating)								

If you use the importance–performance matrix in this way it can be extremely powerful, largely because it asks two questions that are fundamental to any operation: 'What do your customers really value?' and 'How good are you at providing it?' Don't waste the opportunity to establish these questions as a regular platform for debate in your business. Of course, the matrix may not reveal any total surprises. The competitive factors in the 'urgent action' zone may already be known to be in need of improvement. However, using

Figure 9.8 The importance–performance matrix for Remedas Logistics

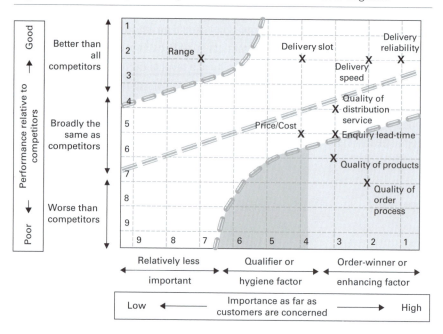

the approach is still useful, first because it helps to discriminate between the many factors that may be in need of improvement, and second because it can give purpose and structure to the debate on improvement priorities.

Dig underneath the measures

An implicit assumption of prioritizing by using the importance–performance matrix is that each aspect of performance is independent of each other. For example, if Remedas Logistics improves its performance in the delivery slot it offers its customers, it will not affect other aspects of performance, such as delivery reliability. However, at some level, different aspects of performance can affect each other. When it comes to improving performance overall, there can be a 'trade-off' between various aspects of performance; improving one aspect of performance may only be achieved by sacrificing performance in another. So, for example, you might wish to improve your cost efficiencies by reducing the variety of products or services that you offer to your customers, or you might try to improve delivery reliability by extending your quoted delivery lead-times. The key issue here is whether this kind of trade-off between different aspects of performance is inevitable, or whether there is some way of securing improvement at doing one thing, while avoiding any deterioration in others. In other words, can operations overcome performance trade-offs?

Overcoming performance trade-offs

The idea of trade-offs is not difficult to understand. One of the best-known summaries of the idea came from Professor Wickham Skinner, who said:

> most managers will readily admit that there are compromises or trade-offs to be made in designing an airplane or truck. In the case of an airplane, trade-offs would involve matters such as cruising speed, take-off and landing distances, initial cost, maintenance, fuel consumption, passenger comfort and cargo or passenger capacity. For instance, no one today can design a 500-passenger plane that can land on an aircraft carrier and also break the sound barrier. Much the same thing is true in... [operations].[2]

By this 'law of the trade-off' there is no such thing as a free lunch. Improvement in one place must be paid for elsewhere. The art is largely a matter of getting the balance right between the various objectives. Skinner's view emphasizes the idea of 'repositioning' performance objectives by trading-off improvements in some aspects of performance for a reduction in performance in others.

This is not the only view of how trade-offs work in operations. Put simply, the alternative view emphasizes the idea that operations managers should be devoting more of their energies not to repositioning trade-offs but to overcoming them. They key questions according to this view are, 'What is it about the way we design or run our operation that makes one aspect of performance trade-off with another? What makes one thing deteriorate when another gets better? Is the type of process technology that we use inflexible? The way we schedule activities? Is it the assumptions we build into how we make operational decisions? What exactly are the constraints? Once the constraints to overcoming trade-offs have been identified, how can they become the target of our improvement process?' In fact, according to this view, the whole purpose of operations improvement is to overcome trade-offs.

Improvement means 'moving the pivot' of the trade-off

Which view is right? Well, both are, actually, and most businesses at some time or other will adopt both approaches. The trade-off argument is such a seductive one because there really is some truth in it. For example, one way of guaranteeing fast deliveries to your customers may be to invest in high stocks of finished goods; but it is not the only way. Sacrificing one aspect of your performance to improve another may be the most convenient solution, or it may even be the only thing you can do in the short term, but it is rarely the only way and it is certainly not the best way to gain a long-term operations advantage. It is like thinking of operations performance as a seesaw where the only way to elevate one side is to lower the other. It is a view that is intrinsically limiting. Just because it is possible to trade-off between objectives does not mean that it is always inevitable.

Think instead of each trade-off not as a conventional seesaw, but rather as one where the pivot as well as the beam can be moved. As with all seesaws, raising one side will indeed lower the other; and true enough one way of making an improvement in one area is by diverting resources away from, or relaxing standards in, another. Here, by applying managerial effort and imagination to moving the pivot upwards, both sides of the seesaw can be raised while preserving the ability to trade-off between them. Alternatively, moving the pivot could allow one side of the seesaw to be raised without lowering the other. The pivot of this analogy is the structure, constraints, assumptions and culture of the operation itself. Raising it may be a long-term task that involves challenging long-held ideas about what really is achievable, expanding the constraints of technology, work practices and systems, and persuading the whole operating function that changing the 'pivot' is not only feasible but also vitally necessary. Figure 9.9 illustrates this pivot effect using the two aspects of performance: 'variety' of products or services and the 'efficiency' with which they are produced.

Partly then, the difference between these two views of trade-offs is time-related. In the short term, trade-offs are very real. There is little time to tackle the 'pivot' of the trade-off seesaw. Trading off is probably the only

Figure 9.9   The 'raising the pivot' analogy of trade-offs

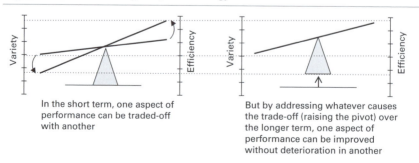

In the short term, one aspect of performance can be traded-off with another

But by addressing whatever causes the trade-off (raising the pivot) over the longer term, one aspect of performance can be improved without deterioration in another option. Operations cannot achieve outstanding performance in all aspects of performance. Yet in the long term, overcoming trade-offs should be the imperative for all operations managers.

CASE STUDY Did Ryanair go too far in its cost–quality trade-off?[3]

Ryanair is the best-known budget airline in Europe. It was not the first to make a success of running with very low operating costs; that accolade goes to Southwest Airlines in the United States. Like Southwest, Ryanair organized its operations strategies ruthlessly around providing a low-cost 'no frills' service.

To some extent these strategies included trading-off levels of service for reduced costs. Complimentary in-flight services were kept to a minimum; secondary and sometimes less convenient airports were used; and one standard class of travel was offered. In other ways also, Ryanair attempted to overcome trade-offs by using a standardized fleet of aircraft, focusing on key processes (such as passenger handling) while outsourcing more peripheral processes, concentrating on direct sales, and reducing aircraft turn-round time at the airports.

To keep focused requires clarity of vision. Ryanair's boss, Michael O'Leary's policy on customer service was clear. *'Our customer service,'* he said, *'is about the most well-defined in the world. We guarantee to give you the lowest airfare. You get a safe flight. You get a normally on-time flight. That's the package. We don't, and won't, give you anything more. Are we going to say sorry for our lack of customer service? Absolutely not. If a plane is cancelled, will we put you up in a hotel overnight? Absolutely not. If a plane is delayed, will we give you a voucher for a restaurant? Absolutely not.'*

The low-cost strategy was wildly successful. Ryanair's operating expenses excluding fuel (conventionally measured as cost per available seat kilometre) were €0.02, while more traditional 'full service' European airlines such as Air France averaged around €0.07 in 2015, according to analysts at JP Morgan.

Then came the backlash with a host of negative press and passenger complaints, perhaps encouraged by the airline's reluctance to apologize, or sometimes even comment. Ryanair was even voted the worst of Britain's 100 biggest brands by readers of the consumer magazine *Which?*. Then, after a drop in its hitherto rapid profit growth, coupled with some shareholder concern, Ryanair announced that it was to reform its 'abrupt culture, and try to eliminate things that unnecessarily annoy customers'. Included in these annoying practices were fines for small luggage-size transgressions and an unpopular €70 fee for issuing boarding passes at the airport rather than printing them out at home (it was lowered to €10). Yet Ryanair insisted that such charges were not money-spinning schemes, but were designed to encourage operational efficiency that kept fares low. O'Leary admitted that Ryanair's brand needed to go through an 'evolution': *'Now that we're carrying over 100 million passengers a year the brand needs to evolve away from being cheeky chappies and deliberately irritating people.'* Part of a move, said some commentators, to help persuade passengers that low fares do not necessarily mean poor service.

Practical prescriptions

- Make sure that everyone understands that performance measurement is not an end in itself. Its main function is improvement – to make the operation better. If it is not doing this, something is wrong with what is being measured or how the measures are being interpreted.

- Do not allow discussion of which aspect of performance should be prioritized for improvement to be dominated either by its importance to customers, or performance against competitors alone. Both are needed for true prioritization.

- Parts of the businesses that compete in different ways should want different things from their operations. Never assume that one set of importance indicators will apply to all products and services produced by the operation.

- Always make a distinction between order-winners and qualifiers. Some aspects of performance are order-winners in that the better the operation is at them the more competitive advantage it gains. Others are qualifiers – they have to be above a certain (qualifying) level not to lose business, but improving them much above that level will not result in significant competitive advantage,

- Check to see whether any of your products or services have any 'delights' – value-adding for customers, but unexpected aspects of performance. More importantly, debate how quickly delights, order-winners and qualifiers will erode over time.

- Continually pose the question, 'What capabilities are we developing that will delight customers in the future?'
- Be careful about what standards of comparison you use to judge performance measures. Different standards have different strengths.
- Benchmark your performance against competitors. Can you really not be interested in how you compare with competitors? Don't let it become an end in itself, and don't let an internal empire grow to do it.
- Benchmark your methods; preferably against other operations that are not direct competitors but nevertheless use the same or similar processes.
- Do not neglect to benchmark internally if comparable parts of the business exhibit different levels of performance.
- Bring your assessment of the importance of different aspects of competition (as customers see them) and their performance (compared with competitors) together to indicate improvement prioritization. Use a formal technique such as the importance–performance matrix.
- For aspects of performance that are priorities for improvement, examine whether any could be improved by trading-off with another aspect of performance that could reduce its performance without impacting overall competitive performance.
- In the longer term, examine what is the 'pivot' of the trade-off to see how the trade-off could be overcome.

Notes

1 Sources include: *The Economist* (2016) The great escape: What other makers can learn from the revival of Triumph motorcycles, 23 January

2 Skinner, W (1985) *Manufacturing: The formidable competitive weapon*, Wiley, Chichester

3 Sources include: Powley, T (2015) Low-cost airlines drop upstart image and dress to impress, *Financial Times*, 5 November; *The Economist* (2013) Ryanair's future – Oh really, O'Leary? 19 October

Position your improvement process

10

Is it really necessary to justify why operations improvement is important? Why wouldn't you want to improve? Improvement means making something better than it was, or would have been if it had not been improved. Who doesn't want to get better? Not just for the sake of excellence itself, although that may be one factor, but for the impact on your business – on achieving an operations advantage. The problem is that we are often too busy doing stuff to think about how things are done. It is important to carve out time to devote to improvement, to treat it as an investment. The good news is that all operations, no matter how well managed, are capable of being better. Surprisingly though, improvement has not always been the central role of operations managers. At one time they were expected simply to 'run the operation', 'keep the show on the road', and 'maintain current performance'. No longer. The emphasis for the best operations has shifted, quite rightly, towards improvement being central to operations management. In part this is down to what, in most industries, is a perceived increase in the intensity of competitive pressures; it is also down to a more optimistic view of what is actually possible. We sometimes forget that it is not just new technologies that have disrupted operations practice; it is also the upheaval in improvement methods and advice that has introduced new ways to improve the way we run operations.

Your operation will never improve to its full potential without you devoting some thought as to how you are going to do it. Allowing improvement to happen in a haphazard manner is a sure recipe for disaster. This is why it is necessary to distinguish between two aspects of improvement (and why we treat improvement in two chapters, see Figure 10.1): 1) how we want to think about the way we 'position' our improvement efforts, and 2) the detailed 'mechanics' of making improvement happen.

This chapter guides you through some of the things that should be decided before you get down to the details of improvement. It does not mean your improvement efforts needs to be bureaucratic or over-engineered. It does

Figure 10.1 This chapter looks at how to position your improvement process

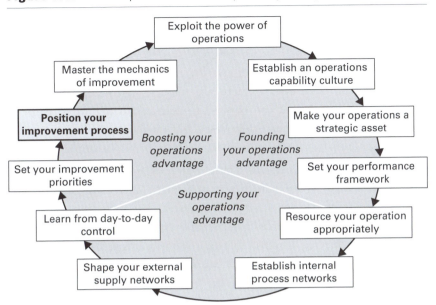

mean that the 'how' and 'why' of improvement need to be understood and shaped to fit with your operation's particular circumstances. There is plenty of advice out there on how you should do this. The general interest in operations improvement has resulted in the development of plenty of new ideas and approaches, which is a good thing. The more ways there are to improve operations, the more interest there will be in operations improvement.

The positioning of the improvement process

It is also the problem. There is a sometimes bewildering amount of advice, hints, techniques, processes and beliefs put forward to help us make sense of how we tackle operations improvement. There certainly is a whole industry devoted to it. So it's not surprising that, along with an overload of advice, there is also no shortage of confusion about how businesses should position themselves in this 'universe of ideas'. A good part of this confusion is because we often mix up four distinct, but related, aspects of improvement:

1 Broad *approaches* to improvement – these are the underlying sets of beliefs that form a coherent philosophy and shape how improvement should be accomplished. Some improvement approaches are far from new; for example some work-study approaches have been used for over a century. Others are more recent, for example Six Sigma.

2 Individual *elements* contained within improvement approaches – these are the individual primary ideas of what improves operations. They could be called the 'building blocks' of improvement and include such ideas as reducing process variability, synchronizing process flow, using problem-solving cycles and waste identification.

3 Improvement *techniques* – there are many 'step-by-step' techniques, methods and tools that can be used to help find better ways of doing things; some are mathematically based, but the most popular are usually more qualitative such as cause–effect analysis, or brainstorming.

4 Ideas of how the *management* of the improvement process should be handled – many of the failures of improvement are because of failures in how your improvement efforts are managed. The improvement activity must be organized, resourced and generally controlled for it to be effective at actually achieving demonstrable improvement. It is at least as important as understanding the approaches, elements and techniques of improvement.

Another source of confusion is the widespread misconception that the various approaches to improvement are different in all respects. In fact, they often have both elements and techniques in common, even if some are particularly associated with one approach or another. This idea of overlap between improvement approaches is illustrated in Figure 10.2. We will deal with this idea in more detail later in this chapter.

Figure 10.2 How the four aspects of improvement: approaches, elements, techniques and management, relate

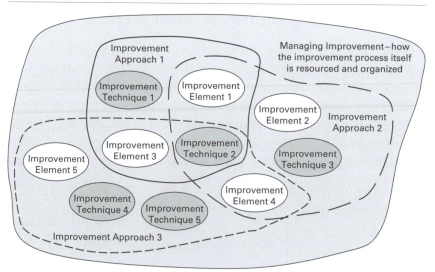

Although different approaches may share some common elements and techniques, they have their own individual set of attitudes to what is important in improvement, so it is essential to understand the relationship between the four aspects of improvement. Unless you do, it is difficult to decide which approach to improvement you should choose: a 'pre-packaged' approach such as business process re-engineering (BPR), or 'lean', or Six Sigma, or whether you should 'pick and mix' from all the available elements.

This is called the 'positioning' of your approach to operations improvement. It establishes the overall purpose, approach and view you take of improvement, what attitude you take to the improvement process generally, and how you choose the most appropriate mix of elements, techniques and overall philosophy. Positioning is the strategic view of improvement. Although most operations improvement is likely to take place at an operational level, it must be placed in some kind of context if it is not to be directionless. You should be clear *why* improvement is happening as well as what it consists of. This means linking your improvement to the overall strategic objectives of the organization. It is also why we are treating operations improvement in two parts. There are two distinct aspects of operations improvement, and two sets of questions to answer.

Top-down and bottom-up improvement

This chapter deals with how an operation's 'top-down' strategic improvement objectives should influence the positioning of its overall approach. It means sorting out which approach is right in what situation. Improvement is essentially a hands-on activity, so the next chapter moves on to take a more bottom-up view of the mechanics and management of what and how your improvement process should be organized. It deals with the more detailed mechanisms of improvement. In particular, it looks at how the tried-and-tested idea of the problem-solving improvement cycle can be adapted to form the basis of operational-level improvement. It also will look at how to manage the improvement process. Figure 10.3 shows these two aspects of improvement. Do not be tempted to jump straight to the next chapter. Without a sound understanding of the why, what and how of improvement, no amount of attention to the detailed steps or techniques will make them fully effective.

In this chapter we deal with the idea of positioning your improvement process. Here are the key questions:

- What is your approach to improvement trying to achieve? Is it to do more or less what you do now, or is it to finish up doing something fundamentally different?

Figure 10.3   Top-down (positioning) and bottom-up (mechanics) operations improvement

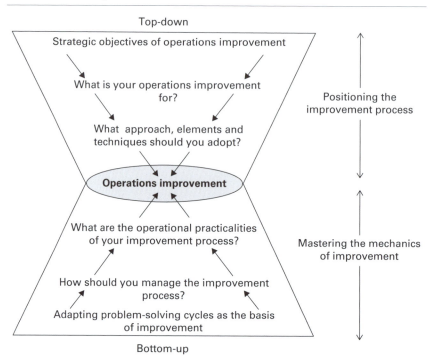

- Do you want your approach to improvement to be cautious and incremental, or radical and innovative?

- Do you want your approach to improvement to be prescriptive in what changes you should make, or to supply a methodology that allows you to work things out for yourself?

- Do you want to adopt a 'packaged' approach with a clear underlying philosophy (eg, lean, BPR, Six Sigma), or devise your own improvement 'package'?

What is your improvement trying to achieve? Better or different?

There can be fundamental differences between the strategic objectives that your operations may have as you shape your improvement efforts. Not necessarily in terms of the various aspects of performance that you may want to enhance, but rather in how you want to be positioned in comparison with the rest of your industry. There is an essential difference between whether you want to operate in broadly the same way as competitors but do it better, and whether you want to operate in a fundamentally different way. Look at the six businesses described in Table 10.1. All are successful (at least at the time of writing) and all are successful largely because of the way they run their operations, but there is a clear distinction between the ways these businesses have reached their status.

Table 10.1 Companies that have successful operations that are either better than or different from competitors

Companies whose operations are essentially the same as competitors', but *better*	Companies whose operations are fundamentally *different* from competitors'
Toyota – Seen as the leading practitioner of lean operations, the Toyota Motor Company has progressively synchronized all its processes simultaneously to give high quality, fast throughput and exceptional productivity. It has done this by developing what it calls the Toyota Production System. This has two themes: 'just-in-time' (defined as the rapid and coordinated movement of parts throughout the production system and supply network to meet customer demand) and 'jidoka' (described as 'humanizing the interface between operator and machine'). Jidoka is operationalized by means of fail-safeing, line-stop authority, and visual control. Both ideas are applied ruthlessly to the elimination of waste, where waste is defined as 'anything other than the minimum amount of equipment, items, parts and workers that are absolutely essential to production'.	*IKEA* – IKEA is the most successful furniture retailer ever, partly because it developed its own special way of selling furniture. Its stores' layout means customers spend far longer in the store than in rival furniture retailers. Its philosophy goes back to the 1950s when Ingvar Kamprad built a showroom on the outskirts of Stockholm where land was cheap. It was innovation in its operations that dramatically reduced its costs; for example, selling furniture in flat packs (reducing production and transport costs), and its 'showroom-warehouse' concept, requiring customers to pick up the furniture themselves (which reduced retailing costs). Both these operating principles are still the basis of IKEA's retail operations. Stores are designed to facilitate the smooth flow of customers, from parking, through the store, to ordering and picking up goods. There is also an area where smaller items are displayed, and can be picked directly. Behind the company's public face there

(Continued)

Table 10.1   *(Continued)*

Companies whose operations are essentially the same as competitors', but *better*	Companies whose operations are fundamentally *different* from competitors'
Toyota claims that its strength lies in understanding the differences between the tools and practices of lean and the overall philosophy of its approach to lean.	is a complex supply network. Close partnerships with its suppliers promote both supply efficiency and new product development. It closely controls all supply and development activities from Sweden.
Four Seasons – The Four Seasons Hotel Group has properties all over the world. Famed for its quality of service, the group has won countless awards for the quality of its service. From its inception the group has had the same guiding principle, 'to make the quality of our service our competitive advantage'. The company has what it calls its Golden Rule: 'Do to others (guests and staff) as you would wish others to do to you'; a simple rule that guides the whole organization's approach to quality. 'We are always looking for better ways of serving our guests. All employees are empowered to use their creativity and judgement in delivering exceptional service and making their own decisions to enhance our guests' stay,' say the company. Four Seasons believes that its greatest asset is its people. It pays considerable attention to selecting staff with an attitude that takes pride in delivering exceptional service. Extensive training programmes and career development plans are designed to support the individual needs of employees as well as operational	*Amazon* – Founded by Jeff Bezos in 1995, it started as a place to buy books, giving its customers what at the time was a unique customer experience. Bezos believed that only the internet could offer customers the convenience of browsing a selection of millions of book titles in a single sitting. Its initial success was followed by continued growth based on a clear strategy of technological innovation. Among its many technological innovations, Amazon offers personalized suggestions, book discovery through 'Search Inside The Book', convenient checkout using 1-Click® Shopping, community features like Listmania and Wish Lists that help customers discover new products, and Amazon Prime. In addition, Amazon operates retail websites and enables other retailers and individual sellers to sell products on its websites. It may not be glamorous, but Amazon has focused on what have been called 'the dull-but-difficult tasks' such as tracking products, managing suppliers, storing inventory and delivering boxes. Fulfilment by Amazon allows other companies to use its logistics capability including the handling of returned items, and access to Amazon's 'back-end' technology. Amazon Web Services, its cloud

(Continued)

Table 10.1 *(Continued)*

Companies whose operations are essentially the same as competitors', but *better*	Companies whose operations are fundamentally *different* from competitors'
and business demands. The company's Guest History database is vital in helping to achieve this. All preferences and specific comments about service experience are logged on the database. Every comment and every preference is discussed and planned, for every guest, for every visit.	computing business, provides the computing power for small and larger high-profile customers such as Spotify's digital music service, and Netflix's video streaming service.
Pixar – Pixar Animation Studios are makers of CGI-animated films using technology modified from the industry-standard. Begun in 1979 as part of the computer division of Lucasfilm, Pixar is owned by The Walt Disney Company. It has produced many successful feature films, and has earned several Academy Awards. Pixar is well known for its adoption of some lean principles in managing creativity. It has encouraged continuous advice and criticism from its production line workers to improve its performance in the same way as practised by lean manufacturers. It also devotes a great deal of effort into persuading its creative staff to work together. In similar companies, people may collaborate on specific projects, but are less good at focusing on what's going on elsewhere in the business. Pixar, however, tries to cultivate a sense of collective responsibility. Staff show unfinished work to one another in daily meetings and so get used to giving and receiving constructive criticism.	***Zara*** – The fashion retailer is known for its 'virtual' vertical integration. It offers cutting edge fashion at affordable prices because its operating model exerts control over almost the entire garment supply chain (retailing, design, purchasing and logistics). Low inventory in the stores means they are reliant on regular and rapid replenishment of newly designed products. Zara minimizes the risk of oversupply by keeping production volumes low at the beginning of the season and reacting quickly to orders as new trends emerge. Design takes place at the company's La Coruña HQ, where inspiration comes partly from its stores passing on customer reaction. Design teams work on next season's designs while simultaneously and continuously updating the current season's designs. Zara manufactures far more of its products than its competitors in its own network of factories. Speed is an over-riding concern for Zara's integrated logistics system. It even buys some of its fabrics undyed to allow faster response to colour changes.

Toyota, Four Seasons and Pixar, all great companies whose operations have much to teach us, basically do the same thing as their competitors, *in broadly the same way*. Visit Toyota and you will see an automobile plant that, at first glance, looks like most others. It uses the same type of assembly line arrangement as Ford, VW, or any other large auto operation. Its advantage lies in its success in incrementally improving how it operates its processes over decades of consistently applying a coherent improvement philosophy. Similarly, Four Seasons is like any other hotel operation in that it keeps its guests warm and dry and looks after their various needs, but it has significantly refined the idea of what quality of service can mean for its target market. Pixar makes movies – great movies. So do other animation studios, yet Pixar has managed to reach levels of creativity envied by its competitors by encouraging its animators to utilize concepts borrowed from the auto industry. In fact, each of these companies has succeeded in pulling away from competitors, not by being radically different but by refining common operations practices.

Not so with Ikea, Amazon and Zara. Like the other companies in the table, they are all successful, and again successful largely because of the way they organize their operations. However, in their cases the path to operations success was by breaking with what was common practice in their industries. They were convinced that they needed to be different from competitors, at least in their operations practice. Ikea combined economies of scale, hitherto untried in furniture retailing, with a radical redesign of its in-store processes and clean economical design. This allowed it to trade-off what customers really wanted (low cost, high variety, availability and clean design) against what they were willing to tolerate (queuing, self-service and picking up from the warehouse). The Ikea operation was different, but it offered what customers wanted and it changed the way we shopped. Amazon was similarly radical. It spotted what promised to be an industry-changing technology in the internet and developed an integrated operational infrastructure around it. Again, it changed the way we shopped, as well as the way other sellers could use its services. If Zara has not changed the whole of fast fashion, it has developed its (largely vertically integrated) supply chain in a way that no competitor has managed to emulate.

Better or different defines your improvement trajectory

This distinction between better and different is important, not only in a strategic sense, but also in defining two approaches to how operations improvement can be tackled and two types of improvement trajectory. Figure 10.4 illustrates this. Assuming that we currently do not organize our operations in a fundamentally different way to our competitors, and assuming that we are not so much better than them that we are unconcerned about improvement, then most of us will be positioned in the bottom-left quadrant of Figure 10.4. Presumably, most of us will want to move into a position where we are better than competitors; there are two trajectories to get to that position. One is to improve in a largely incremental manner, accepting that our fundamental way of working will remain essentially unchanged, but progressively moving towards a better use of our resources and processes. The other is to take the radical path, challenge the underlying justification for how operations are organized, and create an original model of how operations resources and processes are arranged and run.

Of course, there are inherent risks to the radical trajectory. The examples we have used here – Ikea, Amazon and Zara – have been successful in their attempts to create novel operations models, but there are many attempts that you will not have heard of because they crashed and burned before they could offer any improvement. Their radical operations models failed. More positively, a new model can go on to realize its potential and give a superior performance to competitors, but if you want to take this route, you should check that two conditions are fulfilled. First, your new operations model must be feasible and effective in its own right. Second, whoever is implementing it will need to learn fast. It is very rare for a totally different operations model not to need adapting as it faces the realities of day-to-day operating.

Figure 10.4 Which improvement trajectory are you aiming for?

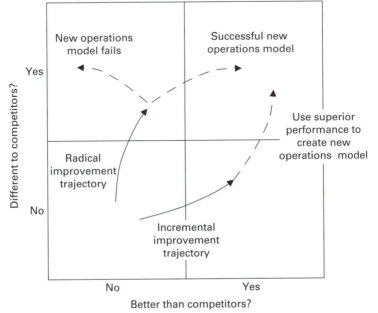

Of course, it is possible for operations taking the more incremental improvement path to finish up in the same place as a successful radical trajectory. Incremental improvement may succeed in moving an operation to the point where its superiority in performance over its competitors is so great that starting to radically change its operations model becomes less of a risk.

Do you want to be cautious and continuous, or radical and innovative?

The first move in positioning your improvement process is very much connected to this distinction between 'being better' and 'being different'. If your overall strategic objective stresses 'being better', it implies a more gradual, incremental type of improvement with many relatively small changes. On the other hand, 'being different' implies a radical and innovative style of improvement, with fewer but larger changes.

Yet if you choose gradual, incremental improvement you are not being cautious simply for its own sake. It does not actively avoid more radical change but it does see small improvements as having one great advantage over more radical ones – you can follow them relatively painlessly by other small improvements. If you treat improvement as truly continuous, it can become embedded as the 'natural' way of working within the operation. While there is no guarantee that such small steps towards better performance will develop a momentum, the whole philosophy of continuous improvement attempts to ensure that it does. In fact, it is your momentum of improvement rather than your rate of improvement that is important. It does not matter if successive improvements are small; what does matter is that every month (or week, or quarter, or whatever period is appropriate) you really do make some kind of improvement. It is a style of improvement that essentially exploits the potential of your resources and processes that already exist. Because of this, its benefits tend to be relatively immediate and predictable, as well as fitting better into an existing strategic framework.

Choosing radical, innovation-based improvement is a very different proposition. It assumes that your main vehicle of improvement is a major and dramatic change in the way your operation works. The impact of these improvements will be relatively abrupt and will represent a step change in practice (and hopefully performance). You will be more concerned with the exploration of new possibilities and you will have to search for, and recognize, new mind-sets and ways of doing things. This type of improvement is rarely inexpensive, usually requires significant investment, often disrupts the ongoing workings of the operation, and frequently involves changing processes and process technology. It will involve you in experimentation and the simulation of possible consequences. It can also be risky. Big change usually means you moving to a new set of operating practices and/or technologies, which in turn means increased uncertainty and introducing a whole pack of potential troubles and tribulations. So benefits are likely to be long term and possibly difficult to predict. You will have to be prepared for any benefits or discoveries to be so different from what you are familiar with that you may not find it easy to take advantage of them.

Can you be both continuous and radical?

Can you adopt a position in between the two extremes? Pure continuous improvement and pure radical improvement are clearly the two ends of the spectrum. Can you mix them? Can you be both continuous and radical at the same time? The answer is, probably yes, but it's difficult. The skills, attitudes and capabilities to be successful at the slow, patient and incremental approach to improvement tend to be different from those that are needed for the radical exploration of innovative ideas. In fact, the two interpretations of improvement may actively conflict. A focus on creating and thoroughly exploring totally novel choices will probably eat up the managerial time, effort and finance that could otherwise be used for continuously fine-tuning existing ways of doing things. Equally, if existing processes are incessantly improved over time, what is the motivation to experiment with new ideas? In other words, the two approaches to improvement may compete both for resources and for management attention. So is it just not possible to have both a continuous and a radical style of improvement at the same time? This is where the notion of 'organizational ambidexterity' comes in.

Organizational ambidexterity

Organizational ambidexterity indicates your business's capacity to address two organizationally incompatible objectives equally well. In this case it means the ability of your operation to both exploit existing processes in a continuous manner whilst exploring innovative solutions as they seek to improve.[1] For example, you may want to compete in mature markets where continuously paring away at costs by improving existing resources and processes is important. Yet at the same time you may want to be competing in new technologies and/or markets where novelty, innovation and experimentation are valued.

Academics who have studied firms that try to achieve both types of improvement seem to fall into two camps: those who think it can't be done, and those who think it can – but it's really difficult. Those who take the more positive view put forward three ways in which it might be possible (shown in Figure 10.5):

1 *You can adopt different types of improvement in different parts of your operation.* There is some evidence that those businesses that did succeed in achieving some degree of organizational ambidexterity tended to organize separate operations that had very different strategies, structures, processes and cultures focusing on either continuous improvement or radical innovation. It is sometimes called 'structural ambidexterity'.

2 *You can adopt different types of improvement at different times.* The basis of this idea is that different times (and therefore conditions) will demand different responses from your business, and that means different types of improvement. Sometimes markets and competition require innovation, sometimes more steady consolidation. So, for example, as a product or service moves through its life cycle from its introduction through to maturity, it will move sequentially from depending on high levels of innovation and improvement at the beginning of its life, then progressively require more steady (and probably cost-based) continuous improvement as it matures.

3 *You accept the challenge of mixing both types of improvement simultaneously.* Both the previous approaches to mixing the two types of improvement rely on separating them, either organizationally or in time. This idea (called 'contextual ambidexterity') could be summarized as, 'OK, we know that it takes very different mind-sets for each type of input, but that is the way of the world, get used to it.' Sometimes you don't have the luxury of compartmentalizing the two types of input; you just have to get on with doing both at the same time. It will lead to conflicts in resource allocation and in attitude, maybe, but this approach says 'embrace the conflicts'. Let the ambiguity and the paradoxes implicit in mixing both types of improvement provide the creative tension that improvement needs. As I said – a challenge.

Figure 10.5   Three potential ways of achieving organizational ambidexterity

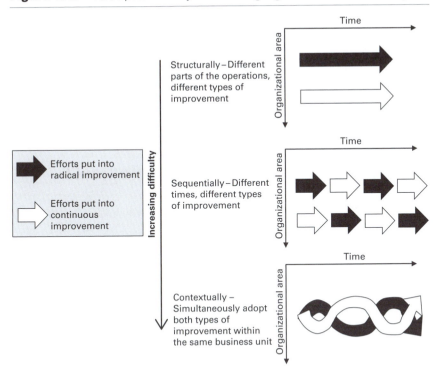

CASE STUDY   Anarchy at 6Wonderkinder[2]

How can a firm organize itself so it can keep some kind of control over its costs and day-to-day activities, while not inhibiting the creativity of the people being paid to be creative? This was the problem faced by 6Wonderkinder, a Berlin-based developer of 'Wunderlist', the task management tool. Now owned by Microsoft, in its early days when it was founded with only six people, it was relatively easy to foster a creative and innovative atmosphere. As the company grew, it became more difficult to preserve that 'start-up spirit'. Increasing size meant more formal processes and attention to incrementally attacking waste. As Chad Fowler, the company's chief technology officer, said, '*Probably every single company wants to maintain the feeling of being in a start-up, no matter how big they get.*'

So, as the company grew it tried several means of preserving its 'start-up spirit' in addition to the more conventional control of its operations. One was its yearly 'Wunderkamp', when all staff spent a week away in Bavarian forest cabins or on the Baltic coast. Another was 'Sexy Friday' when developers got a day a week to pursue their own passions, the aim being to challenge established patterns of working and encourage novel thinking. Christian Reber, the firm's chief executive and co-founder, said: *'On an assembly line you always get the work you expect. People do the stuff you tell them to do. What we, here, try to achieve is that we regularly get the 'wow' factor... if everyone acts like a CEO, they make the decisions; [if] they are responsible for their own projects, then it completely changes [the] dynamics.'*

Do you want improvement that is prescriptive or methodological?

Review any of the many sources of advice on improvement and you will find that there is a distinct difference between the advice that prescribes the specific actions that you should take to improve, and the advice that tells you, not what to do, but how you should approach making the decision about what to do. Some improvement advice has a firm view of what is the best way to organize the operation's processes and resources. It is prescriptive. Other advice will offer no particular view on what an operation should do; rather it focuses on the practice that should be adopted if the operation is to be improved. It is methodological. Table 10.2 lists some of the better-known elements of improvement, classified by whether they are largely prescriptive or largely methodological.

Table 10.2 Elements of improvement classified by whether they are prescriptive or methodological

Elements of improvement that are largely prescriptive (they tell you what to do to improve)	Elements of improvement that are largely methodological (they tell you how to approach improvement)
• Design end-to-end processes • Synchronize process flow • Eliminate all types of waste • Emphasise customer-driven objectives • Reduce variability • Demand prompts activity • Put decisions where work is performed • Prevention better than inspection • Organize around outcomes not tasks • Reduce inventory	• Emphasize evidence-based decision making • Establish systems and procedures • Adopt problem-solving cycles • Emphasis on education • Start with a 'clean sheet of paper' • See perfection as the goal • Use a process-based analysis • Involve everyone in improvement • Analyse processes by the value they add • Aim for continuous improvement

You need to understand how approaches to improvement differ

By an 'approach' to improvement we mean the underlying sets of beliefs that form a coherent philosophy and shape how improvement should be accomplished. Over the last few decades there have been quite a lot of them; here are the better known:

- TQM – Perhaps the granddaddy of them all is total quality management (TQM). It was one of the earliest management 'fashions', with its peak of popularity in the 1980s and early 90s, and has suffered from something of a backlash in recent years. Don't dismiss it too readily. The general principles embraced by TQM are still, quite rightly, hugely influential. In particular, the total, or holistic, view of TQM is both powerful and attractive. At its simplest, it provides an outline 'checklist' of how to go about operations improvement. It is also capable of being developed into a more prescriptive form. The best example of this is the EFQM Excellence Model.[3]

- Lean – Originally known as just-in-time, the idea of lean operations spread beyond its Japanese (and manufacturing) roots and became fashionable in the West at about the same time as TQM. Although its reputation has not flagged to the same extent as TQM, some of the enthusiasm once associated with the approach has waned a little. Now, lean has undergone something of a renaissance as an approach that can be applied in non-manufacturing and internal operations. In particular, the idea of waste elimination has become the most significant part of the lean philosophy, where waste is any activity that does not add value. In fact, some interpret the lean approach (mistakenly) as consisting almost exclusively of waste elimination.

- BPR – An approach that emerged in the early 1990s but provoked a backlash relatively quickly is business process re-engineering (BPR). It was Michael Hammer who proposed that rather than using technology to automate work, it would be better applied to doing away with the need for that work in the first place ('don't automate, obliterate'). His intention was to warn against institutionalizing non-value-added work, making it even more difficult to identify and eliminate. BPR proposes that all work should be examined to check that it really adds value for the customer. If not, processes should be redesigned to eliminate it. This was reflecting very similar objectives to far earlier ideas like scientific management and more recently lean, but BPR (unlike earlier approaches) advocated radical changes rather than incremental changes to processes.

This radical aspect of BPR was summarized by one commentator who held that, 'Today's firms must seek not fractional, but multiplicative levels of improvement – ten times rather than ten per cent'.[4]

- Six Sigma – The electronics firm Motorola conceived Six Sigma, which was originally a more 'technical' approach to improvement, during the 1980s. Initially focusing simply on removing manufacturing defects, it soon came to realize that many problems were caused by latent defects, hidden within the design of its products. It figured that the best way to eliminate these defects was to make sure that design specifications were tight (narrow tolerances) and that its processes exhibited little variability relative to design tolerances. The name 'Six Sigma' was used to indicate that the natural variation of processes should be half their specification range, but the name proved far more attractive than its strictly technical interpretation. It has a 'scientific' feel to it, and indeed the definition of Six Sigma has widened to well beyond this rather narrow statistical perspective. General Electric (GE), which was probably the best known of the early adopters of Six Sigma, defined it as 'A disciplined methodology of defining, measuring, analysing, improving, and controlling the quality in every one of the company's products, processes, and transactions – with the ultimate goal of virtually eliminating all defects'. It is now a broad improvement concept rather than a simple examination of process variation.

Of course there are other approaches to improvement in addition to those very briefly explained here. One could easily have extended this list to include Total Preventive Maintenance (TPM), Lean Sigma (a combination of lean and Six Sigma), and so on. Whichever improvement approaches you are thinking about, it is vital that you don't consider using them without a full understanding of what they are made up of. If operations management does not understand these approaches, how can the rest of the organization take them seriously? The details of Six Sigma or lean, for example, are not simply technical matters. They are fundamental to how suitable any approach could be in your particular circumstances. Not every approach is right for every business.

CASE STUDY   Saint Goran's hospital[5]

The ideas behind 'lean' operations practice have become particularly influential in healthcare. Take, for example, Stockholm's Saint Goran's hospital, which is run by the private company, Capio. It is the setting for one of the more successful examples of lean management in healthcare services. Britta Wallgren, the hospital's chief executive and an anaesthetist by training, admits that she never heard the term 'lean' when she was at medical school. Yet now it is the central philosophy driving St Goran's approach to organizing its medical care.

The hospital's lean concept is based on the two lean principles of 'flow' and 'quality'. It has reduced waiting times by increasing throughput. Everything is done to try to 'maximize throughput' so as to minimize cost and 'give taxpayers value for money'. Hospitals should not be in the hotel business, it says, so to minimize the time patients spend in hospital it invests in preparing patients for admission and providing support after they are released. Before the adoption of lean principles, doctors and nurses used to 'work in parallel'; now they work together in teams. No longer do staff concentrate exclusively on their field of medical expertise: they are also responsible for suggesting operational improvements.

The drive to save costs also runs to how patients are treated. The hospital has been called the medical equivalent of a budget airline. There are four to six patients to a room and the decor is 'institutional' rather than opulent. Similarly, staff are included in establishing improved working practices, many of which are relatively 'low tech'. For example, staff used to waste valuable time looking for equipment such as defibrillators. Then someone suggested marking a reserved space on the floor with yellow tape and insisting that the machines were always kept there.

If you want to understand how the various approaches to improvement differ (and how they do not) you can use the 'radical-innovative' versus 'gradual-incremental' distinction and the 'prescriptive' versus 'methodological' scales to position each improvement element and the approaches that include them. This is illustrated in Figure 10.6. You can see that the various approaches do indeed differ. BPR is very clear in recommending that all processes should be organized on an end-to-end basis. Its focus is *what* should happen rather than *how* it should happen. To a slightly lesser extent lean is the same. It has a definite list of things that processes should or should not be – waste should be eliminated, inventory should be reduced, flow should be synchronized and so on.

Contrast this with both Six Sigma and TQM that focus to a greater extent on *how* operations should be improved. Six Sigma in particular has relatively little to say about what is good or bad in the way operations should be organized (with the possible exception of emphasizing the negative effects of process variability). It concerns itself largely with the way in which improvements should be made: using evidence, using a particular problem-solving cycle (the DMAIC cycle; we will look at problem-solving

Figure 10.6 Four improvement approaches and their main elements

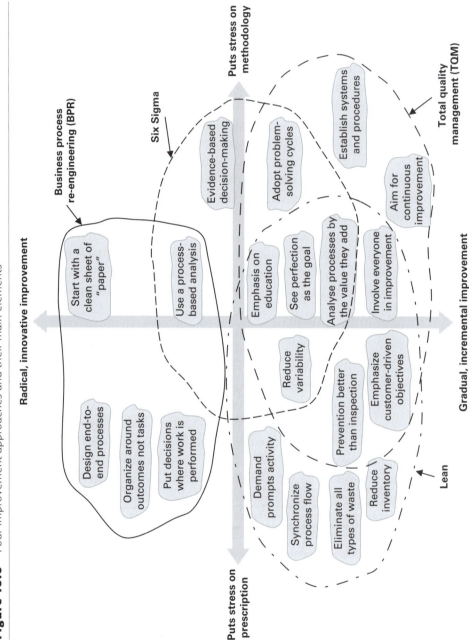

cycles in the next chapter) and so on. The various approaches also differ in terms of whether they emphasize radical or gradual change. BPR is explicit in its radical nature, while both TQM and lean incorporate ideas of continuous improvement. Six Sigma is relatively neutral on this issue and can be used for small or very large changes.

In other words, the 'centres of gravity' of each of these approaches is different. BPR tends to be prescriptive and radical. TQM is continuous and incremental whilst being methodological in nature. Six Sigma can be either radical or incremental but is largely methodological.

... and how they don't

Do not think that approaches to improvement are different in all respects. Look again at Figure 10.6: there is some significant overlap between the approaches to improvement. There are many elements that are common to several approaches. In other words, TQM, BPR, lean, Six Sigma, and so on are all 'packages' that select from common 'ingredients'. There is also a tendency for keen advocates of each of these approaches to draw the boundary of the approach somewhat wider than we have shown here. This has the effect of producing an even greater overlap between the different approaches. Also, as these approaches develop over time, they may acquire elements from elsewhere. A good example is Six Sigma. It has developed beyond its process control roots to encompass many other elements. This is not a criticism of this, or any other, approach. Even if many of the elements are held in common, the differences in each approach's centre of gravity still make some approaches more rather than less appropriate for your operation.

What improvement approach is right for you?

Here are some pointers as to whether you should be favouring radical-innovative or gradual-incremental improvement:

- Go back to the discussion on 'better' versus 'different'. What do you want to be? If you are aiming for an operation (or part of an operation) that is broadly the same as competitors, but better, then an improvement process based on incremental and continuous improvement is likely to be better for you. If you are seeking to explore pioneering and original ways to organize your operations, then it is the radical-innovative route.

- How urgent is your need to improve? Gradual-incremental improvement, by its nature, takes time to establish significant gains. Radical-innovative improvement may be more risky but it can lead to faster results.

- Do you operate in a predictable or uncertain and dynamic environment? If your competitive environment is stable and predictable, the slow but steady approach of gradual-incremental improvement is likely to be appropriate for you. A more dynamic environment is more likely to require new innovative solutions to cope with new circumstances.

- How averse to risk are you? If you cannot tolerate mistakes or if the consequences of mistakes are particularly serious, the improvements implied by a gradual-incremental approach are unlikely to cause you serious concern. Conversely, if you are prepared to take a risk in order to get novel solutions, the radical-innovative approach is more suitable.

- What is the natural or default approach to organization and control in your business? If your natural approach is tight, hierarchical and ordered then it is unlikely that radical-innovative improvement approaches thrive. This kind of organizational culture is ideal for gradual-incremental improvement.

The questions you need to ask in deciding whether you should emphasize prescription or methodology are different. Here are some pointers:

- Does whatever approach you are considering map well onto what you believe to be your own operation needs? The prescriptive nature of some improvement approaches means that there must be a good fit between what is being prescribed and what is appropriate for your particular business. Do not adopt a prescriptive approach unless you are convinced that its advice is appropriate for you.

- Are your circumstances and improvement needs clear and relatively unambiguous? Generally, more methodological approaches are better at coping with ambiguity.

- Do all parts of your business have the same improvement needs? If so, then prescriptive approaches can be appropriate. If not, then the more 'general-purpose' methodological approaches can be more appropriate.

- Are your circumstances and improvement needs likely to change in the future? If they are then the appropriateness of whatever prescriptive approach has been taken may suffer. Methodological approaches do not rely as much on stability.

- How capable are your people of using what can be relatively sophisticated, methodological approaches? Prescriptions can be relatively easy to follow. Methodologies can be more difficult to adapt to specific circumstances.

Adopt a 'package' or devise your own?

It should be clear from the previous discussion that the well-known approaches to improvement are, in fact, pre-packaged 'solutions' made up by selecting from a set of common ingredients. Does this mean that anyone can simply pick out whatever elements that appeal to them and construct their own improvement approach? Well, to a certain extent, yes, but there are two caveats. First, remember that all these pre-packaged approaches do have a centre of gravity. TQM is incremental and methodological, lean is incremental but more prescriptive, BPR is radical and prescriptive, and Six Sigma is methodological. None of these approaches tries to be everything to everybody. Each has a focus. So if you are going to do-it-yourself do not be tempted to spread all over the space defined in Figure 10.6. Second, each of these approaches does have something of an underlying set of beliefs that binds its elements together. BPR is defined by its original radical slogan 'don't automate, obliterate', Six Sigma by its rational focus on evidence, TQM by its inclusiveness, and lean by its emphasis on value-added flow. This gives them one particularly important advantage – it makes them relatively easy to explain.

So, if you are going to do-it-yourself in constructing your own approach to improvement it is important to base it on an underlying philosophy that suits your culture and your strategic aspirations. However, its centre of gravity should be guided by your answers to the questions posed previously. Provided you understand the differences between approaches, don't worry too much about adapting the 'standard' ones to your circumstances. Even those businesses that declare their allegiance to a particular approach have often only cherry-picked some of its key elements – and there is nothing necessarily wrong with that.

Improvement approaches are not operations strategies

One final point concerning your choice of improvement approach – they are not in themselves operations strategies. So (contrary to what one sometimes hears from COOs) the answer to the question, 'What is your operations strategy?' can never be, for example, 'Six Sigma' or 'lean'. The essence of an operations strategy is that it is individual and specific to one organization at one point in time. By contrast, these approaches are generic in nature. That is why they are attractive: they offer generic advice that is broadly applicable across a range of businesses. That is also why they are not strategies, and senior managers who adopt them as operations strategies are deluding themselves. Yet, none of them is incompatible with a sensible operations strategy. They can all be considered as part of a strategy. Indeed the choice of which, if any, approach you adopt is an important strategic decision – but it is not a strategy.

Practical prescriptions

- Accept the truth that, even if your operation is, and always has been, successful, it can still be improved.

- Also accept the fact that you need to put some work into understanding the nature of operations improvement, especially the differences between the various approaches, the elements that are contained within improvement approaches, the techniques, methods and tools that can be used to help find better ways of doing things, and how the improvement process should be handled.

- Be clear in what your approach to improvement is trying to achieve. Is it to do more or less what you do now, or is it to finish up doing something fundamentally different?

- Based on this, decide whether you want your approach to improvement to be cautious and incremental, or radical and innovative.

- If you want to try and do both styles of improvement (incremental and radical) in the same operation, think about whether different parts of the operation should focus on one style of improvement, or should the operation adopt different styles at different times, or should you expect your operation to adopt both styles simultaneously.

- Similarly, decide whether you want your approach to improvement to be prescriptive in what changes you should make, or if you want it to suggest a methodology that allows you to work things out for yourself.

- Review, then decide whether you want to adopt a 'packaged' approach with a clear underlying philosophy (lean, BPR, Six Sigma, etc), or devise your own improvement 'package'.

Notes

1 It is an idea popularized by O'Reilly, C and Tushman, M (2004) The ambidextrous organization, *Harvard Business Review*, **82** (4), pp 74–83

2 Vasagar, J (2014) Experiment with a bit of anarchy, *Financial Times*, 28 January

3 The EFQM model (the organization was originally called the European Foundation for Quality Management) is fully described at, http://www.efqm.org

4 Davenport, T (1995) Reengineering – The fad that forgot people, *Fast Company*, November

5 Sources include: *The Economist* (2013) Schumpeter, Sweden is leading the world in allowing private companies to run public institutions, 18 May

Master the mechanics of improvement

The positioning of your improvement process, covered in the previous chapter, is largely an intellectual exercise. It is a necessary prerequisite before any improvement process can become firmly established, but the mechanics of making improvement happen are far more dirty-handed. It is a practical activity, with its roots in the accumulated experiences of all those practitioners who have tried (not always successfully) to make operations improvement a routine part of what it does. This means you have to get involved, not only in the high-level positioning of the improvement process, but also in getting to grips with the methods and mechanisms that are used to solve the myriad (relatively) small problems that inhibit improvement. It means focusing attention on specific techniques and prescriptions while not losing sight of your 'overarching' purpose, as defined in your positioning of your improvement process. Figure 11.1 places the topic in our overall model.

Jeanne DeWitt, Chief Revenue Officer at UberConference, had the right idea.[1] She said: 'spend time doing the work that your team actually does. Not only does this help establish you as someone who leads by example, but you also learn first-hand about all of the different challenges that people experience every day.' Few would disagree with her. 'Practising what you preach' and 'leading by example' have almost descended into management clichés. Most experienced managers know how difficult it is to do it consistently. It should not be about doing the work of your team all the time (although giving a hand in busy times can be a good move); that is not your job. Admittedly, getting directly involved with the improvement process takes time, and time is limited and you cannot get involved in everything. Yet devoting time to the improvement process can be one of the best investments you can make.

That is because improvement is different. It is the bridge between the day-to-day routines of the operation and the overall path of how the operation

Figure 11.1 This chapter looks at how to master the mechanics of improvement

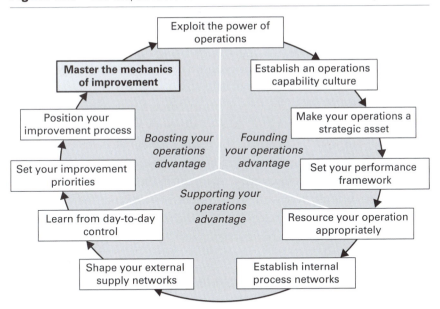

should develop in the future. It demonstrates that improvement rates highly in your priorities, and it helps you focus on learning what the real improvement issues are. Devoting time to it and getting your hands dirty in the improvement process are not only good for improvement, they're good for you.

What exactly is 'the improvement process'? It is the steps one goes through to make improvements and the way going through those steps is managed. Those are the two sets of issues addressed in this chapter. First, we will look at the steps in the improvement process in the form of a problem-solving improvement cycle.

Improvement is not a linear process, it's a cycle

Do not think of the improvement process as a linear set of steps. Think of it as a circular process of continuous problem solving. Improvement, after all, is a matter of continually overcoming the barriers to making things better. It is a repeating problem-solving activity, not a one-off. Even radical, innovative improvement is eventually followed by another radical, innovative improvement. So a model of improvement that learns the lessons from one improvement and starts to think about the next one makes sense. Using a cyclical process really does work. It provides the structure from which even creative problem solving benefits. It also stresses the importance of a literally never-ending process of repeatedly questioning and re-questioning the details of your problems.

There are several improvement cycles to choose from. Probably the two that are the best known are the PDSA (plan, do, study, act) cycle and the DMAIC (define, measure, analyse, improve, control, pronounced De-Make) cycle,[2] but there are plenty of others. Although purists might disagree, they are all fairly similar. They all start with a definitional stage and move through investigation, analysis, solution generation, implementation and, if they are sensible, a learning stage – after which, the cycle starts again. The cycle that we will use here is shown in Figure 11.2. It is not radically different from many others, but it does cover all the main stages and, unlike some, it includes formalizing a learning stage.

Can this problem-solving cycle be used for both radical and incremental improvement?

Yes, and no. Yes, the stages that are required by both types of improvement are broadly the same. Any type of improvement, whether incremental and continuous or radical and innovative, needs to start by defining the problem, collecting data, investigating the root cause of why an improvement is needed, generating possible improvements, implementing the chosen one,

Figure 11.2 A generic problem-solving cycle

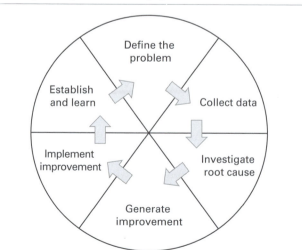

and drawing lessons from the whole cycle. What do differ are aspects of how you will probably need to use the cycle:

- There are subtleties of exactly how each of these stages is interpreted and applied, particularly in how potential improvements are generated.

- There is likely to be more going back and recycling between the various stages when using the cycle for more radical and innovative improvements.

- The 'speed' of moving round the cycle will differ. Incremental, continuous improvement means moving round the cycle nonstop, repeatedly, frequently and therefore relatively fast. More radical, innovative problem solving, by definition, does not happen too frequently.

We will look at each of these stages in turn.

Define the problem

The very first thing that you *must* do is define the problem in some detail. Your problem definition should be a clear and concise description of the issues that need to be addressed. It is a statement of 'what's wrong with what', 'by how much', and 'the consequences to the organization'. Do not skip or undervalue this stage. It is hugely important. Experienced problem solvers know that a well-defined problem is halfway to being solved, and a perfectly defined problem is not even a problem any more. The idea is to step back, reflect, and invest time and effort in improving your understanding of the problem before jumping into solving it. A good problem definition can not only focus your problem-solving team's efforts and avoid setting off in the wrong direction, but can also create a sense of ownership for the team.
   Your problem definition should:

- State the problem clearly, briefly and unambiguously.

- Describe the size of the problem in measurable terms.

- Identify where and when the problem is happening.

- Justify why the problem is worth solving.

- Identify the stakeholders for the problem and how they will judge whether the problem has been solved.

- Describe the impact the problem is having on the business.

There are dangers in drawing up a problem definition. The most common is to define the problem in too narrow a manner: limiting the scope of the problem can stifle creativity and lead to a solution that is not comprehensive enough. You should not let the problem definition prejudge the rest of the cycle either. It should not make assumptions about the likely cause of the problem, or assign blame.

CASE STUDY   IDEO asks the outliers[3]

When the improvement is on the radical-innovative end of the spectrum the problem definition is especially important. The problem will need scoping carefully, with stakeholder's needs and interests carefully analysed and understood.

This is a point particularly stressed by IDEO, one of the world's most successful and best known design consultancies. Starting by offering product design services (it helped to design Apple's first mouse) it has progressed to designing services. One of the firm's principles is to emphasize the importance of looking at problems from the consumer's point of view. But IDEO often focuses on the outliers rather than 'average' customers. For example, on one assignment investigating how medication was administered and consumed, it conducted comprehensive discussions with patients to understand how they go about taking their medication. What were their habits and routines? When and where did they take their pills? How did they feel about the process? The patients of particular interest, the ones who revealed the most useful information, were those who repeatedly forgot to take their drugs or became confused. These were the people for whom a solution would provide the most benefit.

Collect data

Improvement does not happen 'blind': you need data. You need to know the details of what really is happening, and why something is considered a problem. Yet data gathering can itself be something of a problem. Especially for enthusiastic improvement teams, pausing to gather data can seem like a backwards move. Nevertheless, it is an important step, and one where your approach can make a big difference to the quality of the solution that is eventually generated. Collecting data systematically stops you jumping to premature conclusions, if nothing else.

There are some common-sense pointers to collecting data that are worth following. For example:

- Remain as dispassionate as possible. Engage with the issue, not the personalities.
- Try to quantify data where possible.
- For subjective data, take a representative range of opinions rather than just asking one person.
- Don't be afraid to be naïve. Adopt a state of 'conscious unknowing' and ask questions until you are satisfied with the answer.
- Check data where possible.
- Collect data on the current state and possible future states.
- Most important: when possible, go see for yourself – try the 'gemba walk'.

Gemba walks

Don't be put off by (or be over-respectful of) the Japanese term. It simply means the personal observation of work, when and where it is actually happening.[4] It is basically the idea that there is no substitute for getting out of the conference room and seeing for yourself (or better still, yourselves). When you do observe work being done, do it when and where it normally takes place. It is an opportunity to capture the reality and the issues relating to how effectively work is being done in the depot or warehouse, and on the factory or office floor. Also, interaction with the people doing the work is encouraged. They are likely to know far more about what is really happening than you can ever tell from studying charts in meetings. Hereby lies a danger: the spirit of a gemba walk is not to find fault – it is to learn. The surest way to kill the value of the gemba walk is to use it to directly criticize or even to enforce company policy.

Gemba walks are more than just going for a stroll to see what's happening. They need some structure and some preparation. It is best to have an agreed objective, or at least a subject for your walk. However, it is a mistake to prepare anything approaching a questionnaire beforehand. This is not a research project capable of being replicated; it is a learning opportunity. Any questions should be open-ended. If all you get is a simple yes or no to your questions, it is not ignorance or necessarily a reluctance to engage on the part of those you are questioning; it's more likely to be your approach. Nevertheless, some things are best planned in advance, for example the route of your gemba walks. It is sensible to plan a route that covers all aspects of the work being observed without spending too much time away from significant areas. Finally, remember to record what you see and hear, who you talk to, what your impressions were, and most importantly, where there seems to be waste.

Investigate the root cause

The critical question you should be asking at this stage is 'Why?' Why are things as they are? Why have things gone wrong? Why do we need to improve this? It is the process of tracing a problem back to its origins. It involves digging behind the symptoms to the deeper problem beneath. These 'deeper problems' usually fit into one of three categories:

1 Something physical has gone wrong – technology is not doing what it should.

2 Something people-related has gone wrong – someone has either violated set procedures or made an error in deciding a course of action.

3 Something organizational has gone wrong – a process, system or rule on which decisions are based is inappropriate.

Yes, I know that everything eventually comes down to people, but brainstorming these three categories can help in making an initial list of potential root causes. In addition, there are techniques that can help investigate root causes. The two best known (and most useful) are cause–effect analysis and 'why-why' analysis.

Figure 11.3 A cause–effect analysis by a commercial printer supplier investigating the return of parts deemed 'inappropriate' by customers

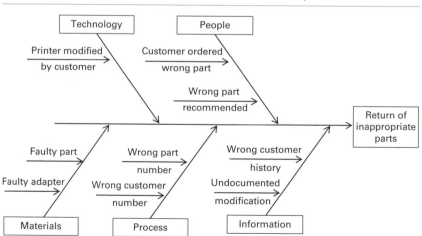

Cause–effect analysis

Cause–effect diagrams search for the root causes of problems by asking what, when, where, how and why questions, but also add some possible 'answers' in an explicit way. They have become extensively used in improvement programmes, partly because they are simple and straightforward, and partly because they provide a way of structuring group brainstorming sessions. Often the structure involves identifying possible causes under the (rather old-fashioned) headings of: machinery, manpower, materials, methods and money. In practice, any categorization that comprehensively covers all relevant possible causes could be used. Figure 11.3 shows an example of a commercial printer supplier investigating the return of parts deemed as 'inappropriate' by customers.

Why-why analysis

This is another method of structuring what is essentially a brainstorming process. It sounds corny, but it can be remarkably effective. There are a number of variants, but why-why analysis usually starts by stating the problem and asking *why* that problem has occurred. Once the reasons have been

Figure 11.4   A why-why analysis of the low return rate of insulating packaging

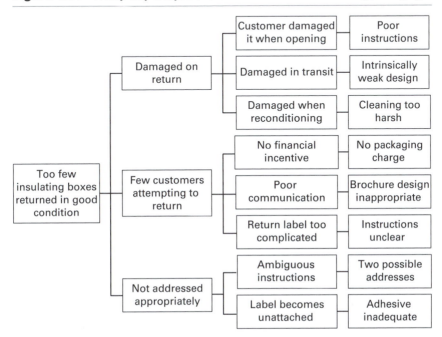

identified, each is taken in turn and again the question is asked *why* those reasons have occurred, and so on. This procedure is continued until either a cause seems sufficiently self-contained to be addressed by itself or no more answers to the question 'Why?' can be generated. Figure 11.4 shows an example of why-why analysis for an internet retailer of frozen food which, for cost and environmental reasons, encourages (not very successfully) its customers to return its insulated boxes.

Generate improvement

A huge amount of creativity has been used in writing about creativity. Advice ranges from 'Some people are more creative than others, so if you want creativity, hire creative people', to 'Creativity is a process like any other process, stick to these rules and you will get creative solutions to your problems.' Believing that only a few people who are 'blessed' with creativity can provide original improvements is surely both pessimistic and runs against common sense. What about the idea that 'creativity is just a process like any other'? Well, a sensible process can help most activities, and searching for creative improvement solutions is no exception. Yet there is more than a hint of 'motherhood and apple pie' about much of the advice as to how to promote creativity. This does nothing to alter the fact that a lack of creativity is down to forgetting about some basic things:

- Recognize that not all problems require the same degree of creativity. Creativity can be disruptive and difficult. Do not treat all improvement as needing radical solutions. Remember the radical-innovative/gradual-incremental distinction we identified in the previous chapter. Focus creativity where it's needed.

- Don't forget that there are many techniques that can be used to promote creativity. Brainstorming is probably the best known. It isn't rocket science, but the rules of first promoting quantity rather than the quality of ideas, postponing judgement, building on others' ideas, valuing everyone's ideas, etc are all useful.

- Make sufficient time, resources and information available for creative activities. People need the room and (paradoxically) the absence of too much pressure to be creative.

- Accept the possibility that everyone has the potential to be creative. It is not just for senior, specialist, or experienced staff. Include everyone in the process.

- Be careful how you use language. There is little more discouraging than (even unintentional) negative reactions such as, 'we can't do that', 'it didn't work when we tried it before'.

- Develop a culture that is supportive of creativity. Encourage novel suggestions. Provide adequate flexibility to pursue possible solutions (within a common vision).

- Remove the blocks to being creative, such as a belief that there is only one way to approach a problem, disparaging new (particularly threatening) ideas, failing to recognize and remedy a lack of self-confidence, or a disenchantment with the whole improvement process.

- Take the pressure off. Let people unwind. Creativity needs the subconscious to take over so that creative ideas can emerge. There is plenty of evidence that switching activities to doing something enjoyable, lighter, and probably unconnected with the task, can promote creativity.

- Do not over-control this stage of the problem-solving process. Allow people the freedom to make their own choices until as late as possible in the process.

Divergent and convergent thinking

Related to the last point above is a particularly useful distinction between two very different ways of thinking while generating improvements. This is the distinction between divergent and convergent thinking.

Divergent thinking means thinking outwards instead of inward, working outwards from a problem to generate a multiplicity of possible solutions. These ideas will be related to the problem, but possibly only in a loose way with each other. As a process it is normally seen as unstructured, spontaneous, uninhibited and 'non-linear'. It requires an ability to elaborate, and imagine any possibility in an unconstrained manner, to diverge from conventional ways of thinking about a problem.

Convergent thinking is the opposite. It means logically narrowing down the possible solutions to a few preferred solutions – or even one. It uses evaluation, reasoning, analysis, criticism and argument to progressively eliminate relatively unappealing options until the best option becomes evident. It requires the ability to marshal facts and data from relevant sources and then objectively use reason and knowledge to make informed decisions that will achieve an explicit objective. (The classic example of convergent thinking is often said to be Sherlock Homes – the ultimate logical puzzle solver.)

Both thought processes are needed to generate potential improvement solutions. Generally, divergent thought is first needed to produce many potential solutions, after which convergent thought narrows the options to find the best option. An example would be the classic brainstorming procedure. However, what you will need to vary is the time and emphasis devoted to each type. Radical-innovative improvement, as one would expect, needs much more effort devoting to the initial divergent-creative stage. Gradual-incremental improvement needs less divergent thought (although it does need some) and more critical convergent thought. This is illustrated in Figure 11.5.

Figure 11.5   The roles of divergent and convergent thinking in radical, innovative improvement and gradual, incremental improvement

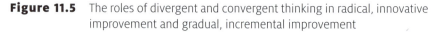

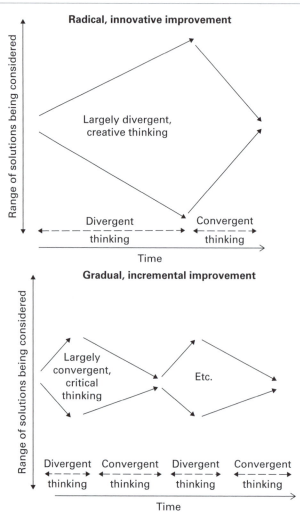

CASE STUDY Brompton Bicycles[5]

The unique Brompton folding bike was first designed and built in London in 1975 by Andrew Ritchie in his flat. It is still made in London today, but now Brompton is making over 45,000 bikes per year and is the UK's largest bike manufacturer. As such, creativity is vital for the company, which designs 80 per cent of the componentry on its bikes itself. To keep its advantage in the market, innovative technical advances need to be made all the time. It emphasizes that it never uses off-the-shelf products just for the sake of simplicity, preferring always to implement the best solution to any design or engineering problem.

Will Butler-Adams, the Managing Director of Brompton Bicycles, stresses the importance of creative problem solving to the company. *'We set aside a small part of our budget to fund experimental projects. Staff can bring forward ideas without the usual drawing-up of a complex business case. If an idea looks good, we will give it the go-ahead and see if it works. This process has generated very successful ideas: Brompton Junction concept stores, a joint venture in China, a clothing range, the Brompton Dock hire scheme. It works because it is straightforward and allows experimentation and innovation. To innovate successfully, you must think carefully about your attitude to mistakes. In some areas of your business, you will have zero tolerance of error. We couldn't afford to put unroadworthy bikes in the shops. But in any area we are seeking to innovate, we expect failures as we are pushing boundaries. If all our experimental projects paid off, it would show we were not being bold enough. We tend to hit obstacles and dead ends trying to do something new and have to discover a different approach. We find out what does not work, which is important R&D information for the future.'*

Implement improvement

Again, how you approach the implementation of improvement solutions depends on whether they are radical or incremental. All implementation needs planning, and all implementation needs monitoring and controlling, but implementing small and frequent improvements is a different task to the implementation of a widespread and radical change.

Large-scale improvements hold the promise of great benefits, but also carry great risks. So risk assessment should be an important part of any

Figure 11.6 Risk, the potential for learning and the value of a pilot depend on the degree of change in both resources and processes

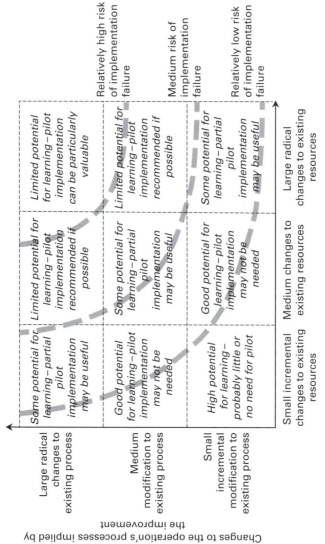

radical improvement implementation. This is when you might want to consider a pilot of the improvement. A pilot can be an effective method for reducing the risk of a radical change, particularly when a possible solution has the potential to be applied to multiple operations. The degree of change, the risks inherent in the change and the need for a pilot, are all related, and the thing that links them is the amount of learning that can take place during the implementation.

Figure 11.6 illustrates this idea. The degree of difficulty in implementing an improvement and the amount of learning that it is possible to gain from its implementation, will both depend on the degree of novelty of any new resources (people, skills, information, technology) required and the changes needed in the operation's processes. The less the new resources are understood (influenced maybe by the degree of innovation), the greater the difficulty of making the change. Equally, the extent to which an improvement requires a modification to existing processes, the greater the difficulty of implementation.

As resource change and/or process change increases, it becomes increasingly difficult to adopt any kind of systematic approach to analysing change and learning from mistakes. It becomes difficult to know what has worked, what has not, and why. Yet this is exactly when the potential of learning through a pilot becomes evident. A pilot performed on a small scale and/or over a short time period is an opportunity to test supposed cause-and-effect relationships and could help to quantify costs and benefits, potentially giving a better implementation with fewer surprises.

Establish and learn

While not wanting to repeat the points made in Chapter 8 on control and learning, it is worth highlighting that the opportunities for you and your operation to learn from the experience of generating and implementing improvement solutions is truly immense. Improvement is about making changes to an operation. Improvement is based on our underlying set of assumptions about how changes will impact on operations performance. So every change that we make in the hope that it will improve our operation is an opportunity to test those assumptions. Every change is, in that sense, an experiment. The worst thing we can do is to see each change purely in binary success or failure terms. Failing to draw lessons from the improvement process borders on gross negligence.

CASE STUDY The Checklist Manifesto[6]

Many improvement methods focus mainly on repetitive operations. Performing the same task repeatedly means that there are plenty of opportunities to 'get it right'. Does this mean that operations involving more difficult activities, especially those that call for expert judgement and skill, need correspondingly complex improvement approaches? Well no, according to Atul Gawande, a physician and author on matters medical. In fact, he thinks that the very opposite is true. Surgeons carry out over 200 major operations a year, unfortunately not all of them successful, but the medical profession overall does not always have a reliable method for learning from its mistakes. Mr Gawande's idea is that his and similar 'knowledge-based' professions are in danger of sinking under the weight of facts. Scientists are accumulating more and more information and professions are fragmenting into ever-narrower specialisms.

He tells the story of Peter Pronovost, a specialist in critical care at Johns Hopkins Hospital who tried to reduce the number of patients who were becoming infected from the use of intravenous central lines. There are five steps that medical teams can take to reduce the chances of contracting such infections. Initially Pronovost simply asked nurses to observe whether doctors took the five steps. What they found was that, at least a third of the time, they missed one or more of the steps. So nurses were authorized to stop doctors who had missed out any of the steps, and ask whether existing intravenous central lines should be reviewed. As a result of applying these simple checklist-style rules, the 10-day line-infection rates went down from 11 per cent to zero. In one hospital, it was calculated that, over a year, this simple method had prevented 43 infections, eight deaths and saved about $2 million. Using the same checklist approach the hospital identified and applied the method to other activities.

Mr Gawande describes checklists used in this way as a 'cognitive net' – a mechanism that can help prevent experienced people from making errors due to flawed memory and attention, and ensure that teams work together. Simple checklists are common in some other professions: airlines use them to make sure that pilots take off safely and also to learn from (now relatively rare) crashes. Indeed, Mr Gawande concedes that checklists are not a new idea. He cites the story of the prototype of the Boeing B17 Flying Fortress that crashed after take-off on its trial flight in 1935. Most experts said that the bomber was 'too complex to fly'. Facing bankruptcy, Boeing investigated and discovered that, confronted with four engines rather than two, the pilot forgot to release a vital locking mechanism. So Boeing created a pilot's checklist, in which the fundamental actions for the stages of flying were made a mandated part of the pilot's job. In the following years, B17s flew almost 2 million miles without a single accident. Even for pilots, many of whom are rugged individualists, he says, it is usually the application of routine procedures that saves planes when things go wrong, rather than the 'hero-pilotry' so fêted by the media. It is discipline rather than brilliance that preserves life. In fact, it is discipline that leaves room for brilliance to flourish.

Give improvement a chance

Some businesses really can be their own worst enemies when it comes to operations improvement. Some improvement processes that are launched, often with high expectations, will either collapse amid recriminations because they have been inadequately designed and resourced, or alternatively fade away before they have had a chance to go on and fulfil their potential.

Reports are released regularly that bear witness to the struggle to actually make improvement happen in a complex operations environment.[7] 'Nearly 60 per cent of all corporate Six Sigma initiatives fail to yield the desired results.' 'Of 500 US manufacturing and service companies, only a third felt their [improvement] programmes had significant impact on their competitiveness.' 'Only a fifth of the 100 British firms surveyed believed their quality programmes had achieved tangible results.' So, do not underestimate the difficulty. Even firms that start off well can fall back into old habits.

What is it that feeds this continuing paradox about improvement? No one disagrees with it, yet we consistently fail to provide the natural support for it to thrive. Practitioners and academics have suggested a number of reasons for this. Their advice is usually given in the form of 'barriers to improvement that need to be overcome', or more positively, 'things you should do to increase the chances of improvement really taking hold'. We take the more positive option here. These 'things that give improvement a chance' are shown in Figure 11.7. Each of them relates to your organization's ability, capacity or aptitude to do the things that support improvement. These 'organizational abilities' are different from the 'constituent behaviours' that support and reinforce them. Unless the appropriate behaviours are present, these organizational abilities will remain empty exhortations. Because of this we will describe, below, each aptitude in terms of some of their constituent behaviours. (These behaviours are also posed in the form of a questionnaire in the Appendix to this chapter.)

Figure 11.7 The organizational abilities that increase the chances of your improvement process succeeding

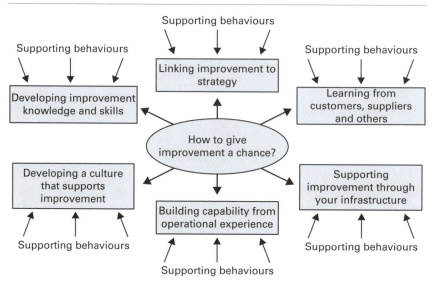

Link improvement to strategy

- Senior management spend time and effort in explaining how strategy shapes improvement priorities.
- Everyone is able to explain how strategy shapes improvement priorities.
- Strategic documents make specific reference to improvement targets.
- Individual and groups assess any proposed changes against improvement objectives.
- Individuals and groups regularly monitor the results of their improvement activity.
- Improvement activities are an integral part of everyone's work, not a separate or parallel activity.

Develop improvement knowledge and skills

- All people and groups demonstrate an understanding of the overall structure and purpose of the improvement process.
- Everyone understands how well-known approaches to improvement fit into the improvement process.

- Everyone regularly uses a common problem-solving cycle.
- All people are trained in the use of simple improvement tools and techniques.
- The improvement process is regularly monitored and developed.
- Everyone understands how his or her improvement activities affect people in other parts of the business.

Learn from customers, suppliers and others

- The individuals and groups who spend the most time talking to customers play an important role in setting improvement objectives.
- The individuals and groups who spend the most time talking to suppliers play an important role in setting improvement objectives.
- The business benchmarks its performance against other organizations within and outside the industry.
- Customers are frequently involved in specific improvement projects.
- The business regularly seeks customers' expectations of our performance.
- The business regularly seeks customers' perceptions of our performance.

Develop a culture that supports improvement

- All individuals and groups actively participate in improvement processes.
- Appraisal procedures reflect a commitment to improvement values.
- Managers lead by example, becoming actively involved in improvement design and implementation.
- Improvement priorities do not change too frequently.
- People frequently cooperate on improvement activities in cross-functional groups.
- There are periodic reviews of the improvement process involving sharing experiences across the organization as a whole.

Support improvement through your infrastructure

- Resources are explicitly allocated to the improvement process.
- Improvement ideas are responded to in a timely fashion – either implemented or otherwise dealt with.

- Sufficient resources (time, money, personnel) are allocated to support the development of novel ideas.
- Individuals' contribution to innovation are recognized and formally rewarded.
- Not punishing mistakes and encouraging learning support experimentation.
- People can identify who 'owns' those processes that cross organizational boundaries.

Build capability from operational experience

- Groups discuss what they have learnt in the course of doing their regular activities.
- There is a formal knowledge management or learning system that is used by all relevant people.
- Individuals seek out opportunities to extend their knowledge and/or personal development.
- All learning leads directly to action and/or changes in practice.
- Learning is deployed across the organization using clear communication channels.
- When something goes wrong, people at all levels look for reasons why, rather than blame individuals.

Avoid being an improvement 'fashion victim'

Before leaving the topic of what helps to secure successful improvement, it is worth noting that improvement has become something of a fashion industry. New ideas and concepts are continually being introduced, and sold as offering a new and better way to improve business performance. Of course, the idea of fashion – what is new, novel and different – is a powerful driver of what we find attractive. We tacitly accept fashion in music, movies, food or clothing. No one is immune. So it is not really surprising that the same applies to management generally, and operations improvement specifically.

Fashion feeds our need for novelty, and given that improving operations is a complex and difficult business, novel ideas can be embraced with sometimes embarrassing enthusiasm. Yet almost all these new ideas follow a very predictable pattern.[8] First, academics, or increasingly consultants, will discover a pattern that seems to show a cause–effect relationship between factors, often in very specific situations. Second, notwithstanding the often-limited relevance of the original study, it will be simplified and its original nuances glossed over. Third, the idea is popularized, often by a management 'guru' or consultancy firm and given a catchy title. Fourth, the idea is universalized to make it seem appropriate in all situations and consultants seek to apply it everywhere. Fifth, evangelical practitioners, for whom the idea has yielded results, enthusiastically embrace the idea and become product champions. Finally, the backlash starts. Doubt and scepticism grow as problems are reported from operations where it has not given the benefits that were claimed for it, or where it was applied inappropriately. The consultants who once promoted the idea now either repackage it or drop it entirely. As one cynical observer puts it, 'What once gave them credibility now makes them look like con-artists; they move on smartly.'

Don't be cynical about fashion – things would stagnate without it

It is a mistake to be too cynical about the role of fashion in improvement. There is nothing intrinsically wrong with fashion. It stimulates and refreshes through introducing novel ideas. It keeps us vibrant; without it, things would stagnate. To popularize anything, including improvement ideas, it needs to be packaged – given a name and given a boundary. Who would buy something called 'Stuff that you put into your coffee, and it sweetens it'? Put it in a bag and give it a name (how about 'sugar' – just a suggestion) and it will sell. It is exactly the same with improvement ideas. They are packages, often using the same or similar ingredients to others, which have been packaged and given an enticing name.

The problem lies not so much with the new improvement ideas themselves, but rather with some managers becoming a victim of the process. They seem to actively want some new idea to entirely displace whatever went before. They become fashion victims. The truth is that most new ideas, even when stripped of the hype, do have something useful to say. None of them is totally fraudulent. However, just as we look at the ingredients when we pick up a new product in the supermarket, maybe we also need to look at what's inside any new (or old for that matter) improvement idea. We would look what it contains and may even try it, at least once. Be careful how and when you try an improvement idea, and don't blame the approach. Rarely are excuses like 'We've tried Six Sigma/BPR/lean, it doesn't work' valid. It's like saying, 'I've tried this tennis racket, and it doesn't work.' Of course it is nothing to do with the tennis racket (or the improvement idea) it's how you are using it. This is why it is your (and any operations executive's) responsibility to thoroughly understand and deconstruct any new idea that comes along claiming to help you to improve your operations.

Without an approach to understanding improvement ideas that 'unpicks' their core elements, the temptation will be to jump from one fad to another with no solid appreciation of their strengths and weaknesses. This is the behaviour of a true fashion victim. Inevitably this will not only generate a backlash against any new idea, but also destroy the ability to accumulate the experience that comes from experimenting with each one.

Avoiding becoming an improvement fashion victim is not easy. It requires you to take responsibility for a number of issues:

1 You should take responsibility for improvement as an ongoing activity, rather than becoming a champion for only one specific improvement initiative.

2 You should take responsibility for understanding the underlying ideas behind each new concept. Improvement is not 'following a recipe' or 'painting by numbers'. Unless one understands *why* improvement ideas are supposed to work, it is difficult to understand *how* they can be made to work properly.

3 You should take responsibility for understanding the antecedents to a 'new' improvement idea because it helps to better understand it and to judge how appropriate it may be for one's own operation.

4 You should be prepared to adapt new ideas so that they make sense within the context of their own operation. 'One size' rarely fits all.

5 You should take responsibility for the (often significant) education and learning effort that will be needed if new ideas are to be intelligently exploited.

6 Above all you should avoid the exaggeration and hype that many new ideas attract. Although it is sometimes tempting to exploit the motivational 'pull' of new ideas through slogans, posters and exhortations, carefully thought-out plans will always be superior in the long run, and will help avoid the inevitable backlash that follows 'over-selling' a single approach.

Practical prescriptions

- No matter what level you hold in the operations function, be prepared to get involved personally in the mechanics of improvement.

- All improvement is never-ending; even radical innovative changes will need more of the same at some point. So think of all improvement as a cycle and formally adopt an improvement cycle model. It doesn't have to be exactly the same as the one used in this chapter, but it should be similar.

- Do not neglect to invest time in defining what you want to get out of an improvement. A good problem definition will focus your efforts and create a sense of ownership.

- Collect the data to support improvement in a systematic manner, preferably by going personally to see what is really happening.

- Use questioning techniques such as cause–effect analysis and 'why-why' analysis to get to the bottom of what the root causes of problems are.

- Creative brainstorming-type techniques can be used to develop creative solutions. Remember that the balance of divergent to convergent thinking will depend on whether the improvement is aiming for gradual incremental or radical innovative.

- Similarly, the implementation of any proposed improvement 'solutions' will depend on whether the improvement is aiming for gradual incremental or radical innovative. Consider the use of pilots or trials of the proposed solutions if they involve significant resource change or process change, or both.

- Learning from the improvement experience is (as ever) important. Always ask, 'What have we learnt from this process, both about our operations and about how we make improvements?'

- Use the questionnaire in the Appendix to this chapter to explore where you could improve your chances of making improvements stick.

- Don't be a fashion victim. Balance healthy scepticism about new approaches to improvement with an interest in what new they might have to tell us.

Notes

1 DeWitt, J (2014) 5 Tips for new team leaders, *Harvard Business Review*, 22 September

2 There are many books that will give you details of these improvement cycles. For the DMAIC cycle see Gygi, C, Williams, B and DeCarlo, N (2012) *Six Sigma for Dummies*, Wiley, Chichester

3 Source: *The Economist* (2013) Back to the drawing-board: Design companies are applying their skills to the voluntary and public sectors, 6 July

4 The original Japanese term comes from *gembutsu*, which means 'real thing', or sometimes the real place

5 Sources include: company website; Hinde, S (2015) How businesses can foster creativity and innovation, *Daily Telegraph*, 13 January

6 Sources: Gawande, A (2010) The Checklist Manifesto: how to get things right, *Metropolitan*; Aaronovitch, D (2010) The Checklist Manifesto: review, *The Times*, 23 January

7 Sources include: Dr Satya Chakravorty, Kennesaw State University; *The Economist* (2010) Was it all worth it? 24 April

8 Furnham, A (2015) Fads and fashion in management, *The European Business Review*, 20 July

Appendix to Chapter 11

Questionnaire: How good is your improvement process?

There are many improvement questionnaires that purport to gauge an organization's readiness or underlying capability to embed operations improvement. Some are better than others. The better ones at least make you think about some of the issues.

The improvement questionnaire included here draws upon the issues discussed in Chapter 11. It is based on the idea that the chances of succeeding with operations improvement depend on a number of organizational capabilities, which are demonstrated through certain improvement behaviours. Try it out. Get your colleagues to do the same. Discuss any differences in perceptions that may emerge. Ask yourself: 'What are the implications of our answers?'

This Appendix asks questions based on the behaviours associated with six capabilities, shown in the first figure. They are:

1 How well do you link improvement to strategy?

2 How good are you at developing improvement knowledge and skills?

3 How well do you learn from customers, suppliers and others?

4 How well does your culture support improvement?

5 How well do you support improvement through your infrastructure?

6 How well do you build capability from operational experience?

Figure App 11.1

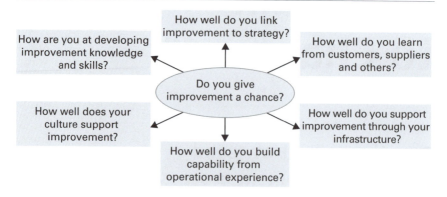

Figure App 11.2

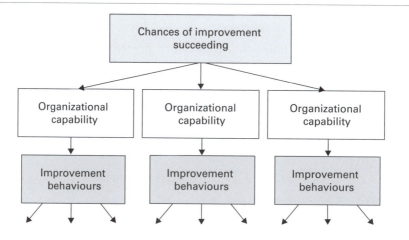

1 How well do you link improvement to strategy?

Consider each statement and rate how true it is for your organization, from 0 (never/no/not at all) to 5 (always/yes/all the time). Then calculate the average score and mark up the polar diagram at the end of the questionnaire.

Figure App 11.3

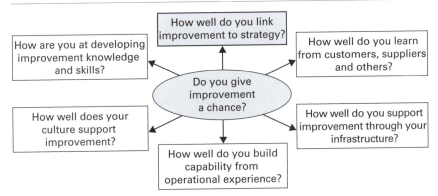

How well do you link improvement to strategy?

How are you at developing improvement knowledge and skills?

How well do you learn from customers, suppliers and others?

Do you give improvement a chance?

How well does your culture support improvement?

How well do you support improvement through your infrastructure?

How well do you build capability from operational experience?

Figure App 11.4

	Never/Not at all/No				Always/ Totally/Yes
Everyone in our business is able to explain how strategy shapes improvement priorities	0 1 2 3 4 5				
Our strategic documents make specific reference to improvement targets	0 1 2 3 4 5				
Individual and groups assess any proposed changes against our improvement objectives	0 1 2 3 4 5				
Individuals and groups regularly monitor the results of their improvement activity	0 1 2 3 4 5				
Improvement activities are an integral part of our work, not a separate or parallel activity	0 1 2 3 4 5				

Average score [ ]

2 How good are you at developing improvement knowledge and skills?

Consider each statement and rate how true it is for your organization, from 0 (never/no/not at all) to 5 (always/yes/all the time). Then calculate the average score and mark up the polar diagram at the end of the questionnaire.

Figure App 11.5

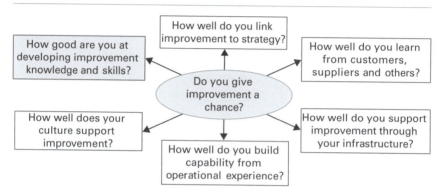

Figure App 11.6

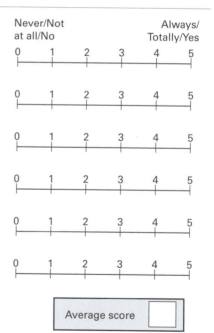

Statement	Never/Not at all/No					Always/Totally/Yes

All people and groups demonstrate an understanding of the overall structure and purpose of our improvement process — 0 1 2 3 4 5

Everyone understands how well-known approaches to improvement fit into our improvement process — 0 1 2 3 4 5

We regularly use a common problem-solving cycle — 0 1 2 3 4 5

All people are trained in the use of simple improvement tools and techniques — 0 1 2 3 4 5

The improvement process is regularly monitored and developed — 0 1 2 3 4 5

Everyone understands how his or her improvement activities affect people in other parts of the business — 0 1 2 3 4 5

Average score [ ]

3 How well do you learn from customers, suppliers and others?

Consider each statement and rate how true it is for your organization, from 0 (never/no/not at all) to 5 (always/yes/all the time). Then calculate the average score and mark up the polar diagram at the end of the questionnaire.

Figure App 11.7

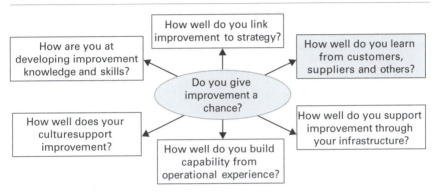

Figure App 11.8

	Never/Not at all/No				Always/ Totally/Yes
The individuals and groups who spend the most time talking to cutomers play an important role in setting improvement objectives	0 1 2 3 4 5				
The individuals and groups who spend the most time talking to suppliers play an important role in setting improvement objectives	0 1 2 3 4 5				
We benchmark our performance against other organizations within and outside our industry	0 1 2 3 4 5				
Customers are frequently involved in specific improvement projects	0 1 2 3 4 5				
We regularly seek customers' expectations of our performance	0 1 2 3 4 5				
We regularly seek customers' perceptions of our performance	0 1 2 3 4 5				

Average score [   ]

4 How well does your culture support improvement?

Consider each statement and rate how true it is for your organization, from 0 (never/no/not at all) to 5 (always/yes/all the time). Then calculate the average score and mark up the polar diagram at the end of the questionnaire.

Figure App 11.9

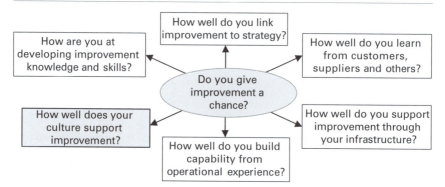

Figure App 11.10

	Never/Not at all/No					Always/Totally/Yes
All individuals and groups actively participate in improvement processes	0	1	2	3	4	5
Our appraisal procedures reflect a commitment to improvement values	0	1	2	3	4	5
Managers lead by example, becoming actively involved in improvement design and implementation	0	1	2	3	4	5
Improvement priorities do not change too frequently	0	1	2	3	4	5
We frequently cooperate on improvement activities in cross-functional groups	0	1	2	3	4	5
There are periodic reviews of our improvement process involving sharing experiences across the organization as a whole	0	1	2	3	4	5

Average score [ ]

5 How well do you support improvement through your infrastructure?

Consider each statement and rate how true it is for your organization, from 0 (never/no/not at all) to 5 (always/yes/all the time). Then calculate the average score and mark up the polar diagram at the end of the questionnaire.

Figure App 11.11

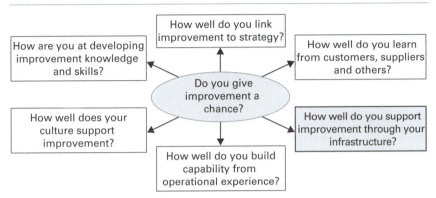

Figure App 11.12

	Never/Not at all/No					Always/Totally/Yes
Resources are explicitly allocated to the improvement process	0	1	2	3	4	5
Improvement ideas are responded to in a timely fashion – either implemented or otherwise dealt with	0	1	2	3	4	5
We allocate sufficient resources (time, money, personnel) to support the development of novel ideas	0	1	2	3	4	5
We recognize and formally reward individuals' contribution to innovation	0	1	2	3	4	5
We support experimentation by not punishing mistakes and encouraging learning	0	1	2	3	4	5
People understand who 'owns' those processes that cross organizational boundaries	0	1	2	3	4	5

Average score [ ]

6 How well do you build capability from operational experience?

Consider each statement and rate how true it is for your organization, from 0 (never/no/not at all) to 5 (always/yes/all the time). Then calculate the average score and mark up the polar diagram at the end of the questionnaire.

Figure App 11.13

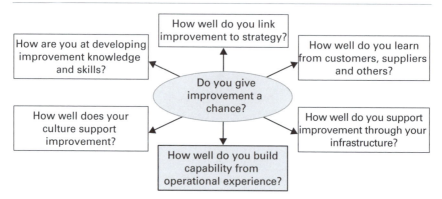

Figure App 11.14

	Never/Not at all/No				Always/ Totally/Yes
Groups discuss what they have learnt in the course of doing their regular activities	0　1　2　3　4　5				
We have a formal knowledge management/learning system used by all relevant people	0　1　2　3　4　5				
Individuals seek out opportunities to extend their knowledge and/or personal development	0　1　2　3　4　5				
Learning leads directly to action and/or changes in practice	0　1　2　3　4　5				
Clear communication channels are used to deploy learning across the organization	0　1　2　3　4　5				
When something goes wrong, people at all levels look for reasons why, rather than blame individuals	0　1　2　3　4　5				

Average score ☐

Bringing it together

Mark the average score for each section on the relevant dimension. What are your strengths and weaknesses?

Figure App 11.15

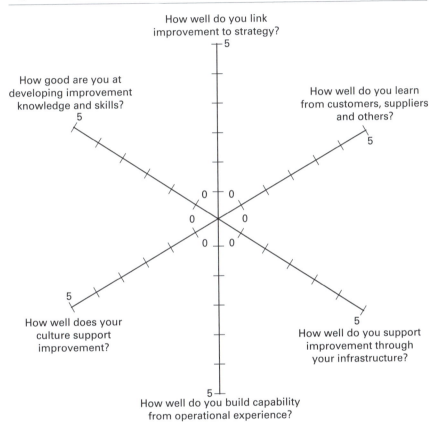

INDEX

Note: *Italics* indicate a Figure or Table in the text.